A

SENSE

of

DIRECTION

Pilgrimage for the Restless and the Hopeful

———◆———

GIDEON LEWIS-KRAUS

ONE

ONE
an imprint of Pushkin Press
71–75 Shelton Street, London WC2H 9JQ

Copyright © 2012 by Gideon Lewis-Kraus

A Sense of Direction was first published in the
United States by Riverhead in 2012

First published in Great Britain by ONE in 2014

Published by arrangement with Riverhead Books,
a member of Penguin Group (USA) Inc.

ISBN 978 0 957548 82 4

Book design by Amanda Dewey
Maps by Meighan Cavanaugh

Printed by CPI Group (UK) Ltd, Croydon CR0 4YY

www.pushkinpress.com

To Harriet Clark,
as promised

And in memory of Richard Rorty

———◦———

ANNIE HALL: Oh, you see an analyst?
ALVY SINGER: Yeah, just for fifteen years.
ANNIE HALL: Fifteen years?
ALVY SINGER: Yeah, I'm gonna give him one more year,
   and then I'm goin' to Lourdes.
                                    —*Annie Hall*

Contents

Prologue

TALLINN

MY FRIEND TOM WAS TRAPPED at home in a tiny, distant city. He had no Estonian visa, and he knew if he left Tallinn he'd be unable to return. More immediately problematic was the Russian stripper he'd been flirting with, or, more specifically, her boyfriend, who had taken to hanging around Tom's front door. Tom pleaded with me to visit, confident the guy wouldn't take on the two of us.

Tom and I didn't know each other all that well then, nothing like later, but it sounded like a fun excuse for a trip. Unlike Tom, I could leave my apartment in Berlin whenever I wanted—I had a German freelancer's visa and no cuckolded Baltic criminals camped out on my stoop—and was, in fact, spending more time away than at home. By that point Berlin often left me feeling at loose ends, and one of the things I had come to like most about living there was how easy it was never to be in town. A lot of my friends had already moved on, had gone back to resume their real lives in New York, and I myself was beginning to wonder if it wasn't time to pack it in. It was unclear where I'd go, though, mostly because nowhere was more appealing than Berlin had once been, should have been still. I'd been living in lovely, provincial San Francisco and had moved to Berlin because I'd felt I was missing out on something exciting, and now I was on the brink of leaving lively, provisional Berlin because I was afraid I was missing out on something serious. A quarter lifetime of anecdotal evidence suggested, however, that once I actually motivated myself to move somewhere I considered serious, somewhere like New York—where I had never actually lived for very long but where, I imagined, I would find myself ready to get on with the routines and attachments that make for a real life (cat, yoga, a relationship)—I would once again regret missing all the novelty diverting people elsewhere. Maybe not New York, then. Maybe Kiev. I'd heard Kiev was cheap and cool. I often reminded myself to look into it.

Tom and I held in common the hope that there might be a geographic ticket out of the problems of indecision, boredom, and the suspicion that more interesting things were happening in more fashionable places to more attractive people. Actually, that last part was my worry; in Tom's version, less interesting things were happening in contemplative places to more industrious people. Tom had moved to Tallinn with the idea he'd be pressed into productivity there, that the constraint of its distance and exoticism would force him to focus on the work he'd been neglecting in favor of video games and the more dissipated varieties of recreation. I'd moved to Berlin precisely for its lack of constraint, hoping that its sense of vast possibility would help me figure out what I wanted. Needless to say, for reasons that went beyond Russian strippers, it wasn't really working out for either of us. Tom's claustrophobia left him desperate for distraction, and my distraction left me desperate for discipline. We were like two ships waiting for a breeze that might float us past each other in the night.

Tom picked me up at the tiny airport in a taxi and brought me up to date. "I was living in Saigon," he said, "and after a year I had to leave because my life was spinning out of control. Then I was living in Rome, and I had to leave after six months because my life was spinning out of control. Then I moved to Las Vegas, and I had to leave there, too, *very quickly*, because my life was definitely once again spinning out of control."

"You were having trouble keeping yourself together in Rome, so you moved to *Vegas?*"

"So I left Vegas and I thought to myself, okay, I need to finish this long-overdue book, so I'll go to a small, distant country with an impossible language and I'll just sit and write all day until the book is done. I came here."

He looked out the window at the looming medieval spires of the old town, where he was paying Manhattan rent to live in the lavishly restored fourteenth century. "And now I can say, with utter confidence, that my life is spinning out of control."

I hadn't known Tom long enough to presume to tell him how to live. Besides, he was a successful writer I admired and had long wished I might one day resemble. He was only six years older than me, not quite enough to make him a paternal figure but enough to make him a guide, and I preferred to think of him as somewhat more together than he liked to suggest. I assumed that despite his life's apparent mismanagement there must be some greater logic to it. Plus he was living out a somewhat distorted but still recognizable version of my own fantasy: skipping club lines with future Baltic dictators, then until-dawn depravity with minor Baltic celebrities. The best thing I could do for him, I decided, was to provide him with company and reverence.

What I chiefly remember about the four-day jag that followed is waking up in my bed, peering at my uncharacteristically unread email, and realizing that I was back in Berlin. I had vague recollections of sitting in an idling cab outside a Soviet-era tower block on the outskirts of Tallinn, and of spending an evening in the company of some Siberian dancers and the man being groomed to lead Estonia's next nationalist front, and of gazing through a bobbing porthole at some gray sea while Tom let his forehead cool against a Formica table. I looked at my camera to discover a few blurry images of what I have come to believe was probably Helsinki. The only other clue was a page in my little notebook, where I'd managed one note in four days: "Camino de Santiago—sense of purpose—June 10." I'd underlined "purpose."

This Camino business sounded vaguely familiar. The internet dutifully reported that in the year A.D. 813, the alleged bones of the apostle St. James the Greater were unearthed in Santiago de Compostela, in far northwestern Spain. St. James had supposedly evangelized as far afield as Galicia—unlikely, Tom says—before he was martyred in first-century Palestine. His relics were said to have arrived at the Atlantic coast, then the presumed end of the world, in a stone boat, where they remained buried under a hermitage until their discovery eight centuries later. A pilgrimage to the site started up within the next hundred years, probably along the old trail of a pagan death cult. (The Iberian Celts walked to the end of the earth to watch the sun perish nightly into the sea.) Around 1140 the Codex Calixtinus appeared, a book that's part how-to and part spiritual advice, and that has come to be regarded as the world's first travel guide—the route is also credited with the invention of the souvenir tchotchke—and since that time the Camino de Compostela has seen a more or less continuous parade of redemptive aspiration. Over the past twenty years, in no small part thanks to the efforts of a dopey German television comedian, the pilgrimage has become popular with a secular crowd. It's about nine hundred kilometers, or a little less than six hundred miles, depending on where you start and whether you continue to the sea, and takes most people about a month to walk.

The book Tom had moved to Estonia to work on was a record of his visits to the far-flung tombs of the apostles, and by the time I was done reading up on the Camino, which had an immediate appeal for reasons I only dimly understood, I'd retrieved a faint memory of Tom's having said he planned to spend the following summer strolling across Spain, starting on the French side of the Pyrenean border. I didn't know what to make of my "June 10" note, though, so I called him up on Skype. He hadn't slept since I'd left, but he sounded chipper, happy to hear from me.

"I miss you, man," he said. "I'm lonely again and wish you were still around."

"Me, too, buddy." I paused. "So, Tom, what's going on June 10?"

"That's the day we start," he said. "It worked with both of our schedules."

I had no schedule to speak of, so I couldn't argue with that. Then again, neither did he. The notion of something working with our schedules made me suspicious.

"The day we start what, Tom?"

"Our walk across Spain. You don't remember? Strolling through hills by night, just you and me and the long path ahead. I told you any hotels we stay in are on me. You had that whole rousing speech about how we'd wake up each morning full of the simple, broad purpose of moving forward. You pounded your fist on the table and shouted to the whole bar that you were one hundred percent in. A few Estonians even clapped, though maybe they were just trying to get you to be quiet. Then we promised some girls we'd send them postcards from Santiago."

Part I

BERLIN

M Y LITTLE BROTHER, Micah, hadn't finished college and he was already making more money than I was; he was playing semi-professional poker, day trading with his cardroom winnings. Partway through the winter quarter of his senior year, he applied for a fancy tech job for which he was highly underqualified. Each successive interviewer told him this, and he replied the same way every time: "I'm an engineer who knows how to write a clear and grammatical sentence." They made him a generous offer.

He was going to move to San Francisco, which I was then preparing to leave, and where, in fact, I'd never meant to settle in the first place. I'd moved there right out of college for the sake of a relationship, had spent three years idly wondering why I was there and not somewhere else—pretty much anywhere else, but especially somewhere that paid slightly less attention to heirloom produce. The long relationship had ended—technically I'd initiated the breakup, though only after she'd moved on to take a job in Peru—and the city was suffused with memories of her. I couldn't even go enjoy the farmer's market at the Ferry Building anymore, and I hadn't even liked farmer's markets until she'd made us go to them all the time. I was mad at her for having made me like farmer's markets and then ruining them for me. I dated somebody else for a while—somebody who liked natural history museums instead of farmer's markets—but I pretty soon realized that I was just in a relationship because I was used to being in relationships. They helped me know when to go to bed at night and when to get up in the morning, and presented me with somebody else's problems to fix. I was ready to go. I wanted to be in a place that felt more like a choice than a by-product of other decisions.

"Let's get a place together," Micah said.

"But I'm leaving San Francisco," I said.

"But we could get a really nice place."

"I'm frustrated here, and I'm bored and restless. I feel like I've frittered away my early twenties at farmer's markets and natural history museums and Tartine." Tartine was the bakery where I read each morning from nine to twelve under the negligent gaze of the world's comeliest baristas. In order to maintain my self-respect, and in order not to alarm those baristas, I spent my afternoons reading at a different venue, at Atlas or Dolores Park Café. I was paying almost nothing to live in the maid's quarters of a middle-aged Dutch high-end housecleaner named Jouke. Jouke lived six days a week in Sacramento with his boyfriend, Rex, so I didn't see him much. Rex had Farrah Fawcett hair and told me each time he came to visit that I ought to give up trying to be a writer and instead use my typing talent to become a court stenographer, like him. Jouke's walls were crammed with Erté prints and stained kimonos. Two porcelain ponies nuzzled at the top of the stairs. Every Monday I'd give them an inch of breathing room, and every Sunday Jouke would return and re-nuzzle the pair.

Micah ignored my complaint. "Your life is economically non-viable. You write book reviews and work part-time at a literary journal not even Mom reads. I have a proposal to make."

"Hm?"

"Find us a really great apartment, wherever you want. Make it a three-bedroom so Mom can stay with us when she visits."

"What about Dad?"

"You're joking."

"I'm joking." Our dad and his partner, Brett, liked to come out for Halloween or Pride and stay in seedy Castro guesthouses. We'd make plans to see each other, but we were often thwarted. Once I called my dad to fix a time for dinner. His speech was slurred, incoherent, and Abba deafened in the background. Brett took the phone and said he'd meet me in the parking lot of the Castro Safeway to return the keys to the car they'd borrowed from me. As Brett saw me approach, the sun falling behind Twin Peaks at his back, he dropped his cigarette and crushed it with a wide, slow swivel of his boot. "I'm sorry," he said, still crushing the butt. I couldn't tell if he was sorry he'd been smoking, sorry my dad was so drunk, sorry that they were in love, or sorry they'd canceled plans once again.

"Anyway," Micah continued, "I'll pay three-quarters of the rent—"

"And you'll expect me to do all the cleaning and the laundry?"

"How'd you know?"

"Ever since you were six and I was nine, you've been waiting for the day you'd make me do your disgusting laundry."

"The offer's on the table. Take it or leave it." Micah hung up.

I took it. Micah called me each afternoon as he left the office to tell me he'd be home around five thirty. As he changed from office casual into running clothes, he'd tell me about his day, about how some idiot supplier in China was stalling again; and as I changed from pajamas into running clothes, I'd yell at him for forgetting once more to clean out the cat litter. We jogged up to Golden Gate Park, bought seasonal citrus on the way home, spent an hour arguing indecisively about where to eat dinner. We began weekend evenings separately but almost always met up at Taqueria Cancún when the bars closed. Neither of us tended to like the other's objects of affection, but it didn't much matter. We dated without any real urgency; after all, we could always kill a long Sunday afternoon together. When I broke up with a girl with whom I'd gotten halfway through the second season of *The Wire*, I made Micah spend a weekend watching sixteen straight episodes so we could continue together. When we needed time apart, he'd play golf or, worse, watch golf on TV. I only ever got annoyed with him when he asked me to pick up his dry cleaning, the implication being that I didn't have anything better to do during the day. In the end I always picked up his dry cleaning, mostly because I didn't have anything better to do during the day.

A year passed and I couldn't remember ever having been happier, but I also couldn't remember the last time I'd done anything that felt exciting or youthful or new. I bought a ticket to visit an old friend who'd been living in Berlin for six years, paying a hundred euros a month to live in an unrenovated prewar apartment. Delia had a wide balcony and no discernible line of work. It was midsummer, when Berlin endures only three or four hours of actual darkness, and the air is soft and heavy with desire, clear with vast possibility. In the early evenings we lolled around, drinking cheap beer on the overgrown grass fringe of the canal in the stalled sunset radiance, thick with the scent of untamed green, and later we went out, each night until long past dawn, biking all over the city with a rotating cast of international dubiety—paint-spattered people with unidentifiable accents—dancing at Rio, at WMF, at Bar25, at Club der Visionäre, at Weekend, the last of which had just been written up in the most detailed Berlin-is-the-place-of-the-now sally the *New York Times* had yet produced. I cannot account for what we did during the day, if we did anything at all. I couldn't account for what I did during the day in San Francisco, either, but in San Francisco it felt as though there was something wrong if you had daytime available to pick up your little brother's dry cleaning. In Berlin it was the usual course of things, though in the three years I was in Berlin on and off I don't think I ever got a single thing dry-cleaned. I didn't want to come back to San Francisco.

"I'm going to move to Berlin next year," I told Micah when he picked me up at the airport.

"I knew you'd get sick of doing my laundry."

I told him his laundry, unappealing as it was, had very little to do with it. I had two main reasons. One was that everyone I encountered in Berlin seemed to have the freedom—economically and culturally—to do exactly what he or she pleased. What was important was what was happening *right now*. Nobody seemed to hold anybody to account. It wasn't like San Francisco or New York, where the first question anybody asked at a party was what you did for a living, and the second was where you lived and how much you paid to live there. The other reason was that, perhaps because of that freedom, Berlin felt like the center of something surprising and important, and I couldn't help thinking it would be a good place for an aspiring writer. The rumors of a new Lost Generation were a terrible cliché, but it was hard to resist them.

"That doesn't make any sense," Micah said. "So on the one hand you want to go to Berlin to do nothing at all, and on the other hand you want to go to further your ambition. You're an idiot."

I applied for a Fulbright, figuring I could do with at least the imprimatur of institutional legitimacy. My proposal—some essay I planned never to write about contemporary young German novelists, about whom I knew exactly nothing—was the sort of thing I'd been advised the committee wanted to hear, and I got it. A year later Micah took me to the airport and we stood there and cried.

. . .

TWENTY-SEVEN was an unusual age to move to Berlin, but I'd always had a precocious sense of crisis, and my decision to go was spurred at least in part by my fantasy that I might be able to stave off future regret. I felt like I owed the experience to some subsequent self. Everybody else in Berlin was either twenty-two, just out of leafy liberal arts colleges and in flight from the responsibilities ahead, or they were thirty-nine, just out of a career or a relationship and in flight from the responsibilities behind. For my part, I moved there as a kind of preemptive strike, reasoning that if I bolted while I could, in my late twenties, I wouldn't bolt when I couldn't, in my forties, or maybe more specifically at approximately forty-six, when my dad left his marriage and moved in with Brett, a lovely guy he met at the gym, and Micah and I could never get in touch with him about car insurance or baseball games because the two of them were always disappearing to the nightclubs of Key West or Palm Springs. They emailed self-portraits in sailor suits from themed Atlantis cruises down Baja. My dad's justification for this, in those moments when he felt as though he needed to produce one, was that he was claiming the outré adolescence he'd been denied. He'd lived a life long on sacrifice and short on pleasure, and had begun, at last, to live the life he deserved. "Deserved" was his word.

More than anything, his two mistakes—first, not living the life he wanted; and, second, believing this had been a sacrifice that freed him from all future sacrifices, like having dinner with his children when he wanted to stay longer at the bar, or treating their mother with any respect—were what I hoped to avoid. I explained my fear of regret in terms of how unusually clearly my dad's life—in which a bad, perhaps even cowardly decision made in his twenties became a thirties of anxiety, a forties of resentment, and a fifties of abandon—

exemplified the great cost of not having acted as one wished when one still had time.

I cannot now say what, exactly, I was afraid I was going to regret. I was just afraid of the idea of regret in general, and thought my determination to avoid it was a form of being considerate toward those I might otherwise one day resent. I wanted my twenty-seven-year-old self to take good care of my forty-six-year-old self, and I wanted my forty-six-year-old self to be able to look back happily and be proud of my twenty-seven-year-old self. I thought that perhaps my dad's problem was that he hadn't had enough experience, that he'd chosen a career and a marriage before he knew what else was out there, and I didn't want to make the same error. Experiencewise, I wanted what I thought everybody wanted: to go to secret parties with artist/DJs that people in Brooklyn hadn't even heard of, or to sleep with as many people as, say, Tom, so that when I got back into a committed relationship it wouldn't be for the mere sake of being in one but because I'd chosen that person. Those were the reasons I gave for moving to Berlin. Or at least, those were the excuses I gave for moving to Berlin.

I arrived in time for a few days of lingering late summer. I took the U-Bahn from the airport, dropped my stuff at a sublet, spent my first euros on a pack of cigarettes, and walked slowly down the Karl-Marx-Allee toward Delia's apartment feeling alone and free and already different. My first night in town was Delia's send-off, which seemed cruelly unfortunate at the time. (Later I understood it was a common enough coincidence: every day somebody arrived and somebody else left.) I arrived at her apartment to find the German national women's Ultimate Frisbee team running around in their underwear in the living room while the men smoked on the balcony, trying to decide where we'd all go later, if the women decided to put their pants back on.

In Berlin it thus seemed, from that first night's demented relaxation into morning, as though everything was up in the air at all hours; no possibility was foreclosed. The local custom was to commit to as little as possible, and by "local custom" I do not mean "German custom." If the twentieth century had taught anybody anything at all, it was that Germans had lousy customs. Hence Berlin's appeal: there was no cultural arbitration. My colleagues in Paris had the futile errand of trying to resemble the French. Those in Beijing competed in the absurd contest of trying to *understand China*. In Tokyo, or in London, or in Moscow, your sunlit hours had to have some nontrivial relationship to the economy. Berlin was an experiment in total freedom from authority, an infinitely long weekend with your parents out of town. It felt like an anti-gravity chamber. The old crimes licensed you to ignore the claims of the past; the low cost of living licensed you to ignore the demands of the present; and the future was something that would happen when we moved back to New York, where many of us would once more live in uncomfortable proximity to our actual parents, and where people talked about real estate and restaurants.

It was not that I did not like talking about restaurants. It's normal to like talking about restaurants. But in Berlin when we talked about restaurants, it was the cheap kebab places; this was part of the ritual by which we acknowledged the aspects of our Berlin existence that differentiated us from our friends at home. We, and now I mean the people I came to love in Berlin, David Levine and Alix and Emilie, often felt like survivors whose home planet had become glutted with condos bought by people who waited in line for cupcakes, and we congratulated ourselves and one another on having gotten out just in time. This gave our decision to do as little of consequence as possible—with this ocean of space and profligacy of hours—the legitimate pretext of cultural and economic protest. We rebelled against the authority of rent and cupcakes.

In theory, this chartered us to do whatever we pleased whenever we wanted. In practice, it meant we spent a lot of time wondering what we wanted to do, and if we wanted to do anything at all. Or maybe that was just me. Part of my anti-regret crusade involved making sure I was always doing just what I felt like, which mostly meant keeping myself open for things that might come up, saying yes to whatever distraction happened along. It was an extremely active kind of passivity and it went swimmingly at night, when things were always coming up: there were gallery openings and bars and clubs, all elbowy with asymmetrical people proving provocative until breakfast. The daytimes were another matter; then it was less clear what the most vital and necessary and memorable experience available might be. I went to Berlin with a whole shelf of unread books, books like *Middlemarch*, but every time I sat down hungover in a café at eleven a.m. with that copy of *Middlemarch*, the whole day open before me, I inevitably thought to myself, Why move to Berlin to read *Middlemarch*? I could read *Middlemarch* in San Francisco (though, naturally, I hadn't). The whole point of living in Berlin was being an agent in the world of total possibility. Was reading *Middlemarch* the thing I most desired to do in that particular hour? It wasn't easy to say. Ordinarily I had to put the book down and go on a walk to think it over, to make sure I was maximizing the value of my experience. These often turned into some pretty long walks. When I got back to the neighborhood from my walks, I sat around the Turkish bakery with Alix, or I went with her to check out the newer galleries up in Wedding. When I was with Alix, I felt as though there was nothing else in the world I'd rather be doing. When she was busy I went to see *Wings of Desire*.

Part of the point of Wim Wenders's 1987 film, which I must've seen a dozen times in that first year, is that Berlin before the fall of the Wall had long been an inertial place, a sort of vacuum. There was no industry in the West; factory owners were afraid the Soviets would blockade the city, as they had shortly after the war. The banks were in grimy Frankfurt, technology and automobiles were in bourgeois Munich and arrogant Stuttgart, the press was in wealthy Hamburg, the provisional government in boring Bonn. West Berlin was merely a symbol of resistance, a great series of photo ops, and America was happy to help pay for it as long as it continued to provide such good press. East Berlin was just as unreal. It was a Communist set, the utopian socialism of the future, but it was also a big, expensive mock-up. The rest of the country was bankrupted by the purchase of ornamental tile for the wedding-cake palazzi that lined the Stalinallee (now the Karl-Marx-Allee I walked to Delia's Frisbee-underwear going-away). The Fernsehturm, or TV Tower, at Alexanderplatz, the city's only height of note, had been built in 1969 as a present to the *Volk* from their twenty-year-old puppet government. They'd had to use Western technology and Swedish engineers, and the people were already picking up TV signals from the free side of the city. After the Wall went up, in 1961, there was never anything of true geopolitical importance at stake. Its construction wasn't an escalation but a diffusion: it made the conflict not political but rhetorical, for the benefit of the media.

The movie follows two angels as they bum around the city. One of them becomes smitten with a doleful French trapeze artist, and his feelings for her convince him to leap from eternity into time. Peter Falk, playing himself as a former angel, encourages Damiel's transition. In the scene where he first wakes up as a mortal, he asks a passerby for help. The man teaches him the words for the colors in the graffiti on the Wall—his life until then had been in black and

white—and then gives him change for his first hot coffee and pack of
cigarettes. He gulps the black coffee, his eyes wide.

This had always evoked what felt like a disproportionate response in me; it wasn't the sort of movie that was supposed to make
you cry. On some level it was probably just because I was lonely and
indecisive, sitting yet again by myself on a Tuesday at one in the
afternoon at the Kino Babylon or at the Moviemento, and because it
ends with the inevitability of an enduring romance, which already
seemed impossibly remote in libertine Berlin. But it wasn't just that.
The citizens of divided Berlin were marooned on an island outside
of time. Their ability to do what they wanted to do was thwarted by
their historical circumstance. But once they, like the angel, were able
to pass through the Wall, they would leave behind their suspended
existence and enter the swift current of *life*.

When the angel wakes up as a mortal, he strides away from the
Wall with the assurance and the joy of the convalescent. He's so
giddy to have time—to have finite time, time that now counts for
precisely something because its quantity is fixed—that he knows just
how he's going to use it. I'd been so entranced by this image that I'd
missed the crucial prelude, the process by which his desires crystal-
lize and he understands *why* he wants to be free: to share a fleeting
life with his trapeze artist. In moving to Berlin, I was working (or not
working, as the case may have been) on the assumption that a grand
gesture was itself enough—that, in the wake of the decision to up-
root myself, my true desires would emerge to fill the vacuum. In the
nineties Wenders made a sequel to the movie that I'd never seen; the
last thing I wanted to know was what happened next.

But I realize now I should have known what would happen next.
One of the very first things I'd heard upon arrival in Berlin was a line
from the 1920s feuilletonist Karl Scheffler: *Berlin dazu verdammt, im-
merfort zu werden und niemals zu sein.* Berlin is damned always to be-

come and never to be. It was such a seductive idea, that the city would never grow fusty or calcific and that, by proxy, *you* would never become fusty or calcific. And if a place was always becoming, there was no time for belatedness, no great era you'd missed out on, no cost to frittering away your time doing this or that. But we were, I was, so easily seduced, I missed the part about *damned*.

For a while there, at the beginning, starting with that Frisbee panty party, things were genuinely fizzy and I didn't at all mind spending my days just walking around and my nights saying yes to whatever happened to present itself. Just being there felt glorious, or, more than glorious, felt like *enough*. We felt like participants. The cigarettes, those endless stockpiles of cigarettes, and the coffee really did taste different, as they always do in a new place, and drinking coffee and smoking cigarettes felt like sufficient acts. Cigarettes marked off the time. For the few minutes one lasted, you knew exactly what you were doing: you were smoking that cigarette. When it was done, you would figure out what to do next, or you would just light another.

I arrived in Berlin with ten email addresses. The first person I met, Emilie, looked at my list and said I needn't bother emailing the rest; she knew them all, and I'd see them the next day at the big gallery opening. Her friend Alix was coming along, and I'd love her.

We met at Emilie's place first, in a cobbled and uncharacteristically pretty street behind Arkonaplatz. Alix's name was pronounced in the French style, *ah-LEEX*, and she arrived with a duffel bag big enough for a body.

"Where did you just come from?" I asked. "A trip? Hockey practice?"

"Nowhere," Alix said. She's thin and angular and striking, with pointy elbows, long, nervous fingers, and deep-set almond eyes. She has a soft rumpled tide of unruly hair and glows with a cold marmoreal light. She opened the bag and changed in front of us, into a billowy unbelted stained silk dress and Thirty Years' War–vintage combat boots tourniqueted at the ankles.

The economic, cultural, and psychological draws of Berlin—the sheer amounts of time and space that in other cities would be taken up by day jobs or the steady emotional drain of long-standing friendships; the almost religiously shared belief in the possibility of personal reinvention; and an addiction to the promise of the new—made for a robust art scene, at least according to various multilingual periodicals. This opening was at the new outpost of a huge London gallery. The room, or rather the space—nothing took place in something as banal as a room—had the size and character of a well-swept munitions depot, and probably had served as one once. Everything in Berlin happened in a former somewhere: the former sanitation-technology factory in the Ritterstraße, the former pretzel factory in the Prenzlauer Allee, the dome of the former post office in the Oranienburgerstraße that now had a restaurant/club that would only take reservations via text message to a secret number, the former department-store-vault club that was now in the former basement of the former (current?) power station, and of course the former dentist's office, which the white tiles heated up like a sauna. All of these rooms had been liberated from their erstwhile indebtedness to productivity.

In the former munitions depot, people dressed in lab coats angled through the crowd with purpose, and I assumed they were caterers. Once I'd become a little more familiar with art, I'd look back and wonder if they hadn't been part of the installation, or, once I felt as though I knew even more about art, if they'd possibly been *both* caterers *and* part of the installation. After the opening we got into a cab and went to a party in Kreuzberg hosted by a fragile, fey artist in a black feathered boa and his bloodshot gallerist, who was wearing a T-shirt that said "Vulva Vaginal Scent" and chewing on lollipops. I texted a friend in San Francisco, described these guys, and asked if they were anybody I should feel pleased to be at a party with. He wrote: FAMOUS GUY SAATCHI ART CAVE OF DICKS. I tried nonchalantly to ask Emilie what CAVE OF DICKS meant and she said that the guy in the black feathered boa had once made a cave of dicks. Actual live dicks. They hung down from unsuckably distant glory holes in the ceiling.

A sometimes-celebrated young conceptual artist who, I was told, was always on the prowl, found out I was a writer and asked me to help him craft a text message to a chick photographer on assignment for *Vice* in Stockholm. He had thick tortoiseshell glasses and whined with refinement. He assumed I was an art critic, as most everyone did when I introduced myself as a writer, and asked me about magazines.

"Have you ever written for *Domus*? No? But you've heard of *Domus*, right? What about *Precept*? Not that, either? Yeah, it's weird, me neither, I hadn't heard of them until recently. There are just all these magazines, and it's weird, all of them profile me. And you're, like, *what are you*, you know? Are you art magazines or fashion magazines or what, when you profile me?" He named more magazines. "*Uovo. Texte zur Kunst. 032c, Bidoun, Monopol, mono.kultur.* So many. *Texte zur Kunst.*"

Alix swooped in and delivered me onto a roof to smoke, though of course you could smoke inside too. She rolled her eyes and promised that there was more to the art scene here than naming magazines. There were, to be fair, some very fine artists. There was Omer, a gruff Israeli who made multichannel video installations; there was the pretty much just Danish guy who made a big deal about being

Icelandic and had a dirigible hangar and eighty pretty assistants; there was Maxime, a French kid in his early twenties who shot the kind of harsh and tender photographs one might have seen on Nan Goldin's Facebook page; and there was Ignacio, who'd spent ten years in an office job making private artworks out of thousand-cell Excel spreadsheets. However, with the exception of Maxime, who had to stay out late enough for his friends to start tattooing each other so he could take pictures of them to put online, the really good artists didn't seem to go out that much.

"Let's get out of here," Alix said, and took me to Bar Drei, where we sat until seven o'clock in the morning. There was no art space in Berlin more interesting than Bar Drei, and it wasn't an art space at all. It looked like a gallery that had dispensed with the pretext of art entirely in favor of the unimpeachable idea of charging money for the free drinks. It was a fishbowl on a lonely corner behind the Volks-bühne and had no sign save a large "3" stenciled on the door. The bar itself was a trapezoid of black Formica countertop in the center of the room, its vertices rounded off, so sitting at it made you feel as though you were a member of some deliberative post-tribal council of the future. The walls to the street were enormous windows. Everyone went there after the openings, or, as you got smarter about things, you skipped the openings and went straight to Drei, which was like an opening but with chairs. That was all anybody wanted at an open-ing, anyway, were chairs. The only other furnishings at Drei were black spherical bulbs that hung on cords at even intervals over the bar, like soft interrogation lamps; they weren't fixed to anything and the only thing that would get you kicked out was pendulating them. Drei hired mostly artists, both Americans and Germans, as bartend-ers, and part of their art practice—I assumed this had something to do with the art world's recent infatuation with something called "re-lational aesthetics"—was never keeping precise tabs. At the end of the night there was always a tense but pleasurable negotiation about the matter of what to pay.

Drei, I came to see as I became part of it, had an astonishingly regular clientele. Berlin was a city where three-quarters of the population couldn't drag itself out of bed before noon, but if there was one place that made people reliable, it was Drei. It was safe to assume that on any given evening, between the closing of the openings and the opening of the clubs, most of the people I came to know would be there. Some people I knew I saw only there. I met David Levine at Drei; and Zhivago, a beefy and voluble half-Danish, half-Syrian installation artist who grew up between Sacramento, Paris, and Valletta, and spoke at least eight languages, all of them fluently, none of them natively; and Carson, the gentle czar of the international-art-expat scene, who ran a noncommercial space devoted to intersections of art and architecture, dressed in sheer and tasteful varieties of drapery, and was always off to Osaka or Cap d'Antibes or Istanbul for a biennial or panel; and the other David, who painted surgically enhanced women in oils with textbook anatomical precision and spent three hours each day at the gym and seven hours each night smoking; and the style bloggers; and the Norwegian video artists; and, a little while later, the younger guys with the internet-based work. In the summer everyone sat around on the monument outside, the one to all the lost and forgotten monuments, and in the winter the smoke was so thick inside that nobody had to smoke at all.

B UT BAR DREI DIDN'T OPEN until nine thirty at night, which still left the matter of the daytime. As far as doing nothing was concerned, if you couldn't be an artist, you could at least be Jewish; in a way all the Americans in Berlin were honorary Jews. (Many of them were actual Jews.) In the first quarter of the twentieth century the saying used to go that "every Berliner comes from Breslau," from the shtetls of the Pale of Settlement. They also said that "the Jew comes from the East and has no time." He was an avatar of restless commercial modernity. These days the Jew comes from the West and has more time than he knows what to do with. He is an avatar of restless noncommercial modernity. I got by in that first year by writing up cranky little dispatches for a web-based Jewish magazine out of New York that allowed the Jewishness of my content to be glancing.

The main trouble, it seemed to me, was that American Jews and Germans felt as though they needed to say something to one another, but never quite knew what. My mom, a rabbi and a psychoanalyst, came to visit for my first Thanksgiving, and we toured the standard Jewish monuments and memorials. Her feeling about the monuments and the memorials, like her feelings about anything in general, was that it was important to keep the conversation going, that the only way toward healing is through talk. I told her that of course I tended to agree with her, but that the problem in Berlin was that the conversational partners just didn't match up. It often felt as though Germans over a certain age—twenty-five, say—wanted something from you, some sign that everything had finally become okay. I mostly *did* think that everything had become okay, but I never felt entitled to say that. After all, I hadn't any personal connection to the Holocaust. The people who could offer real forgiveness were dead, or they were dying.

The ubiquity of these conversational templates made it impossible to forget I was Jewish. In the States it was something I'd never thought much about, which had always struck my friends as strange. They assumed that I, as the son of two rabbis, would have a strong religious commitment. But my parents had been savvy enough to know that if they made a big deal out of observance, we'd certainly end up defecting; so—with the exception of weekly Shabbat dinners at home and High Holiday attendance and large annual seders—they left it up to us, which meant we'd ended up mostly like normal, suburban, disaffected cultural Jews. Our Jewishness meant Woody Allen and latkes, like anybody else's.

But in Berlin this ambivalent patrimony was foisted upon you. It was immediately clear that Jews had a certain purchase in Berlin; as David Levine let me quote him in one of my first columns, "They really know how to torque it." I decided at a certain point that I liked those Jews best who were a *little* interested in the Holocaust, who liked to talk a few minutes of Holocaust now and then, technical stuff, mostly. These were often academics, like my friend who was writing a dissertation about the few exiles who returned, against their wives' protests, to help rebuild German universities after the war. But a healthy relationship to the Holocaust wasn't the norm. Melodrama was easier, more cheaply satisfying, and it was one way to explain to yourself what you were doing in Germany: just existing there was an act of defiance and strength. Being a Jew in New York is a mark of some considerable banality, but being a Jew in Berlin makes you special. You have the Holocaust in your pocket, the run of a city you rightly deserve.

There was the feeling that the Holocaust got you off the hook, only furthering the idea that you were in Berlin to do just as you pleased, sleep with whomever you felt like, even if she had a boy-friend. It allowed you to be contemptuous of the Germans, gave you an excuse to ignore the local culture. Or you could be obsequious, make a big deal out of how little you cared about the Holocaust, how much you despised the "Shoah industry," how awful the histrionics of Libeskind. Jews like this were ambassadors; they found it in them-selves to congratulate the Germans for having gotten over the past, which often—counterintuitively—meant congratulating themselves for having overcome their own fraught Jewish-American identity. It was a gesture of forgiveness that had everything to do with the forgiver and little to do with the forgiven. It was forgiveness as power, as arrogance.

This was all true, in an inverse way, about the Germans too. They reveled in their powerlessness. For them simply not being a Nazi counted as an accomplishment. For decades they had done really fine work not being Nazis—unlike the Austrians, who were still basically Nazis. The Germans had made not being Nazis into a central plank of their identity, and, as with the Jews, that meant they could be absolved of other ambitions.

As uncomfortable as it made me, it was often easiest just to give in to the sense of Holocaust-related entitlement. Sometimes this took the form of standard guilt. When the synagogue in the Rykestraße reopened to great fanfare, I felt I had to go at least hear Kol Nidre, and I did, though I left after fifteen minutes. Other times it took odder forms, like the habit I developed of walking around listening to Paul Celan read "Todesfuge" on my iPod. But most of the time these feelings were desublimated, more crassly manifested. At a birthday party for an Icelandic artist a young and beautiful German Goth reclined in a bathtub. The bathtub was in the kitchen; it pulled down from a closet between the sink and the stove, like a Murphy bed. She lolled against the dry porcelain and told me she'd just finished her degree in Anti-Semitism Studies, with a focus on the post-Shoah relationship between West Germany and Israel. My friend Max was tall and handsome and obviously Jewish and made a habit of this sort of thing, and I pulled him aside to ask for the encouraging advice I knew he'd give. "The only way we—Germans and Jews alike—will heal these old wounds," he said, "is if we take seriously our duty, difficult as it may often be, to take women like that home."

. . .

T HE PERSON who pulled off the bohemian thing most con-
vincingly—that is, neither self-consciously nor apologetically—
was Emilie, which was funny, because Emilie was also the only one
of us who had an actual job—in fact, a whole series of them. The rest
of us had come to Berlin to escape the authority of work, but Emilie
hustled. She was always on the phone, screaming at someone in German customs to free up a six-foot carved totem from Uttar Pradesh
in time for an opening that night; or running a gallery while her boss
languished in Moabit Prison on charges of fraud (later acquitted); or
curating a genuinely good group show in a former brewery, featuring
work by some of our friends and later written up on the style-and-
art-blog circuit by other of our friends. But she also managed to
party as though it were her job. She worked harder than anybody
I knew.

Emilie's life may have been in a constant state of crisis, but it was
never an *existential* crisis. They were practical crises. Some of them
might have landed her in bureaucratic labyrinths or trapped her on
Baltic islands with street-art-dealing aristocrats, but none of them
ever seemed to make her wonder *why* she was in Berlin, which was
something she could be specific about: she sold art. One of the nice
things about Berlin was that you didn't have to be specific if you
didn't feel like it. If somebody asked you what you were up to in
town, you could say you were an artist or just interested in art and
leave it at that. They didn't need to know anything more, didn't have
to worry you were withholding anything, because in part what you
were communicating was that you probably weren't a hundred percent sure what you were doing there. But your erstwhile interrogator
almost certainly wasn't sure what she was doing there, either, so everybody could get away with being broad-brush about things. This

obtained in general. Part of the liberation of Berlin in Berlin was the permission to be vague.

Emilie was different, though. She was good at the specific thing she did during the day, knew the right ways to talk to artists and collectors. She paid taxes, had been audited, had an expensive couch she tried not to get too many cigarette holes in. She was also loyal, and loyal in a way nobody in Berlin ever seemed to try very hard to be. She had principles, made a point of never sleeping with anybody her friends had slept with, and never cheated. Rarely cheated. All of these things were of a piece. The rest of us, at a certain point, began to worry that we were going out too much, felt mildly concerned that we were somehow betraying our true selves by not feeling held to account, not getting enough done—enough of *what* done we could rarely say—but Emilie never had that problem. She got done during the day what she had to get done and she did at night what she wanted to do. She was comfortable with her desire for some things because she was obligated to do others; she was able to oblige some things because she desired others. She bore the same relationship to us that Micah bore to the friends he had in Shanghai—shortly after I abandoned him he put in for a transfer overseas—who were always arguing about whose Mandarin had the best tones. Micah just went to the factory in Suzhou or Zhuhai or Taiyuan and got on with it.

Emilie, so confident about how she spent her time, was the closest thing we had to a true doyenne, and she could have posted up at Bar Drei with the rest of us. But she was cut out for demimonde grandeur, and was delighted to include anybody who wanted in. For a while Emilie dated an endearingly feckless East German named Kevin, a sweet case study in the most extreme psychological effects of the nanny state. Kevin was notionally a DJ, but sometimes he was so busy partying he would forget to play music; when he remembered, though, everybody had a good time, and even when he forgot, it was okay. At the beginning we'd hang out in his studio—he was also, notionally, a photographer—and he'd spin records. He and his studio-mate called the place the Bernsteinzimmer, the "Amber Room," after the alleged hoard of still-missing Nazi gold. His DJ name was Kevin9/11 until Emilie forced him to change it. Then he called himself Kevolution. Emilie sighed and gave up.

They had a pretty good relationship for a while, one mostly based on mutual respect for the intensity with which the other could party. Their terms of endearment were party related. *«Du bist das Partymäuschen»*, they would say with affectionate accuracy. "You are the little party mouse."

At four thirty one December weekday morning, at the close of what felt like my first semester in Berlin, we left Kevolution behind at the Bernsteinzimmer to play or not play records as he continued to see fit. It was Alix's birthday and we were near the Prenzlauer Berg–Pankow border. Emilie had heard about a new club, and six or ten of us were wandering around in the chilly dark looking for it. As we walked past one of the entrances to the Mauerpark, a disputably green zone where a strip of no-man's-land once was, she noticed a single votive candle on a sidewalk. She swerved into the black lane. Someone asked where she thought she was going.

"There's a party in here," she said, gesturing ahead of us into the dark. Someone asked how she knew.

"Did you not see the votive candle? Whenever you see votive candles, you follow them, and they take you to a rave." We followed the votive candles a kilometer into the park. The tree branches stitched a starless canopy against the black sky. Somebody picked his or her way along in heels. We tried to turn back.

"Do whatever you like," Emilie said, "but I'm going to this party."

"This is bonkers," Alix said, and shivered.

We walked for twenty more minutes, rounded a corner, and

came through a copse to a Weimar-era toolshed. Inside there was a spectacular rave, with several rooms of music, an enormous amount of barely nibbled Turkish *Fladenbrot*, hundreds of people.

"This is bonkers," Alix said again, and we went to dance. We left Emilie there at eight thirty in the morning and took the M10 tram in a wide arc back to our side of town. The streets were just beginning to steep in the squalid sub-lactic half-light of a winter Thursday. Commuters read nationalist tabloids of anti-immigrant sentiment. Alix folded herself under my arm and fell asleep, I had nothing to do for the rest of the day, and life to me felt almost unbearably full.

ALIX AND I LIVED in the same neighborhood for a while, on the east side of Kreuzberg near the river, and we would sit outside the Turkish bakery and watch the elevated orange U-Bahn grind by as we shooed finches from our crumbs. Alix was probably the smartest, certainly the most alluring, and probably the strangest person I knew in Berlin. She talked in big impressionistic clouds and then gesticulated in their vicinity to disperse them. She was in the middle of applying to grad school and was writing about art; she wrote about the new gallery shows each month for a magazine out of London. She was one of the very few critics around who said anything interesting about what she saw, though she could also be pretty opaque, about art and in general.

She was American but most people thought she was French and she didn't discourage that. She wore ballet slippers that Maxime, the young crooked-grinned amateur-tattooing photographer had given her, and a very tight and short lacy alabaster one-piece we called the "ivory TK," after the typesetter's code for a descriptor to come later. No proper word did ever come later, but somehow the infinitely deferred description made sense. Alix went on to acquire a denim TK, which was like a cross between a tent and a jean onesie, and then several other TKs, many of them from the closet of the Long Island home of her crazy aunt Terry, a high school art teacher and the relative she most longed to resemble.

Alix had lexical idiosyncrasies, told hammy old jokes, dazzled, and made oblique references. Her basic reaction to the world was to call it bonkers. It was hard, in fact, to spend as much time with her as I did—or any time at all with her, really—and not become convinced that everything was indeed bonkers, not least of all Alix. She was nearly incompetent logistically, could talk in whole paragraphs about trends in analytical Marxism but could only under very unusual circumstances catch a train. She'd ended up in Berlin, in fact, due to logistical mishaps. She'd been at Oxford, then worked as a labor organizer in London and overstayed her visa. One February she came to Berlin, about six months before I did, to draw some panels for an opera—she was most relaxed when she was drawing, which she does quite well—and was deported upon her attempted return to the UK. They'd made her sit in a deportation lounge with an entire Cypriot village. She'd come back to town and spent a year always on the verge of leaving. Neither of us had any furniture.

Her place was in a nonresidentially zoned converted factory with old concrete walls painted the color of newer concrete. It was thousands of square feet and nobody was ever sure how many people, or which ones, were living there at any given time. Sometimes Alix would come home and there would be new walls blocking out fresh rooms. Alix's favorite roommate, Thilo, was an East German whose family had escaped to the West when he was a kid—they'd been separated during their flight, though, and he'd gone years without seeing them; he didn't like to talk about it—and he was now a makeup artist. He did high-end fashion campaigns for magazines and TV commercials, cut hair, and sold drugs when he had them, often to the people whose hair he was cutting. It wasn't ever clear if it was an outrageously overpriced haircut with complimentary drugs, or a standard price for drugs along with a free haircut. The drug-haircut thing was only to support his real passion, though, which was working on splatter films. There was only one bathroom, and it had a shower on a faux-marble pedestal and a high-backed antique couch in it. An unlit air shaft lined with decapitated mannequins ran from behind the shower to Alix's room. You could hear the U-Bahn trains screeching around the bend in the tracks before they disappeared over the bridge.

Alix often communicated via annotated press release. She'd forward the emails she got from the galleries and highlight sentences like this: "By exploring a system in which the traditional Hegelian linear progression of time is replaced by one that is cyclical and self-reflexive—in which the mechanics of chronology are rendered inoperative—we approach a logic of preemptive action and calculated risk that has taken hold of Western politics at large." That one was for a group show called "Back to the Future," which was based on the Robert Zemeckis film of the same name. More than anything, though, the press releases were interested in the French philosopher Jacques Rancière, and frequently something called "object sexuality." It was unclear if anybody had actually read Rancière, but they knew that he had written a famous essay called "The Emancipated Spectator," and that phrase in and of itself was some comfort. Nobody liked to think of himself as a fettered spectator.

Object sexuality, perhaps relatedly, described people who fell in love with, and sometimes married, objects. The most famous of these people, their de facto international spokeswoman, had once married the Berlin Wall, and a young Norwegian video artist made a haunting film about it for a Berlin Biennial. The film was shown on a loop

in a trailer in an empty lot where the death strip had been, and Alix
and I jogged through the late-spring snow to see it at least half a
dozen times. A few months later we went to see the spokeswoman
talk, and someone asked her how she knew the Berlin Wall loved her
back. "I do not hold him to human standards," she said, "just like I
would never expect him to hold me to object standards." Everyone
else nodded in agreement and Alix dug her nails into my palm to
keep from falling off her seat.

This was around the close of my first year in Berlin, when the
novelty had largely worn off and the cigarettes were once again just
cigarettes. I no longer wrote home when I was invited to a party in
an abandoned S-Bahn station or underneath a stalled produce truck.
That early shipwrecked period—when everybody you met had a
history you neither knew nor cared much about, when all that mattered was that you were in it together—had come to a close, the press
releases and "emancipated spectator" and "object sexuality" had
started to seem less transgressive than ridiculous, and among the few
things that felt real and important to me were Alix's conspiratorial
nails in my hand.

Sometimes Alix would disappear for a few days at a time, sometimes with her boyfriend, sometimes not. Her phone was always
broken, or it had no credit on it, and she was never particularly forth-
coming about where she'd been when we weren't together. She'd hint,
leave wineglasses out on the table, happen to mention having seen
dawn in a strange part of the city. This was a sort of obliqueness that
made me anxious in a way I found familiar. I've never been good at
waiting for people, wondering where they are and when and if they'll
want to hang out again. When I was a kid my dad used to disappear
for whole weekends, referring vaguely to new friends he'd met in
New York that maybe he'd tell me about one day. Then he'd come

home in a black mood and expect us—Micah and me—to drop whatever we were doing and attend to his demands.

But my dad's gestures were real, and Alix's were at least in part my own creation. His seemed caught between secret and invitation, or rather they were invitations to know that there were secrets, stuff you had to know you didn't know about. Indications of another life that didn't involve you. As a kid I did not know how to ask about this secret life to which he so often alluded.

One of the things I wanted out of Berlin, or rather out of the provisional life I was leading there, was that it might make me into somebody who didn't have to ask, somebody who could accept a vague response without pressing the issue. Someone who was strong enough to allow for privacy or uncertainty without taking it personally. One problem was that it worked too well: I genuinely didn't care about the secret lives of most of the people I met there. Amid the clamor of the shipwreck, you take people at face value: you accept their broad-brush reasons for doing what they do, being who they are, because all you have together is right now.

Perhaps this is why in those years I was always getting involved with unavailable women. I thought I might find a way to feel intimate without the relentless accounting that was my custom. One Sunday afternoon I slept with a friend of mine and walked her along the canal, past the noisy swans on the hospital knoll, to meet her boyfriend. We were half an hour late but we didn't rush. She told me she couldn't wait until I had a girlfriend and we were late to meet *her*; I said when I had a girlfriend we would no longer be sleeping together, and she let go of my hand. I put it in my pocket. I'd never done anything like it before, never thought of myself as somebody whom an attached woman might even *want* to sleep with. I'd always seen myself as a husband, not a lover. I'd never wanted to be the person who

cheated—it was important to me that I'd never cheated on anyone—
but I certainly liked being party to the deception. I liked the know-
ingness. Or, rather, I liked feeling as though I was the secret itself.

When we got to the boyfriend's apartment he was outside, looking at his watch, and all I could think about was whether there was
enough light left to go running. Feeling like a lover rather than a
husband made me want to go for a long run, and then I thought I'd
have a beer by myself at the canal-side club with the floating rafts. I
didn't look down on her boyfriend; I just didn't think anything of him
at all. They were going on vacation somewhere for some amount of
time. I'd see her again, or I wouldn't, and we'd sleep together, or we
wouldn't; I didn't feel like I minded either way. Some months later,
six or eight, she and I sat at the terrible faux American diner across
from the Sony Center, Berlin's pathetic answer to Times Square, and
complained about the nachos. She said she didn't think we should
spend nights together anymore but wanted to stay friends. That
sounded fine to me. We went to see some American romcom across
the street. We stayed friends.

But when that feeling of consequence crept in, the need for detailed explanations returned. One day at the Badeschiff, the swimming pool sunk into the river and buffered with a fake beach that all
the visitors from New York liked to write home about, Alix raised
her sunglasses to read to me from a press release. It mentioned that
the artist had "tattoos that lead us to fancy that he descends from the
Incas or else some historical family that fought against colonialism."
Alix did not even bother to roll her eyes.

Sometimes she would go on studio visits to conduct interviews.
It was her attempt to do an end run around the people who wrote the
press releases, but all too often the press releases had been leaked to
the artists in advance, so the artists knew precisely what to say about
the relationship between colonialism and their tattoos. Whenever

she went on studio visits I thought of a line of Geoff Dyer's: "For the writer the artist's studio is, essentially, a place where women undress. Van Gogh may have said that 'painting and fucking a lot don't go together' but the smell of white spirits and paint is suggestive of nothing else so much as afternoon sex."

Alix tied slow bows of black ballet-slipper ribbon around her ankles and calves. She got up from her towel, put her copy of Jerry Cohen's *Karl Marx's Theory of History* away in her duffel bag, and said she had a studio visit to make.

"So, what's the deal?" I said in an attempt to be casual, in an attempt not to care. "There are canvases against the walls and the complete works of Rancière in messy piles and then the artist makes love to you on the floor?"

She was getting on her bike, put off by my ugly posturing. "No," she said as she began to ride away without looking back, "on the bed."

THERE WAS SOME PRETENSE, in Berlin, of sexual adventure as part of the never-ending audition in recklessness. A close friend, Jordan, complained that his cohort, all the pretty young ubiquitous art boys, had developed an orgy habit, and that he wanted no part in it. He was conservative, he said, and did not like to sleep with his friends; he just wanted a monogamous relationship with a nice man. He was twenty-three and modeled part-time; he spoke seven or eight languages, including Arabic and Polish and Japanese, and I was constantly telling him to quit his gallery job and get into a linguistics PhD program, where he belonged.

Jordan seemed to have a healthy, unconflicted relationship to his sexuality, and we spent a lot of time talking about my dad. I told him that the main thing that had changed since my father came out was the innuendo. Actually, "innuendo" isn't the right word, as it implies subtlety. There are many things for which you, or, more specifically, I, could reasonably blame my dad—deceit, say, or the sustained fantasy that a decade of complete and utter irresponsibility was the least the world owed him—but subtlety, especially about sex, is not one of them.

When I was a kid, there had been signs—mostly in his flickering moods—that he had another life. After he came out, everything was explicit. When I was in my early and mid-twenties, during the periods in which we were talking to each other, I would come through New York and we would meet for dinner or a drink in Chelsea. We would walk past a bar with blacked-out windows and a studded leathery stegosaural bouncer and he would roll his eyes and say something like, "Oh, God, the Rawhide. You really gotta keep your back to the wall in there."

These stories made good anecdotes to trot out for my friends and girlfriends. They worked because they relied on the idea that I might have been expected to feel bad but instead took in the whole thing with detached amusement. My wacky gay-rabbi dad and his crude hijinks, I would imply, as if I were starring in the most progressive of sitcoms. I did not experience detached amusement. The innuendo always felt to me like bragging—bragging about the open eroticism of the life he led now, in contrast to his old, straitjacketed existence at home. This was, to some extent, the transparency I'd always wanted from him, but now it only made me feel lonely.

In turn I made a big deal about my endurance. The first time he took me to a gay bar, a New Jersey mansion dive in teak paneling and threadbare velour with the characteristically unimaginative gay-bar name of the Raven, I asked for a beer, he bought me a Cosmo, and then he walked off to greet some friends he and Brett had met at a club in Fort Lauderdale. I stood in the corner and sipped my Cosmo—I figured he was watching out for my carb intake—and did my best to avoid eye contact with what I was later told were called trolls. The next morning I called my then girlfriend, the one I'd hung around in San Francisco for, to complain about how exposed I'd felt under so much perverse late-middle-aged male scrutiny. "Welcome," she said, "to what it's like to be a woman *every single day*." I told that story for years, and the moral I made of her punch line was that everybody feels vulnerable sometimes and you ought to just get over yourself. In Berlin I went to gay bars all the time—which wasn't hard, as in Berlin even the convenience stores often felt like de facto gay bars—to prove that I'd gotten over myself. For me this was the point of my dad's Rawhide references: Get over yourself.

When I talked to Jordan about this, I was both looking for sympathy and trying to needle him; I was in part proud of my dad's candor, his ability to be so unashamed of his desire, his apparent lack of hang-ups. "Jordan," I said, "aren't you selling out the revolutionary promise of homosexuality? What about the idea that the ethics of sexual loyalty is a hetero hang-up your kind has gloriously overcome in favor of the ethics of betrayal?" What about Genet—what about his sense that the traditional monogamous relationship was "something of a protection racket," as Adam Phillips put it in a review of an Edmund White memoir. I promise to pretend as though you're the only thing that could possibly make me happy, it says, and you promise the same thing, and we'll surely make each other miserable. Genet's counterproposal on behalf of his generation of homosexuals? An intimacy of anonymity. His idea, Phillips writes, was that "so-called relationships were the place where one needn't take anything personally."

Jordan was unfazed. "You just say that because you only fuck girls with boyfriends and you want to find some intellectual reason to think that's okay, and because you know you yourself are dying for exactly that protection racket. You can't stop looking for the perfect girl. Anyway, as far as gay people my age are concerned, what you're talking about is the big problem with what your dad's generation did to our generation. They grew up trying to be straight, so when they could finally fuck men, they went all crazy about it, and they still can't stop fucking, and they've saddled us with the idea that gay life should always be this creepy free-for-all of fucking. But I've been gay since I knew how to talk, and all I want is my boyfriend and my dog, Miss Tilly, and a nice duvet and some DVDs. If you want to call that a protection racket, go right ahead, doll face. It's what I want."

But there was still a part of me that felt as though I had to grow up and into the ethics of betrayal, that part of coming to Berlin was getting over petty jealousy and the childish desire for an impossibly complete presence, and what felt so terrible so often wasn't the old sadness and jealousy but the guilt about still being hung up in the same old ways.

T HE ONLY ARTIST who made work that seemed to address, in a serious and useful way, what was going on in Berlin—the absence of authority, the tyranny of desire—was David Levine. David was tall and muscular and perpetually stubbled, his jaundiced eyes open wide in frequent disbelief, and he spoke with a dark, feathery rasp. In summer he wore frayed wifebeaters and in winter thermal undershirts and motorcycle boots with the ringed trusses clipped off. You could imagine him smoking while working out, smoking while swimming. We had friends in common in New York, as everybody else did, and he had impressive and successful ex-girlfriends.

David was an experimental theater director and conceptual artist who thought the two worlds had something to learn from each other. Performance art had given up on the idea of rehearsal because it thought that authenticity could only derive from spontaneity, from unself-consciousness, which could make a performance feel uncanny and novel. But the authenticity part is always a red herring, David used to say. Well-acted, well-directed, and well-rehearsed theater could be just as moving, or as alienating, as any given performance-art tantrum. If you rehearse, if you employ all the traditional techniques the theater uses to create credibility, and only *then* take away the scaffolding, you could perhaps make something that would split the difference. Art doesn't want to be seen as trying very hard, but the trick of the theater is that sometimes it's only when you're trying as hard as you possibly can that you seem effortless. David practiced forms of ritualized improvisation, or improvised ritual.

His first really big piece—called *Bauerntheater*, it had been written up at great length in the "Arts & Leisure" section of the *Times*—closed shortly before I arrived in town. He'd rehearsed an actor in the role of a potato farmer in a previously untranslated Heiner Müller play about East German agricultural collectivization in the fifties, then put the guy in a field about an hour outside of Berlin and had him plant potatoes in full costume in the regional style of the day. He'd gotten a large grant from the German cultural ministry to do this, and it had gotten him a lot of good press. An arts journalist friend of his wrote yet another thing about Berlin artists for a Manhattan magazine, and the big pull-quote was David's. It concerned the differences between being an artist in Berlin and New York. "In New York," he said, "if you're not making a hundred grand and sleeping with a lesbian, you're nothing."

At Bar Drei one night after the story came out, he seemed distracted and I asked him why. "I'm worried," he said, "that the story is going to piss off the lesbian I sleep with when I'm in New York."

Alix put her cigarette out. "And I wonder if it'll also piss off the German cultural ministry that made *Bauerntheater* possible by giving you a hundred grand."

. . . .

D AVID LEVINE'S NEXT PROJECT after *Bauerntheater*, the first one I was around for, was called *The Gallery Will Be Relocating over the Summer*. It was a fake art opening that took its name from the fact that the real gallery that hosted it was supposed to be relocating over the summer. Then the gallerist had a kid with a young Spanish artist, started posting about the Andalusian weather on Facebook, and was never heard from again. The fake opening was a final project for David's students in a class he was teaching at the Freie Universität. Each student spent an entire semester studying the habits and affects of an art-world person—an artist, curator, gallerist—and showed up in character for the performance at the gallery, in the Brunnenstraße. All the newer galleries back then were in the Brunnenstraße and they would coordinate their monthly openings in a way that turned the street into a block party. These were my favorite evenings of that first year—drinking free beer in the nine p.m. sunlight, parading around in the street, knowing that everybody you knew in the whole city was on that block and was going to an afterparty where everyone was there and nobody ever left—though the art was rarely very accomplished. David liked to say that the Brunnenstraße was where everybody got a chance. He didn't mean that cynically.

"The most important thing to remember," he said to me through the smoke at Bar Drei the day before his fake show was set to really open, "is that every artist is always making the best art he or she possibly can. You can call it bad art, if you want, and most of it is bad the way most of anything is bad, but there's no grace in impugning the motivations behind it."

I felt greedy and often impatient for these lopsided moments with David, moments of instruction and clarifying tenderness and even the occasional reprimand. Over time I tried harder not to press him into a vigilance he was neither interested in nor prepared for, and I was eager for chances to reciprocate, to show him I was just as interested in friendship as I was in oversight. So I was happy when David asked Alix and me to write the fake press release for his fake show. We took the job very seriously, spent hours outside at the Turkish bakery working on it, but in the end our draft wasn't all that distinguishable from the real press release.

The fake opening had fake-real art on the walls, inspired by the real art of the characters under study, and real free booze, and a non-negotiable locked-door duration of four hours. At seven p.m. David bicycle-locked the front door of the gallery. The only person inside in character as herself was an arts reporter in town, a friend of a friend whom we'd introduced to David at Bar Drei. He'd invited her to appear in the piece as herself, and she was flattered. "You're like Peter Falk in *Wings of Desire!*" I said. She frowned.

The real opening, i.e., the opening of *David's* show, was in the courtyard outside, where we milled and drank the same free booze the fake people were real-drinking inside. Occasionally we looked in through the window to see what the fake attendees were up to. What they were up to looked largely the same as what we were up to, which was part of the point, but we were afraid that they were having a better time. After all, they had been licensed by hard work and careful direction to spend a few hours being different people, which meant they were drunkenly rolling around on the floor and wrecking the artwork and making the most of it. This made an even better point. We were ourselves at a real event, which meant our hearts weren't in it, not the way theirs were. We were freer, but they were surer of their roles and we couldn't help but look over our shoulders at them.

The night was warm and there were a lot of free drinks and the after-party sounded increasingly auspicious and it had been a while, I realized, since I'd had such a nice time out at yet another art function in Berlin. The doors to the fake opening were unlocked at eleven. The New York arts reporter playing herself came out and held up her BlackBerry. Someone we knew in New York, or someone some of us knew and others had heard of, had gotten three-quarters of a million dollars for his novel, which apparently included whimsical drawings. This was somehow not surprising, that news of ambition and focus and whimsy-related success in New York had come via the one New York media reporter playing herself inside a well-directed fake art opening in Berlin. It was the real toad in the imaginary garden.

The real news from the fake opening had seemed an ill omen. I'd been in Berlin for a year and had no better idea what I was doing there than I had when I arrived; the mere lifting of constraint had not infused my life with purpose, and I did not feel any freer than I had in San Francisco. I'd come to Berlin at least in part to escape what I saw as a kind of generational malaise, and had discovered there a slightly different kind of generational malaise. It had simply become a nonstop moral holiday, and we lived in it, and there was always someone in town from New York to show off for. This is an alternative to waiting in line for cupcakes, was the implication. Two friends visited and had a threesome with a tied-up Swede. Another friend came and cheated on her boyfriend with a twenty-one-year-old male model who was writing his undergraduate thesis on Heidegger. They came to see dawn and to cheat and we took them out and in the process allowed ourselves a great time we didn't have to take full responsibility for. But as time went on we felt less and less great about it. We finished the night at seven in the morning, long after the sun had risen too early and too hot over the river at Bar25, at eight in the wintry morning coming out of Berghain long before the sun painted its gray on gray in the slushy sky, at ten in the morning at the Mauerpark flea market before you've been home to sleep, at eleven in the morning taking a regional train to a crummy Baltic beach to doze it off. The visitors were always ready to go home after an amazing week. It was their vacation but it was our life, and it no longer seemed like what I'd wanted. At that time there was a song lyric that did not stop running through my mind: "You spent the first five years trying to get with the plan / and the next five years trying to be with your friends again." I wanted old friends and Micah and meaningful work and to sleep with a woman I was in love with and to wake up in the morning. I wanted the innocent life I'd had in San Francisco but this time having had the experiences I'd had in Berlin.

Even the spaces felt different to me. I no longer saw the aesthetic appeal of the postindustrial. We'd been pleased that the dilapidated buildings still stood, thought that the ruination—as opposed to Belle Époque elegance, or geometries of steel and glass—was a mark of our cold grit. But once things started to go bad, it seemed to me that we'd let the past persist merely to burlesque it. We sent up its quaint striving with athletic derangement. We kept the past around not for the sake of continuity but for the sake of rebuke. For a few months when I was out on my *Middlemarch*-avoiding walks I was drawn to the posters at bus stops asking for donations to shore up the Kaiser-Wilhelm-Gedächtniskirche. It had been built by the second kaiser in honor of the first one, and was mostly wrecked during the war. Since then it had been fastidiously maintained in its ruination, that it might stand as a warning. Every time it got too ruined, they had to beg the public for money to fix it up a little. It was a lot of effort to preserve an ideal state of decay. The effort involved seemed so pointless.

"I think I'm having a crisis," I said to David as we walked to his after-party. I felt sheepish about casting him once more in the mentor role, especially on the night of his big success, but it was probably exactly that big success that made me feel I needed so much from him.

David fished a cigarette out of his pocket and lit it for me. "Of course you're having a crisis. Look, everybody is having a crisis all of the time. You either feel like you're too tied up and thus prevented from doing what you want to do, or you feel like you're not tied up enough and have no idea what you want to do. The only thing that allows us any relief is what we tend to call *purpose*, or what I think about in terms of direction."

You deal with the crisis that is life by obeying some authority you despise, the authority of money or the authority of relationships or grad school or the authority of cupcakes, and in that case you're freaked out all the time because you feel like you're always being thwarted, or you deal with it by renouncing all authority, and in that case you're freaked out because you're entirely thrown back upon yourself all of the time in a way pretty much nobody can handle. The main problem with desires, Berlin made clear, is that they're not nearly as authoritative as we wish they were.

A sense of purpose allows for both the comfort of obedience and the dignity of autonomy. It represents relief from feeling servile and relief from having to worry at every moment about what we think we might want right now, what costs we're willing to pay. The question is: How can you find some structure that allows you to begin to understand what you want without forcing you to pay constant attention to the fluctuation of endlessly conflicting desires? And how can you realize that, whatever the situation, you're probably already getting what you want on some level, whether you know it or not?

"Everybody is in a crisis all the time," David finished, "and everybody, at the same time, under some sort of cover, is also pretty much doing what they want. Life *is* the crisis of doing what you want.

Which means: Hold people accountable, but try to be understanding. Nobody gets off the hook just because they're in a crisis, but you can have sympathy for them as they hang on it. The hook, I mean." We reached the bar and he lit another cigarette.

Just before we entered the bar, he turned to me one last time.

"You are in a crisis, and you are also doing what you want."

EVENTUALLY OUR CRISES BEGAN to resolve themselves, or maybe it was just that we'd grown bored of these particular crises and were ready for different ones. After one long week of inventive partying, Emilie called Kevolution from their apartment and asked when he would be home. It was ten to midnight on a Friday. "I'll be home in twenty minutes," Kevin said. He walked in at ten on Monday morning. Emilie threw her glass of orange juice at his head, narrowly missing an Alec Soth print worth ten thousand dollars, and asked where the fuck he'd been.

«*Unterwegs*», he said. Under way.

Emilie broke up with him then, or maybe it was a little later, and Kevin was furious. He took back all he'd said before. «*Du bist nicht das Partymäuschen. Du bist eine Scheiß-Ami-Bitch*». It was cruel, but he knew he'd lost something good. She moved on to a guy with a job, a guy who could afford to go on actual vacations instead of trying to live in one.

Alix, for her part, was also moving on, going to graduate school in New York and some measure of stability and routine that, she feared, would drive her bonkers. She kept her place in Berlin, though, just in case. At the time I was happy for her and sad for myself. I'd thought I'd gotten used to the transience of the place, the constant new crashes and rescues that changed the demography of the shipwreck, but I hadn't. At least not in her case.

Right around the time she was leaving they were closing the Building, some sort of artist-run space with wishy pedagogical ideas in the back basement of a supermarket wedged in between some East German tower blocks. For their final weekend of events, the people who ran the Building had invited their constituents to take an hour and do whatever they wished with it. Alix called her hour "The Event at the Building: Pedagogy as Potentiality in Reverse" and wrote a press release for it. It was to be listed as a lecture with a voguish description. The audience would file in and Alix would hand out boards and paper and charcoal and present a live model, and the people who expected a lecture on Rancière would have an hour of drawing from life.

Unfortunately for Alix, the Building's press release, which Alix had long relied upon for its inanity, was in this case perversely clear: it went ahead and revealed the surprise. Alix tried to cancel the class, no longer saw a point, but her nude model was insistent. Alix wrote me a frustrated email. "The model won't *not* get naked. It's part of her art practice, she says." Until then nobody knew the nude art model had an art practice.

The nude model with the new art practice asked if I would document her nudity textually as part of a future project she was considering, on intimacy. Weren't there going to be photographers there, I asked, not to mention a whole room of people drawing your nude figure? Yes, she said. But she wanted a *text*. Sort of like a live blog without the internet.

I shouldn't have been at all surprised, but by then I was so tired. Everything in the art world required extensive documentation. They didn't believe in preparation, but they did believe in proof. I wondered then if the difference between people who believed in preparation and those who believed in proof, like the antagonism David described between those who believed in rehearsal and those who believed in spontaneity, wasn't the difference between those who worked constantly for something that would endure and those who sought to capture something that occurred once. In Berlin photographs were taken of performances. Writers wrote about the photographs. Bloggers posted about the writers. Installation artists installed pieces about the bloggers. Performance artists performed in the installations, hoping to get photographed. Photographers shot pictures of the bloggers, hoping to get in magazines. The Berlin Wall had existed primarily on television and in magazines. Berlin galleries existed primarily in *Frieze* and the social diary of Artforum.com.

Despite the confusion of the uncharacteristically lucid press release for the Event at the Building, most of the people were somehow surprised by the revelation that the fake lecture was going to be a real drawing class, which led one to believe that Alix was actually the only person reading these press releases in the first place. Everybody took it seriously. These were people who were very comfortable with their spectacular emancipation, but it had been years since they'd drawn from life, if they ever had. Everyone was quiet and absorbed and Alix shone like her crazy aunt Terry as she directed the changes in pose. She was immensely pleased.

At Bar Drei afterward we all felt clearer than we had in some time. David was inspired, and talked about his own version of a drawing class. He said he always thought about going back to actual theater directing, if he could do what he wanted. We ran out of cigarettes and walked out, past the Volksbühne, where he'd recently taken me to see Frank Castorf's version of *A Streetcar Named Desire*. He called it *Endstation Amerika*—the Williams estate refused to let him use the name—and it lasted five hours. Kowalski was a grizzled Polish biker with roots in Solidarity. There was nudity and barbershop-quartet

Britney Spears, and at one point Mitch forced Blanche to read off some stage directions from the supertitles. The actors may have been drunk. We'd both found it a shade too long.

"You know what the single most radical thing I could do in the Berlin theater would be?" David asked as he looked up at the stolid engaged columns of the Volksbühne. "I'd put on an old-fashioned naturalistic staging, in full period costume, of *The Cherry Orchard*."

But pulling that off was going to take some time and a lot of preparation. The last show David put up while I still had an apartment in Berlin was called *Hopefuls*. It consisted of a few thousand headshots and cover letters seeking actor's representation, which he plastered with hidden logic on his gallery's walls. The point of all this was to represent the actor's commitment to plasticity, to potential. One of the cover letters said that the actor had been told his range extended from Hayden Christensen to Halle Berry. This was because he was, he went on, "ethically dubious." These were people campaigning vigorously for direction, and we needed to see them as gauche because we so acutely felt the same way. They were all doing the best they could to do something they cared about, and very few of them would succeed. We were doing as little as possible and pretended being in Berlin made us better than them. I stood in the room full of headshots and each one seemed to say, "I must change my life."

We took out our frustrations on Berlin's attempts to resemble New York. A lounge called Tausend opened up under the S-Bahn tracks near the Friedrichstraße station. *Tausend* means "thousand," and it was not at all a Berlin name. A Berlin name would be "One" or "Two" or, at the very most, "Six." Tausend also had a strict door policy, which was unusual. The night it opened David sent me a series of texts. "SHOCKINGLY NY 90S." "I'M SITTING ON A GRAY FELT BANQUETTE." "BLACK LEATHER CAR COATS

OVER WHITE V-NECK T-SHIRTS, AND ONE PORK-PIE HAT." "JAMIROQUAI."

The whole point of Berlin was that there was nobody from college who worked in finance and asked if you rented or owned, nobody who blogged about media gossip, and no places like Tausend. Which meant that when a place like Tausend opened, it suggested that perhaps Berlin was *over*. But then Emilie would take us to the Damensalon, a former cosmetician's in Neukölln with a bare interior, a plywood bar, and a vast subbasement dance floor, and it was clear that nothing was over, that the very idea of a place being *over*, just like the very idea of a place being *hip* in the first place, was absurd. It had everything to do with the person saying it and nothing to do with the place itself.

What the word "over" really means is that your expectations of a place, your fantasies of who you might have become there, have been confounded by the persistence of you. You want a place to be strong enough to resist the patterns you force onto it, and there are places that can do that for a while. As it became increasingly clear that my era of inconsequence was not going to end in Berlin, as I'd anticipated, and as it had for Wenders's angel, with the new taste of coffee—with, that is to say, the ability to feel as though what was in front of me was enough, the strength to sit alone in a room and not wonder what was going on in other, secret, more crowded rooms—I began to hope that it might end *with* Berlin. If moving to Berlin had not left me altered, alert and grateful and decisive, perhaps moving away would. Or perhaps just moving with direction would, waking up each day knowing I had committed myself to spending daylight walking as far as I could toward Santiago de Compostela. I didn't actually care about what it meant to arrive there, or at least not the way a religious Catholic might. The word "pilgrim" comes from the

Latin *per agrum*, "beyond the fields," and for a long time in a lot of places it was pretty much the only pretext you had to leave home. I didn't need a pretext to leave home, but I did want an excuse to have a series of structured days. I thought it might be a redemptive exercise in pointless direction, and I hoped in the end it might give me a better sense for where I stood.

Part II

CAMINO

I T'S JUST AFTER SIX in the morning on the tenth of June, around the time that the sunlight through the windows of the clubs in Berlin gets too enterprising to ignore, when Tom and I follow our first yellow arrow en route to the end of the world. The yellow arrows are dashed out in spray paint every ten or fifteen feet. Sometimes they indicate turns; mostly they just remind you to keep going. There are far more of them than any pilgrim would really need. Right away we begin to gesture at the hidden and the faded ones, worry when it seems like we haven't seen one in a while.

The arrows free you from needing a map or a sense of the terrain. They're not symbols of direction; they *are* directions. They free you from needing pretty much anything. You can literally show up and start walking. You just let yourself be ushered forward by the arrows, and by the third or fourth one it already feels great to make zero decisions about where you're going or when you'll get there or what you'll do when you arrive. The manic Berlin of cigarettes and openings feels inconceivably distant, but Santiago does as well.

A deep fog ahead of us obscures the looming mountains. For the next eight hundred kilometers we will join fellow pilgrims in the ritual of ruing the misery of the first day, the seven or nine or eleven hours of unbroken uphill. "But in the end," they would always smile and say, "as hard as it was, it was all worth it for those spectacular views!" Our view is a three-hundred-and-sixty-degree panorama of freezing fluffed velvet fog. John Brierley's *A Pilgrim's Guide to the Camino de Santiago: A Practical and Mystical Manual for the Modern Day Pilgrim*, with which we would soon develop a complicated and hostile relationship, warns against attempting the first day's mountain path in inclement weather. But we just shrug and shoulder our packs and charge ahead into the frozen stifle of mist. We don't see ourselves as the sort of pilgrims who worry about a little weather.

We also don't see ourselves, as we set out, as the sort of pilgrims whom other pilgrims make a habit of passing, but it's a self-image we're quickly encouraged to revise. We see almost nobody else in the six a.m. fog, but over the first hour or two other pilgrims begin to fall in behind us, then consistently and with minimal effort waltz right by, offering cheery greetings of *"Buen Camino"* as they hurry along in droves. Norwegians, Finns, Spaniards, Germans, old people, all bound together by the lazy confidence with which they pass us.

We take a long break at lunchtime, stare into the mist caping the Pyrenees in cold, flocculent silence. I look a little wistfully at the other pilgrims sailing by, pilgrims who slept until noon, pilgrims with prosthetic limbs and debilitating hangovers. Tom narrows his eyes. "This is not a race," he says.

"One time," I say to Tom as we begin to walk again, "I saw an episode of this TV show, *Man vs. Beast*, in which a man and a giraffe were competing in a sprint. The first color commentator remarks that the man's strategy has got to be getting out there and running as fast as he possibly can. The second color commentator responds that the giraffe's strategy has to be *realizing that it is in a race*. And that is the parable of the giraffe."

"I can't say I like what you're getting at," says Tom.

"Well, I'm not serious, or at least not totally serious, but it's comforting to think about this competitively, you know? I mean, at least it presents *a* reason for us to be walking across Spain."

For practicing Catholics, of whom we will meet almost none, the reward for arrival in Santiago is a full plenary indulgence, a complete pardon of the purgatorial debt you've accrued thus far. The rest of us are cagey about what to expect. But almost every pilgrim we meet over the next thirty-nine days admits to some feeling, however muted or vague, of transition or crisis.

An elderly Irish man passes us slowly enough for Tom to strike up a conversation. "So, why are *you* walking across Spain?" Tom asks.

The man slows momentarily, pauses. "Why are any of us walking across Spain?" He speeds up again and soon he is gone. I haven't yet decided how fair it is to ask this question. Is it intrusive? Do these people just want to be left alone? Do they know we're asking them why they're doing it just to help us figure out why *we're* doing it?

For his part, Tom does have some specific reasons, and some specific expectations. Since I last saw him, on our Estonian bender, he's written an entire book (on video games), has found the woman he's pretty sure he wants to spend the rest of his life with, and has taken a tenure-track teaching job in America. He's planning to settle down for the first time, and he looks at this walk as a chance to use up the remaining quantity of his restlessness, to walk himself into the tranquillity he needs to inhabit a stable life shaped by romantic commitment.

Of all the ways of directing yourself, of organizing your days and desires—professional ambition, social status, religious observance, etc.—I'm most drawn to and disgusted by the promise of romantic commitment, White's mutual protection racket. In the memoir Phillips reviewed, White writes, "I'd sit on the bus and look at the man across the aisle from me and wonder if I could be happy for the rest

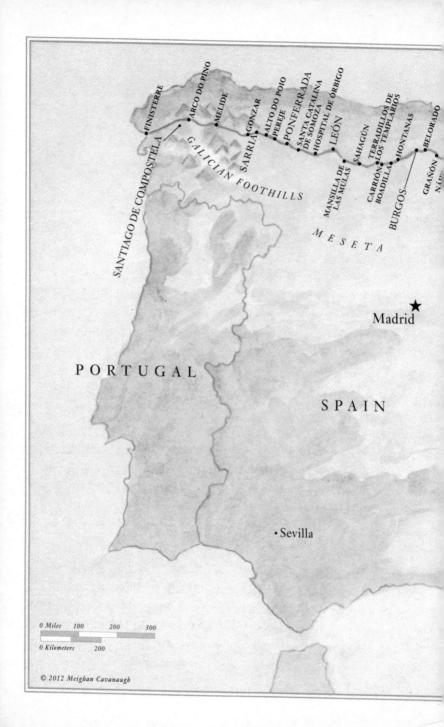

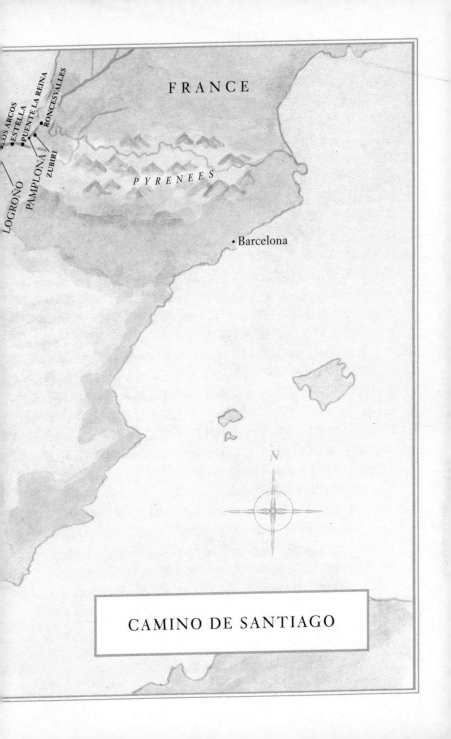

FRANCE

LOS ARCOS
ESTELLA
PUENTE LA REINA
RONCESVALLES
LOGROÑO
PAMPLONA
ZUBIRI

PYRENEES

• Barcelona

N

CAMINO DE SANTIAGO

of my life with him. I'd imagine exchanging vows with him—the idea of true love excited me. Marriage got me hard." I often felt the same way, which is probably why I raged against it when I saw it in others. I'm jealous of it in Tom.

But, at the moment at least, that's not anything I have to look forward to or prepare myself for. For now, my reasons for being here are murkier—they have more to do with the freedom I'm trying to escape, I think, than the stillness I'm hoping to find—so I sympathize with the old Irish man's evasiveness. I also recognize immediately that, like Berlin, this is another place where a broad-brush explanation seems sufficient. We can never really know what other people want—we rarely even know what *we* want—but on the Camino it's clear from our first conversations with fellow pilgrims that that's okay. You trust that the people you meet along the way must have some reason somewhere, even one that's largely obscure to them, and in turn you trust that you've got a pressing motive of your own. "It sounded fun" is as good, and acceptable, an explanation as any.

But it is still an absurd errand, so Tom and I seek solace in our most obvious brief as writers: documentation. Tom looks down at the muddy path and says he's going to describe the sheep droppings as "black scarabs of shit." He stops to write that down in his little black notebook, pleased with himself. It's already late morning and I've taken no notes yet so I stop, too, to write down that Tom is pleased with himself. I've got the same little black notebook. I'm suddenly afraid that he's noticing more than I am, making more unusual and interesting observations about the scenery and the conversation; so, in an effort to catch up, I jot down a bunch of lush descriptions of the mist and the narrow mud path. Our ambition is already narrowing, tailoring itself to this simplified life.

I look at Tom. "Wait, but isn't the point of a trip like this maybe to provide an escape from such self-consciousness? Are we dooming ourselves from the start by constantly wondering why we're doing this, constantly recording the lyrical appearance of every piece of ungulate shit?"

"I have to say, I think I'm less worried," Tom says, "about issues of self-consciousness here, and more worried about the three blisters I already have, and when we're going to get to the top of this mountain, and how I'm going to do this for another month."

We're climbing what, if we could see more than seven feet ahead of us, would surely be identifiable as a sheer rock face. The bleachy mist kicks with the haunches of half-visible sheep. We stroll by something or other commemorating the glorious victory or death of someone or other. Tom develops his fourth blister and I take his heavy pack for a while; he claims I'm just doing it so I can represent myself as a hero later. We achieve the pass after about nine hours, which, according to the helpful and insulting signage, ought to have taken about five. We're finally above the clouds and can see the loping green hills of the Basque country below us. We nap briefly in the sun before heading down the steep, shady downhill to the *albergue*, or pilgrims' hostel.

For this last interim nobody passes us; apparently there's nobody left to do so. The *albergue* at Roncesvalles is a converted chapel, a high and severe vessel of chill gray stone with a few hundred bunk beds in an aisled grid. There's a soft chant playing, and a sanctimonious but not unwelcome air of reflection. We register with a *hospitalero*, one of the volunteer wardens; they're usually former pilgrims themselves, or people who, for some reason, are unable to complete the walk themselves, and they come from all over the world to serve for two-week stints. This *albergue* has a five-euro fee, though Brierley's manual mentions that many of them, especially those run by the local parishes, are by-donation only. There's a mimeographed inscription from a poem written here in the thirteenth century:

> The door is open to all, sick or well,
> Not only Catholics, but pagans also,
> To Jews, heretics, idlers, the vain.
> And, as I shall briefly note, the good and worldly too.

The two of us—a heretic and a Jew, both as idle as we are vain—walk over to the town bar, where there's a small convention of good and worldly people who, at some point during the day, passed us. They've been here for hours, maybe days. There's a puckish little Irishman who looks up from his beer and asks us where we've been.

"I've been sitting here long enough to get drunk," he says, and we immediately dislike him.

"If we ever see that guy again," Tom says, "I'm going to call him Lucky Charms."

WE WAKE AT SIX to thunked-on kliegs and the slow-charged rustle of fabric. Pilgrims leap from their bunks and set about the rustling—of sleeping bags, towels, bandannas—with quiet intensity. We're in no particular hurry. We slept deeply, with strange dreams, interrupted periodically by a death bulletin of a snore. Later on in the day a German couple would tell us they didn't sleep at all. "It was like being in hell," the German woman said. This is the first and pretty much the last religious comment we'll hear on the Camino.

By the time we get out of bed, people are already setting out. We brush our teeth and Tom checks Facebook, updates his status with a cryptic message intended only for his girlfriend, or rather to advertise for the world that he's leaving cryptic messages for somebody. A crowd of pilgrims has collected outside the *albergue*; they're exchanging pleasantries in eleven languages, holding an international colloquium on styles of passing us. A sign says "Santiago de Compostela: 790 km." The first day totaled about twenty-five, which is about what you have to average if you want to finish in a month. We look to the Brierley to see how many kilometers he recommends for today.

It took us only a few hours to loathe John Brierley and his idiotic mystical manual. The book has maps and practical information for each stage—he's broken the walk up into thirty-three stages, one for each year of Jesus's life, although most of the other guides and websites suggest thirty-one—but it's also a daily compendium of treacly, self-righteous meditations on the spiritual renewal this walk is supposed to inspire. Most of these anecdotal lessons begin with John Brierley's having gotten furious with someone, on the trail or in an *albergue*, and later realizing, with great regret, that he ought to have infinite love for all beings. He weeps constantly about bragging. He also brags constantly about weeping. One day he's sitting and drawing a picture of a stork and he starts weeping. Another day he refuses to stay at some dirt-floored shepherd's hut and then finds that the *albergue* is full and he has to walk seven more kilometers, unable to see the arrows through his tears. A third day he meets the devil, who makes him weep.

"I wonder how he found the time to walk, given all that weeping," Tom says.

The path is cut between the bald foothills of the Pyrenees on our right and some lowland pastures on our left. Periodic villages are blocked out in sturdy whitewashed houses of prim stucco. Blue-and-yellow scallop-shell waymarkers are set into walls and poured-concrete bollards. We follow the steady yellow arrows down a rocky hillside, through stately and unidentifiable conifers. The sunlight splashes cool and messy on the path, and Tom stops and takes out his notebook. I make florid pen-on-parchment gestures, assume a falsetto, and mock. "Afternoon sunlight slanting through the tall pines dapples our stony aisle."

"You're a dick," Tom says.

We walk a gradual slow uphill along a wooden fence and I ramble on about how shallow the concerns of Berlin feel from this distance. "I love this," I say. "I want to do the Camino again."

"Gideon," Tom says, "we are *two hours* into our *second day.*"

A few kilometers later we stop and sit in a ramshackle barn above a river and Tom takes off his boots. His right upper heel is gone; in its place is a wide, jagged tear of red, more blister than foot. Or, actually, it looks as though it's skipped the blister phase and gone straight to advanced decomposition. He thought window-shopping in a Michigan mall for a few days would be sufficient to break in a new pair of boots.

"Each day," he says. "has been a different path toward extraordinary pain."

"Tom," I say, "we are *five hours* into our *second day.*"

T HE MAJOR ETIQUETTE POINT en route is the phrase *Buen Camino.* It's a salutation and a valediction, but its most important role is in establishing boundaries. You're walking along and you see another pilgrim; maybe he stopped for a little while—or, more likely, *we* stopped for a little while—and now there's some promise or threat of social interaction. After all, you're both headed in the same direction. *Buen Camino* is the universally respected conversation ender. You might say hello and immediately get a *Buen Camino.* Or you might have ten minutes of conversation about where you're from and where you started—we started in St. Jean-Pied-de-Port, which is more or less considered "doing the whole thing," but some people start in Paris or Arles or St. Petersburg, and lots of people, *despicably shiftless and inauthentic people*, start down the line, in Burgos or León or Ponferrada—and then bam, *Buen Camino*. Or you walk together for a few hours or even a few days or weeks or some people get married. But you can always *Buen Camino* yourself out of a situation at any time. It gives all exchanges a nice, dangerous quality, and contributes to a direct, fearless ambience. The flipside is that if you're not soonishly *Buen Camino*'d, you feel invited to be as candid and probing as you like; on the Camino, two or three exchanges exhaust the possible small talk, and at that point you're either going to talk about your divorce or your layoff or you're just going to stroll on alone. Another version, I think, of the shipwreck, or the flushed early hours of the apocalypse.

We get *Buen Camino*'d with some frequency. First is Fabrizio, a breezily healthy Italian who's been walking already for four weeks, since Le Puy, a medieval hub in central France. He says it's been a little lonely—pilgrims on the long French stretches are much fewer and farther between—but now that he's past St. Jean he's happy there are so many more people to talk to. I can't imagine doing this alone, and I'm grateful to be walking with Tom, who's so funny and agreeable and generous, if a little slow.

"So, why are you doing the Camino?" Tom asks Fabrizio.

"I did it last year, too, and I think it is good to clear the mind and cleanse the blood." He makes a squeegee motion that signals amateur dialysis. "I will probably do it again next year, though next year I think I take the Camino del Norte." There are three main trunk routes: the Camino Francés, which we're on and which is the most popular; the Camino del Norte, which is more rugged and runs along the Cantabrian coast to the north, and which is the one I'd also like to do next; and the Camino de la Plata, which runs more than a thousand kilometers north from Seville and is apparently unwalkably hot in the summer months. "I move to Bologna in the fall to study philosophy."

Tom laughs, apologizes for laughing. Tom has a dim view of the ambitions of Italians.

"*Buen Camino,*" Fabrizio says, and picks up his pace.

On our second day we're sitting in the sun at an outdoor café in the center of a Basque village and making fun of what looks like their national typeface, which is distinguished by a crowned "A." "It looks," Tom says after considering it from all angles, "like a tiki-torch Brady-Bunch-goes-to-Hawaii end-credits font." The kid at the table next to us starts to laugh, and we're flattered he finds us funnier than everybody else seems to. As we get up to keep walking, he adopts us.

His name is Ben and he's from Belgium and he's twenty-three. He says he's hitchhiked from his home, near Ghent, and that it took him two days to get to St. Jean.

"In America," Tom says, "hitchhiking is unusual and dangerous."

"Yes," I say. "When you hitchhike in America, you either get murdered or end up murdering the driver."

"It's a tense contest," Tom says.

Ben looks at us with a rich sort of pity and condescension. Tom changes the subject by asking why he's doing the Camino.

"Well, my mom did it, and my brother did it, and my uncle did it, and you meet people from all over Europe, and it's cheap. I think I can do the entire Camino, one month of travel, for less than five hundred euros." We walk by a little riot of newborn sheep, and throw some unripe figs over a fence to an old goat. We sit on a log in the shade and Ben shares his croissants and Nutella. After ten minutes Ben looks eager to resume the walk, but Tom wants to rest his decaying feet awhile longer.

"There are two main strategies for walking the Camino," I say to Ben. "The first way is to walk quickly but take frequent short breaks, or infrequent long ones. The second is to walk slowly but take few breaks, or only short ones. But *our* way is to walk slowly *and* take frequent, long breaks."

"Buen Camino," Ben says.

B RIERLEY SUGGESTS going another eight kilometers today, but it's very hot and Tom's just about had it. Tom says he wants to skip the *albergue* in favor of a little hotel. He lies prone on the bed, and I tell him what's going on in the world of Basque reality television.

"Tom," I say, with a crappy gentleness, "you need to take a few things out of your pack. I can't just carry it for you all the time."

"Go to hell," he says into his pillow, but he pushes the pack toward me with the foot that still has a little skin left on it. I remove the hardcover biography of Augustine, and the two-volume life of Jerome, and two of Tom's three pairs of jeans. In the morning he'll sneak the Jerome back in, but he'll lose a few ounces by cutting the legs off his remaining jeans.

Back on the trail in the morning, we stop along a lone stone wall in the shade of a village and Tom finds his blister bandages have slipped and taken the rest of his heel with them. I congratulate myself on my sensible sneakers and light pack, pace back and forth along the trail until he's ready to get going again.

We walk along a barbed-wire fence through a jarring industrial valley, some sort of mining operation, where a placard apologizes to pilgrims for the noise and dust. The path is narrow, and for stretches we're walking single file, talking over our shoulders, first about suicide, then about a person's capacity for change.

"David Levine says that the only two things that really change a person are a relationship or a crisis, and given that he thinks we're all mid-crisis all the time, I guess he means somehow realizing that whatever's going on is so bad, it's no longer bearable."

"I think the Camino is already unbearable, and we're only on day three," Tom says, with a strained laugh. "But yeah, maybe that's right. I think that this new relationship I'm in is already stabilizing me. I've never felt so ready to settle down in one place."

I'd had that sort of stability for a while in San Francisco—the happiest I'd ever been romantically—but over time I grew resentful, frustrated and trapped, and in the final few months I'd felt ugly and irritable in a way I never wanted to feel again. Still, I'd lacked the courage to end things until she left the country, and, besides, nothing had ever felt *wrong*, exactly. And then, though on some level it was a considerable relief, I'd sat in the Berkeley Rose Garden with a friend and watched the sun set over the Golden Gate through silent tears. "You *broke up?*" he said to himself, taking care not to look at me as I cried. He wasn't used to seeing me cry. "That's what my kids are always doing." He taught English in a Catholic school, though it wasn't quite what he wanted to be doing; we'd become friends, at eighteen, when his courage to say he wanted to be a musician helped me find the courage to want to be a writer. Now he didn't seem very sympathetic. "These fifteen-year-olds I teach, they're always *breaking up* with each other. It's weird. *We broke up.* You guys *broke up.* Too much." He got married four months later, and at the reception I got so drunk I threw a beer bottle through a banquet hall window. I didn't know why I took it so personally, our diverging lives, but I felt betrayed. Yet I couldn't ever figure out whom I thought he was selling out, with whom I most identified: my friend, his lovely wife, or their blameless children. Naturally this had nothing to do with their actual lives, but since pretty much that moment, as the beer bottle smashed into that window, I hadn't let myself feel accountable to anybody in a serious way, and hadn't put myself in a position where I might initiate rejection, or face it. Real romantic involvement had become something that was always imminent, something I wanted but only once I was absolutely sure that it would be perfect, that it would both electrify and sustain the settled life once I'd adequately prepared myself for it.

We sit in the shade of a dilapidated barn and eat some tomato sandwiches with Basque tapenade. I say it's time to go, but Tom stalls for a little more time, picks up the Brierley, and starts to read. "So Brierley says here that you should stop at least once an hour to take off your boots and rub your feet."

"Yeah, and it also says there that he saw the devil by the side of the road and wept at him! I can't believe you're invoking Brierley as an authority now."

"I'm just saying he says we should stop frequently. Sit down."

"We're already stopping frequently. I sat down last time."

"What, you don't want to stop? Are we stopping too much for you?"

"No, it's fine. I don't mind at all. I'm happy to stop. We're not in any hurry. We can stop whenever you like."

"It's not a race."

T HE PATH CURLS AROUND a hillside over a camouflage-green river, and here and there pilgrims sit on its banks, soaking their feet. We cross the river and come to our first major road; the Camino follows the shoulder for about six hundred meters of awful shock. Apparently as recently as fifteen years ago much of the Camino was on asphalt, but the regional tourist authorities have gone to some effort to make the walk safer and softer for the ever-growing crowds. Something I read said that in 1979 only a few thousand people arrived in Santiago to get their *compostela*, the certificate of completion for walkers or cyclists. These days it's almost two hundred thousand, though that includes people who start way down the line and only walk the final bits. According to the church authorities, you only qualify for a *compostela* if you walk at least the last hundred kilometers or bike the last two hundred, and we've already been warned it gets very crowded near a distant town called Sarria.

"It's amazing," I say. "We've only been walking for some fifty total hours and already I can't imagine what it would be like to ride in a car. Like, it's only ten a.m. right now, and it's going to take us most of the rest of this sweltering day to get to Pamplona, and if we flagged down a car we would be there in literally ten or fifteen minutes."

"Wait, *what*?"

"Yeah, something like that. Twenty at the most."

"You know what I'd do if you weren't around?" Tom asks.

"What, Tom?"

"I'd take the bus."

"No you wouldn't."

"Yes, Gideon, I definitely would. I'm in a huge amount of pain, I'm not doing this for any sort of spiritual reason, I do not believe in God or divine forgiveness, and I no longer really even believe that it's going to effect any sort of secular change in my life. I have no idea at all what the point of this is. It's not a race, no matter what you say about giraffes, and I would not hesitate for one second to take a bus."

But there's no way we're taking a bus. I don't believe in God or redemption, either, but the whole point of this exercise is playing by the rules. They're arbitrary but they don't ask too much of you. "Did you ask me to come along just to prevent you from taking buses? Was I drafted as your conscience?"

"No, you were drafted because I knew I would've been miserable alone and you're the only person I know with even less to do than me. I'm miserable now, of course, but without you I'd be much more miserable."

"I thought you said without me you'd be in a bus."

"Oh, right. So I guess I'd be differently miserable, then, because though I might be alone, I'd be alone on a bus."

"But think of it this way: if we took a bus, we'd be in Pamplona by eleven a.m."

"So?"

"So, then what would we do for the rest of the day?"

"Good point," Tom says.

"Besides," I say, "I just can't imagine what I'd do in a car, how I'd relate to the scenery."

Tom gets angry. "I know what *I'd* do, I'd pay a hell of a lot more attention to it. You can't really pay attention to how the breeze is ruffling the treetops if your feet are literally coming apart."

The trail leaves the road and crosses back over the river to run again along the hillside. We're at a slight downhill and out of the sun, so we're stopping less.

We enter a clearing. "Wow," I say, to no one in particular, though the only person around is Tom, "that's beautiful wheat."

"That's wheat?"

"I think so."

"I don't know the names of any plants."

"Neither do I. And I hate books where the writer name-drops flora. It's such a cheap and easy way to establish credibility. You're like, 'They walked down through the sugar pine and the incense cedar' and all you did was consult Wikipedia's 'evergreen' entry but now you seem like the kind of ruggedly trustworthy narrator who could survive alone in the woods."

"That's sort of what this apostles book is going to be about, the way that the church, before it had consolidated any institutional authority, went about telling these stories that came together to form a compelling tradition, and then how all of those great early stories got rewritten to shore up the subsequent institutional power. It's about how stories that provided some moral or behavioral orientation became dogmatic bullshit."

Tom was an altar boy when he was a kid, and now he distrusts and resents churchgoers in the way only a truly religious person can; part of his project is his attempt to reconcile the stories he loves so much with the crummy personal behavior, at least as he sees it, that the Church inspires. On the very few occasions he and I stumble into a church, he lights up as he explains the iconography. "See Saint Bartholomew up there? He was flayed alive, so he's usually depicted with a big knife, and sometimes he's even holding up a heap of his own skin—you can see that in the Sistine Chapel. And see Saint John? He's always got a book, because he was one of the writers of the New Testament."

Having grown up with two rabbis for parents, I never knew any of this stuff. I've also never felt quite the same sense of conflict between the stories and the doctrine. I'd seen up close and from a young age the human failures of the clergy, their hypocrisy. Authority figures were always going to say one thing and do another. But I think that it was precisely my early mistrust of religious authority that allowed me to enjoy religious ritual. A ritual doesn't *say* anything; it doesn't ask you to believe; it just asks you to do. And it doesn't pretend to know *why* you have to do it, which is what makes it trustworthy.

THERE'S A CROWD of Basques barbecuing kebabs in a park, and Tom is indignant. "Why aren't these Basques at work?"

"It's Saturday."

"So these Basques are enjoying a hot summer weekend after-noon."

"And we—" I begin.

"Are walking across their country." We laugh at how ridiculous this is; these are the best moments.

The grilling Basques, of course, don't think it at all strange; they've been watching pilgrims stroll by for a thousand years. I won-der what that must be like, to do your daily errands and your grilling in a place where part of your routine is watching so many people pass by en route elsewhere. What must this experience look like from the outside, or rather, from the inside? The still procession of porches and windows whose tenants sit and watch pilgrims walk by, pilgrims who have left behind families and jobs, their own porches and children.

We enter the outskirts of Pamplona. The graffitied yellow arrows here are painted high up on drain spouts, or below on the pavement itself, directing an open secret route through the city, a route that has nothing to do with the city's own purposes. Brierley thinks cities are dangerous distractions. He advises us to consider even the smallest city as a lurking Sodom.

But distractions from *what*? From getting to Santiago? Is he re-ally afraid that someone who's chosen to come this far to walk across Spain would get to Pamplona on the third day and think, Oh, well, this city and its pleasures are so nice, I'm just going to stay here? What else could it possibly mean to be distracted?

We follow the steady riddle of sidewalk arrows through the heat and the traffic, and Tom says he's on the verge of losing his temper. We're both heat-stroked and sullen, and every few minutes one of us asks the other yet again what the point of this could possibly be. Tom looks at each bus going by with the affection Robert Frost had for woodpiles. If not for the vivid hallucinations, we'd both be catatonic. Tom finds us a hotel off the square and I hear him telling someone on the phone, it must be his girlfriend, that "a meringue of pus" is coating the inside of his socks. We eat Chinese food in a restaurant-cum-brothel and agree that this walk is degrees of magnitude more difficult than we'd imagined.

O UR DAY OFF IN PAMPLONA, Tom notes, is an emergency vaca-tion from the Camino, which itself is a specific vacation from the general vacation that is our lives; he says he's never been so deeply implicated in vacation before. It sets the precedent for all subsequent days off. It's a city of not insignificant charm, where there is much for an ordinary tourist to see and do, but we haven't the faintest desire to see or do anything but the mall and our email. Tom talks to his girlfriend on the phone for a few hours and I kill time at an internet café, writing my first email dispatch about the walk. I cc Tom on the email and by the time I get back to the hotel he's read it.

"Are you capable of processing an experience without emailing fifty-seven people about it?"

"What, are you mad? Should I not make jokes about carrying your bag, or how messed up your feet are?"

"No, that stuff was funny, and the world ought to know about my suffering and your childish martyr complexes. I'm mad that you told people I checked Facebook."

"You *did* check Facebook. You even updated your status. You have seventeen hundred friends. Did you think no one would notice?"

"Yeah, but you checked Facebook too. You didn't mention that, did you? You made it sound like only *I* checked Facebook."

"You're right. In my next email I'll apologize for that."

"You better. Anyway, did you hear back from anybody yet? Let's go see."

We check my email together in the business center. There's one from my mom, asking if I was serious when I asked her to mail us, poste restante to Logroño, individual packets of Crystal Light to replace Tom's cache, which we've almost exhausted in the first three days. I tell her it's sweet but she shouldn't worry about it. There's one from my grandfather Max, my dad's dad, telling me he and Lois, my grandmother (my dad's stepmother), are following us on a map they put up in their house, and asking if I mind if he forwards the email to his friends. He also asks, gently, if I plan on including my dad on future emails or not. There's one from David Levine, offering solace and good wishes from him and Alix. They say I'm not missing anything in Berlin but the usual. And there's one from Micah, who's taken issue with my parable of the giraffe.

"First of all," he writes, "you weren't even with us when Trevor and I watched that episode of *Man vs. Beast*. You stole that story, you jerk. Second of all, it wasn't a giraffe, it was a *zebra*. Fix that. And third of all, the most important thing was that the color commentator was CARL LEWIS."

"Who's Carl Lewis?" I ask.

"I think he's an athlete," Tom says. "Unlike us."

THEY'RE ABJECT DAYS, these days off, and we wake up at five thirty the next morning in our comfortable Pamplona boutique hotel with a sense of shame and urgency. We wait around for the desk officials to stamp our pilgrims' *credenciales*, the little passport that proves to the *compostela* authorities that we made the journey on foot, and take up once more the trail of yellow arrows, which channel us through and out of Pamplona, through the gates of the old city, along the perimeter of a sleeping park, past the star-shaped dodecagon citadel and finally onto the parade-wide boulevards of Franco's Spain. A light rain falls, but it feels great to be walking again, especially in the city's silent dawn pallor.

The arrows are sparser here, or maybe we're just missing some of them in the dark. "If I'd lived in a city along the Camino growing up," Tom says, "I'd have done nothing but paint fake yellow arrows all over the place. That's just the kind of kid I was."

As we pass the final houses on Pamplona's outskirts, where the path leaves the road and begins to ascend a soft winding rise to a ridge sentried by windmills, I start to feel anxious for the first time since we started walking. As we walk past the final houses of the city, their inhabitants just waking to the usual demands of the day, I make eye contact with a young woman in tears, crouched at a dormer as the sun rises in front of us, and it deepens my sense that something isn't right.

Midway up the long slope, we stop to look past the scrub toward some ruins in the middle distance. Towers of half-toppled sandstone stand in a lime field of early wheat, here and there sad little bursts of vermilion poppy. Atop the ridge we're hailed by the first Americans we've met, a couple in matching yoga pants. We take to them the way naïve co-nationals do, and make our way down the hill in comparative resumé investigation. At the bottom of the hill we stop at a pilgrim dive for *bocadillos*, Spain's tindery staple, a condimentless relative of the developed world's sandwich. I thought I hadn't cared much about food in Berlin, but on the Camino all calories seem more or less indistinguishable. The food is bad and monotonous, but within days we barely notice except to riff on it.

Tom is reading out a passage of Brierley on Christ and Mammon for the completely unamused Americans when he's interrupted by a heavyset Swede. She's doing the Camino for the second time and has a lot to say about these issues of spirituality and, more important, weight loss. Tom and I have had the temerity to tell only one person that the real reason we're doing this is weight loss, but it turns out that it's a pretty common motivation. The Swede is holding a *bocadillo de jamón serrano* the size and moistness of a cinder block and says that last time she lost fifteen pounds. She assures us that we can eat whatever we want en route and will still lose weight.

"When you get to the end, though," she warns us, "you have to say that you did it for religious purposes, *not* weight loss, if you want to get the nice *compostela*. If you write 'exercise' or 'tourism,' you get a crappy one where they don't even write your name in fake Latin."

The Swede has one more piece of advice. "The last hundred miles," she says with the lazy geographical determinism of northern Europeans, "are really crowded with cheating Spaniards and Italians who take a bus from village to village and get their *credenciales* stamped without ever walking more than a few kilometers a day." Tom and I can't believe someone would do that, though I can easily imagine Tom doing that. We are already nursing the sense of outrage we'll feel overwhelming pleasure to experience when the time comes.

After lunch we get *Buen Camino*'d by the Americans, but we're feeling so good that we decide to add a few extra unnecessary clicks to see a thirteenth-century Romanesque church Brierley calls "the jewel of the Camino." It's closed, and will mark the first and the last of our detours en route.

At dinner in the *albergue*, a buffet, Tom has a feral oblivion in his eyes. It's been a seventeen-mile day, our longest so far. He eats his salad like a defensive den animal, shows linguistic difficulties.

"The buffet," I say, "has a second course of chicken and fish."

"I don't know what you want from me," says Tom.

The lounge has some coin-operated internet terminals; we've been surprised to find so much internet on the Camino. Both of us check Facebook, and then Tom gets in bed.

"Don't go to sleep now," I cluck. "It's only seven thirty."

"But I'm so tired."

"But if you go to sleep now, you'll be awake in the middle of the night."

"Leave me alone." He falls asleep by eight p.m. in his soiled clothes, then wakes me up at three fifteen as he shuffles back to bed. I ask him what the hell he was doing and he murmurs something about email; he was afraid his girlfriend would worry if she hadn't heard from him in two days. The night janitor told him that real pilgrims do not check their email at three in the morning and sent him back to the dorm. I lie awake until dawn staring at the sooty ceiling, unable to think of anybody other than my mom and Micah who might be wondering where I am right now.

Andy's been alone for his first few days and Tom says that the only reason he's the first person to go more than an hour without *Buen Camino*'ing us is that he's been driven mad by the isolation. He just graduated from college, in San Antonio, and was backpacking around Europe with some friends. They were off to Paris but he realized that his depleted savings would allow him either four days there or a month on the Camino. He's been slouching his way along, living on crackers and staying only at the by-donation *albergues*, even when that means tacking a few extra kilometers onto the end of a long day. All Andy's got on him is an elementary school backpack (though he carries Tom's for a while when I tire of it), one change of clothes, and a faded paperback copy of *Dubliners*. Tom's thrilled to have him along. I decided on the afternoon of the first day I wasn't going to drink on the Camino—I figured it was a good chance, considering the general slosh of Berlin, to see what it would be like to abstain, and it'd be easier and more pleasant to walk without a hangover—so it's great for

Tom to have somebody with whom he can booze a little, even if he ends up paying for all the beers.

"That's love, homeboy," Andy says, watching me change Tom's bandages before we set off in the morning, thickening his Tex-Mex accent for effect. "It doesn't look like the Camino has messed with your friendship at all."

"Huh?" Tom asks.

"Most of the people I met who started out walking with friends ended up splitting up within thirty kilometers," Andy says.

"Why?" I ask.

"Dunno," Andy says. "Maybe they were bugging each other. My friend wanted to come along with me but I said nuh-uh, I didn't want nobody bugging me out here. It's weird, though, right? Because it's not like you're making any decisions about what to see or where to go. You're just following these damn arrows and deciding how often to stop." Tom and I narrow our eyes at each other. Andy smiles and picks up his bag. "Let's go, then, but don't you two go bugging me."

The first five hours of the day always pass quickly, and now that we've got a companion to share the constant burden of entertaining each other, they go by at an even faster clip. The map shows a "wine fountain" of some kind up ahead, which gives us added incentive to make good time.

We bisect a walled hilltop postcard of a village and leave through an arch of yellow stone weathered soft. There's a fork in the path and we can't find a yellow arrow, but there's an adorable young woman standing there, and our confusion gives us a pretext to introduce ourselves. She's Québecois and is waiting for her friend, to whom she owes twenty euros. We ask when she last saw her friend. "Two days ago," she says.

We ask which way people have been going and she says the Camino goes off to the left, on an old Roman road. Tom consults

Brierley, who loves this next stretch; it gives him yet another occasion to sneer at convenience. "Will the nearby N-128 still be there in two thousand years?" he asks. Tom, for one, thinks so. The cars along the N-128, in a valley just below us, look like they're making great time.

The old Roman road is chunky and uneven and kills our feet after the soft dirt tracks of the morning. Tom stops to write this down, but it's really just an excuse to stop. I write that down, that Tom only writes stuff down when he wants an excuse to stop. Tom looks lustfully down at the N-128.

"What are you guys writing down?" Andy asks. "Is it something about all the stupid things I say?"

"Of course not, Andy," Tom says. "I only write down the stupid things Gideon says." Andy looks over at me for confirmation. I nod.

Mountains threaten along the horizon, and we labor in their shadows for hours; they don't look like the sort of mountains whence cometh help. The foliage is a thick brush with the occasional acre of stunted old wintergreen olive trees. Every once in a while there's a small rock cairn beside one of the waymarkers, a Camino tradition we haven't been able to figure out. In a moment of frustration Tom knocks one over. It makes the three of us feel instantly uneasy.

Two *albergues* with two identical cafés face off across the Camino as it dips through a village called Lorca. Tom falls upon his sandwiches, I check my email to see if anybody else has responded to my dispatch, and Andy hits Tom up for a beer. Postprandially we sit on a bench and I lance Tom's youngest blisters.

Three older Spanish women with whom we've been leapfrogging for a day come over to kibitz. I pull Andy away from finishing Tom's beer to translate.

"Uh, they're Catalan nurses, and Tom's feet are among the worst they've ever seen, and this old one here says when she saw them, she was about to start crying." The younger nurse rushes in.

"Yeah, okay, and she says that she was very moved that you were tending to his feet with such Christian charity, but that you were also tending to them very poorly. Her husband has been driving a van ahead with their stuff, and he's on his way back now with a first-aid kit."

The Catalan nurses are so concerned, they light up a bouquet of cigarettes and hand them around. Supplies arrive and the chain-smoking congress of Catalan nurses sets to work, rotating out only to smoke, rotating in while still smoking. They spray iodine all over Tom's feet, confer in a smoky ring, take out needles and thread, and run them through the blisters. They gesture that this is what I ought to be doing with my Christian charity, dousing Tom's feet in great inaccurate sprays of iodine and then bisecting the blisters with old thread.

In a few hours all of this medical advice will be confidently reversed by a Red Cross medic, who will tell us that this hasn't been au courant anti-blister practice since the Spanish Civil War. Tom's been rereading *Homage to Catalonia* and he finds the archaism appealing, but the medic insists that it will only result in infection. The medic, a gruff incarnation of cosmic wisdom, will also tell Andy, in Spanish I can understand, that he ought to *Buen Camino* the two of us pronto.

For now, however, the nurses are pretty convincing. We stand in the narrow lane, filled with blood and pus and iodine and dozens of pilgrims offering advice and condolences in as many languages, and listen to the kind scolding of the nurses. The adorable Québecoise shows up, smiling and laughing and taking pictures with an antique camera. She can't stop smiling at Tom, a wide and inviting French-Canadienne smile. Even under relatively normal conditions, which in his regular life occur rarely enough, Tom has an aura of a half-dangerous cuddle bear; and, drenched in iodine, his feet mummified in gauze, and cooed over by the anxiously hypernicotined Catalan nurses, he's just too much of a draw, at his most vulnerable and sweetly deranged. I'm jealous as hell.

After lunch we walk more slowly, as usual. Gaining on us is the Tank, Tom's nickname for the cuckoo-eyed block of Bavarian farmer who's been ski-poling herself steadily behind us all day. Despite our best efforts, we can't seem to catch up to the Québecoise, who darts fairylike ahead of us, taking photographs of olive trees and other items that are surely of no interest to anybody but her. She will post hundreds of them to Facebook, will refresh Facebook for years to come with ever more irrelevant pictures of the Camino's plant life.

There's periodic rain, and Tom throws the very last of his energy into sustaining a repartee with Andy. Although I'm too tired to join in, I'm finding it's harder than I thought to share Tom's attention. Jealous was the last thing I thought I was going to feel on the Camino. I'm annoyed too. We're not going to make it to the fucking wine fountain before dark. I bet if I'd been alone I would have.

O N OUR WAY OUT of Estella at dawn the three of us are pretty tired—some bozo kept rustling her space blanket in the dorm—and the Camino runs along a dingy suburban side street, garages and town houses. Tom reads to us out of Brierley to get us angry and raise our spirits. Today's passage addresses the issue of cities and busy roads. Brierley advises keeping your positive pilgrim energy up by singing your favorite pilgrim songs into oncoming traffic. We hadn't known such a genre existed. Such idiocy improves our spirits right away, and soon we're at the wine fountain, which has a webcam. We each have a few ceremonial sips—after all, it's only six thirty in the morning—and Tom, whose feet are still killing him, has a few ceremonial glasses.

The path up and over the hill is soft dirt in the shade, and the sun, slow in rising at our backs, throws shadow runnels in front of us. On both sides are wide, newly plowed fields, and in the northern distance is a glinting uneven height of eroded granite massif. The sun isn't yet obliterative and we walk on and off with some American medical students, everybody feeling light and companionable.

In the day's first village Tom sobers up on a bench while I feed yogurt off my finger to some kittens, figuring the kittens and the yogurt finger will make good props for the Québecoise, whom we're expecting to come around the corner momentarily. But just as she ski-poles up, a Frenchwoman starts feeding the kittens pasta, and the kittens forget all about me and the yogurt, and besides, all feminine attention around is directed toward Tom anyway. You were shitty props, yogurt kittens.

In the terrible heat of midday we're sitting in a combination town square/jai alai court. Andy and I order a round of *bocadillos*. Tom thinks we might have to stop here for the day, but the only *albergue* in town is run by Dutch evangelicals whom Brierley can't recommend highly enough. Then Tom's *bocadillo* breaks apart, spilling dry omelet and potato into his lap.

"I've bottomed out," he says.

"Let's go, Tom," we say.

We help him to his feet. The great thing about Tom is that once he's bottomed out, he has no trouble at all continuing.

The remainder of the day passes in shadeless stupor. A gravel road, each individual pebble like a hot nail, cuts across wide waving fringes of ochre hay. Heat shimmers on the treeless plain, and heatstroke fuzzes the hot brain. Tom mutters something about how we very well might be walking to our deaths under this tyrannical sun.

"I think if you die on the Camino, though, you go straight to heaven or something," I say. "It's in Brierley's appendix."

"It is *not*," Tom says, and begins to lecture with mad ambition.

"There are several distinct species of Camino walkers," Tom begins. He taps his first finger. "There's the tank."

He taps his second finger. "There's the zombie—that's what I am."

He goes to tap his third finger but stops in midair. He stands motionless in the heat. Andy and I try to nudge him forward.

"There are two types of Camino walkers," he says, "tanks and zombies. And I," he concludes, "I am a zombie."

The landscape is the most stunning we've seen so far, a soft, voluptuous swell of green hill, hayfields bedded lightly on the hilly flanks, the gray road a slow ribbon to the horizon.

"Why aren't you guys talking," Tom says into a light breeze that ruffles our burnt necks and hurts our sore feet.

"The scenery is nice," I manage.

"*Scenery?* I just see a bunch of shit you have to walk past!" Tom turns somber. Andy hasn't spoken in hours, readjusts Tom's pack on his back. "Brierley said this was going to be a day wonderful!"

"A day wonderful, Tom?"

"Please don't write that down."

The landscape deliquesces into a hot, blurry bath of scrub and hay and olive hashed with the stark lines of an occasional vineyard. I'll look back at my notebook later and find it scarred with runes. "T claims," I wrote, "he fucking *minored* in meteorology."

We don't even have the energy to wonder why we're doing this.

There's just the shadelessness and the rippling naked nerves of our feet torn by the gravel. We crawl into the *albergue*, stomp on our clothes in the shower, vacantly check email, hope nobody snores.

IN THE MORNING I buy a walking stick and discover my first blister, a little guy about which I'm immediately histrionic. Tom reminds me that his feet, with no fewer than eight blisters per foot, are springlike in their suppurating blooms. "I don't think you're really trying to understand or give a shit about the serious pain I'm in," Tom says. I take this as a wide-ranging criticism and can't stop thinking about it as we walk on in the silent early heat.

We do our best to walk without touching the ground, which of course will mess up our knees and ankles. Andy jogs on ahead a little bit. The Camino runs from deep river valley to broad vista with views of vineyard and scrub. Little decrepit stone huts like bashed-in beehives dot the landscape. The constant up and down, though demanding physically, is actually easier psychologically than the long, unaccountable stretches of flat: they give you a sense of progress. We can see Logroño, where we plan to take our next day off, on the distant plain below. It's ninety-five degrees and Tom sits down on the melting asphalt of the mesa road.

We have lunch along the main drag of a touristy hill town, all built in stone of a burnt-wheat hue. Tom orders a tableful of beers for himself and Andy.

"That's a bad decision," I predict.

"You are predicting wrong," says Andy, awash in free beer.

Eight or ten of their beers later, I return from dunking my head in the historic town fountain and Tom looks at me, sweeps his arms across a table of empty bottles, and says, "You weren't around when

I was quoting myself quoting myself in the future." Tom likes to quote himself as much as the next guy, but rarely with such temporal intricacy.

"You're talking, I gather, about how this pilgrimage experience seems to take place outside of time?"

"That," says Tom, "is what *she* said." He and Andy erupt in a fit of drunken giggles.

I'm shepherding these children through the furnace of the street when we see a woman we'd met the night before at the *albergue*, a schoolteacher from LA who'd told us that she was the first person in America who knew George W. Bush was lying to the American people. Now she looks as though she's going to cry; her face is purple and she can't stop sweating. She left before us and we've been here for two hours.

"I keep telling myself," she says between little choked hiccups, "that I've got all summer to finish this, that I'm not going to give up like I did last time, that I can go as slowly as I want and I'll get there. Someday." We take her bag and help her find the *albergue*. We'll next see her in front of the cathedral in Santiago, where she'll look at her feet and tell us she took the bus.

It's now more than a hundred degrees out, but Tom and Andy are much too drunk to notice as they slalom their way down the path, arm in arm. I'm walking alone, twenty feet or so behind, and can't really hear them. Periodically they solicit my opinion on one matter or another but it's too hot to have opinions, too hot to do anything but put one foot in front of the other, and it's much too hot for that. They look like they're having fun, but they're just distracting themselves, I decide. From what? The idea of a distraction only makes sense in terms of a particular aim; there's no such thing as simply being "distracted." It's always relative to something. They're not distracted from our big agreed-upon end, which is just moving toward, and eventually reaching, Santiago. There isn't any other goal here, I guess, so as long as they're moving, they're technically undistracted. In fact, they're moving faster than I am right now. Yeah, but they're drunk. They're missing something. What, exactly, do you want them to be experiencing more fully? The pain and the heat? Why do you think this experience has to be miserable all the time? If being drunk helps them get through the heat, why begrudge them that? It's the absurdity, that's what it is. They're distracted from the absurdity of this.

"Why are we doing this, again?" I realize I'm whining.

"Gideon." Andy swivels in my direction. "You probably won't know until much later, at the end or maybe even after the end, when you get home, why you did this, and what it did for you, if anything at all. So stop worrying about it for now."

"Andy," accuses Tom, "you just said that because you knew it's *exactly* the sort of thing he was going to write down."

Andy grins a little. "So, what's wrong with that? Knowing you guys might want to write something down makes me try my hardest."

"Andy," Tom says, "why are you succumbing to the crushing pointlessness of it all?" Andy laughs.

"Andy," Tom says, more insistently this time, "why have you joined our bullshit caravan into nothingness?" Andy starts to say something but Tom cuts him off, more serious now. "Andy, are you glad you hooked up with us?"

"You two have made me feel worse about everything: about myself, about others, about the world." Tom looks a little crestfallen, but then Andy starts to laugh. He'll leave us alone the next morning to squander a horrible day off, another day of constantly refreshing our email, moping, and eating *pato de Pekin*, but his stories about his wacky days on the bullshit caravan into nothingness will filter back to us across the overlapping pilgrim generations.

. . .

WE LEAVE THE BOUTIQUE HOTEL in Logroño by five, in time to watch the last drunkards stagger into a kebab place called Döner Berlin. The yellow arrows are easy to notice in this final street-lit hour, and Tom and I agree that the moments just before dawn are the best part of the day.

We walk through a dark municipal park and around a lake, then along a chain-link fence threaded with thousands of crosses made of bark. On the other side of the fence, down an embankment, is the highway we've been paralleling, the one Brierley hates.

Tom pulls the already worn book from his cargo-pant pocket. "He wonders if we'll take the time to stop and 'enforce this thin separation of the sacred and the profane.'"

The crosses, which are snaked through the fence for hundreds of meters ahead of us, are disturbing in the crimson early-morning light. "They remind me of *Pet Sematary*," I say.

"I was thinking *The Blair Witch Project*. Either way, I'm glad that Jesus wasn't beheaded."

But it is the line of yellow arrows, not the bark crosses, that appears as a manifestation of the sacred in the world, what the writer Mircea Eliade calls "hierophany." In *The Sacred and the Profane*, Eliade writes that the sign of the sacred is something that doesn't belong to the world, something that establishes itself as necessarily and self-evidently true; it provides orientation, choreographs our movements. The yellow arrows do not belong to the world of barbecues and errands and idiosyncratic desires. In fact, they ask us to ignore that world, and all of its conflicts and fears, for the sake of their single directive. Eliade describes hierophany not in terms of obedience, as thinkers from Nietzsche to Dawkins have talked about religious devotion, but in terms of simple *orientation*. We orient ourselves with reference to the primal acts of creation, the occasions at which the first decisions were made about the world. Our relationship to the sacred is the story of how the members of our community manage the problem of where to go and what to do there.

Eliade, too, understood that the origin of the sacred, the motives behind the primal acts of creation, could be immaterial. Any old aleatory source will do as long as it has the trust of the people over time. "When no sign manifests itself, it is *provoked*. . . . A *sign* is asked, to put an end to the tension and anxiety caused by relativity and disorientation—in short, to reveal an absolute point of support. For example, a wild animal is hunted, and the sanctuary is built at the place where it is killed. Or a domestic animal—such as a bull—is turned loose; some days later it is searched for and sacrificed at the place where it is found. Later the altar will be raised there and the village will be built around the altar. . . . This is as much to say that men are not free to *choose* the sacred site, that they only seek for it and find it by the help of mysterious signs." And this, after all, is what Tom—in Saigon, Rome, Vegas, Tallinn—and I—in San Francisco, Berlin, Shanghai—wanted, some sort of mysterious sign indicating a way out of the tension and anxiety caused by relativity and disorientation. What's so great about the yellow arrows is that they demand of us no particular adherence. They have the form of command without content. They traffic in pointless direction.

We're following the mysterious signs today with ease, making good time and feeling relaxed and confident. The red-dirt track is wide and wends its way between village and vineyard. I remember this distinctly as one of the nicest days of the entire walk, though there's nothing in particular that distinguishes it. There are other days I remember with vivid fondness for more specific reasons—the day that my feet stopped hurting, say, or the predawn Alina and I spent walking close in silence, or the final approach to Santiago—but I remember this as simply a wonderfully calm and pleasant few hours.

We see almost no other pilgrims. We come over a final rise and see half of the small province of La Rioja spread out before us in a shallow basin, ringed with craggy recumbent mountains tinged a deep Andean green. Low cliffs of red soil hang over the vineyards—vineyards that produce the famous red wines the Spanish love to refrigerate for Tom to drink with breakfast. We stop and breathe.

"This, I think, is as close to nonpharmacological euphoria as I'm ever going to get," Tom says. "Thanks for doing this with me."

A T FOUR FORTY-FIVE in the morning we gather our effects after a miserable night in the municipal *albergue*: endless rows of bunks under a low ceiling where dim-witted pilgrims snored like circus bears, drunk yokels carrying on in the parking lot outside. This *albergue* seems to have had an unusually high proportion of scuzzy types, men and women who clearly identify as pilgrims but look a lot like mere indigents. Apparently these guys have a long history: the more inventive medieval beggars realized that walking to Santiago was a relatively respectable way to go about seeking alms.

We walk silently out of the dorm, the first to embark (not that that matters or anything) into the night. The early starts we've made so far were on our way out of cities, so we could count on an hour of street lamps to help us find the arrows, but leaving Nájera we find ourselves in heavy blue dark. The blue sweep of dark land, sleepy indigo rows of vines under a slim rent of moonlight, is ominous, and we're a little afraid. One or two cars race toward us, underlit and too fast, on the gravel track. We're mostly quiet, a little cross.

"I wasn't sleeping when the alarm went off," Tom says.

"Yes you were. I had to poke you. Twice."

"Don't tell me when I did or didn't sleep. I know when I slept."

We stop at dawn for *bocadillos* and, for Tom, chilled red wine.

The next stretch is the most beautiful landscape of the whole Camino: careful cultivation, alternating fields of hay, vineyard, stubbled fallow, counterpaned yellowing greens and greening blues. From the heights the land below us looks like a sea of inconstant depth, a mossy blur of lime and pea and jade. Shadows of low clouds pool in the valleys and small depressions of the earth.

"These pastures are stunning," Tom says.

"They're fields, not pastures," I reply. "Pastures are for livestock."

"Yeah, well, I smell manure in the air."

"I know. It's so acrid."

"There's a line of David Foster Wallace's where he calls the smell of manure 'blameless.' I've always liked that," Tom says.

"I think there's a lot of fantasy and delusion in the idea that we might interestingly call animals 'blameless.' They don't make decisions. The idea of blame doesn't apply."

We fall silent for a while. I can't understand why I'm being so contradictory. We try to have a serious conversation about religion. I forget how the subject comes up.

"Your vituperative anti-religiosity is just as simplified and hackneyed as those Richard Dawkins tirades," I say.

"Nothing good has ever come from religion," Tom says.

"That's an insane thing to say. I mean, there's not even really such a thing as 'religion.' If you give up the superstitions of the divine—if you acknowledge that we do the things we do, have the habits of action we have, for social reasons rather than supernatural ones—religion just becomes the name for how we talk about and, through ritual, enact our tradition of moral responsibility."

"Right, and that's nothing a secular humanist can't do."

"But what you don't realize is that only Christians can make this argument about humanist universalism. You don't know what it's like to feel as though, secular as you are, the dominant tradition isn't your own. And anyway, if you think no good has ever come from religion, why are you writing a book about it?"

"Well, at least in part it's about exploding the myths that undergird Christian belief. Like the idea that Saint James ever made it to Spain in the first century, or that Saint Thomas brought Christianity to India at the same time."

"Yeah, but who cares about the people who actually believe crap like that? Why bother arguing with biblical literalists?"

"Because I grew up with biblical literalists. You never had to deal with people like that, but if you had, you'd be just as worked up as I am. I mean, look at the ends this Saint James myth has been put to." All over the place we've seen representations of Santiago Matamoros, Saint James the Moorslayer, on a white horse with a flaming sword. It was the chief military propaganda during the bloody centuries-long Christian siege of infidel Spain. "And then, to make matters even worse, the image was taken up by Franco too."

But there's also Santiago Peregrino, Saint James the Pilgrim, who takes vows of poverty and privation and provides a model, along this trail, of humility and gratitude. After all, the two of us are walking this trail right now, and both of us have some hope, however faint, that it'll bring us solace. "Neither of us believes in divine redemption or the story that a fucking stone boat delivered apostolic bones to Galicia."

Tom doesn't say anything. I can tell he thinks we're better off just dropping this for the moment.

"I mean, just proving that the stories are myths doesn't necessarily change how people act. Like, I realize the archaeological record blows some pretty big holes in the idea of the Exodus from Egypt, but I still love my mom's seder every year, and it feels meaningful and resonant for me."

"Yeah, and I derive meaning and succor from a little holiday I like to call Thanksgiving, which doesn't involve a vengeful God who drowns a bunch of Egyptians and later reappears in history to support illegal territorial claims!"

"Tell that to the Indians."

We don't talk for an hour, by far our longest stretch of silence so far. We trudge past the vineyards and along a road through an industrial zone and some parking lots. I find myself in a truly black mood. Tom's made me out to feel like some shtetl dupe, and I've cornered him into a chilly rationalism. The soaring feeling of fellowship that made yesterday so wonderful has dissipated. I've given up on the day, am eager to get somewhere and stop walking, or would rather just keep walking, but our feet hurt and there's no shade and we have to stop sometime.

WE STOP FOR LUNCH in a cute town with a funny little pilgrim welcome center—mostly, we realize, for tourists who are interested in watching pilgrims go by. It has free internet, so we stop to check our email, which we hadn't had the chance to check in at least sixteen hours.

I get an email from my dad. It's Father's Day weekend and he's been thinking about me. "I want you to know I love you very much. I am sorry I've hurt you in the past, and caused you to be angry with me. I am hoping you'll forgive me, and we can reestablish our relationship as father and son, built on mutual trust and respect. I'm sure there have been many wonderful things going on in your life this past year, and I would enjoy being part of your life and these experiences. I hope you will accept my apology and trust my sincerity, please write or call me when you have some time."

It occurs to me that he has no idea that I am making my way across Spain on foot for no reason. We haven't spoken in almost eighteen months, since we got into a sort of clumsy fistfight one Sunday morning in Berlin, when he and Brett and Bubbe, his mother, were visiting. As we struggled in the street near the elevated U-Bahn, a passing German stopped to tell us that "fazzers und zons should not fight, zey should go and talk mit ze ozzer over some beers." But we both said cruel things, and then I jumped into a cab, kicked his grip off my ankle, and pulled the door shut behind me. At the train station, I told the woman behind the ticket counter that I wanted a train that was going (a) as far as possible, (b) as soon as possible, and (c) as cheaply as possible. This is the kind of question that explodes a German's brain.

She thought for a minute. "Do you want to go north, south, east, or west?"

I didn't really have a preference, but I knew I was going to have to answer. "Uh, north or east."

"Do you want to go to the sea or the mountains?"

That was a great question! "The sea," I said right away. She booked me a ticket on a train leaving for the island of Rügen in ten minutes, where I'd take a ferry out into the stormy Baltic to see Friedrich's chalk cliffs. My dad sent me dozens of texts to the effect that he was ready to forgive me for my "outburst" and that if I met him for dinner he would act as if nothing had happened. Which was, of course, precisely the problem, or one of them: his willingness and ability to go on acting as though nothing had ever happened. He wrote, "I have a great partner, great friends, a great job and have never felt better. All I wanted to say was that your behavior toward me was not going to succeed in angering, saddening or depressing me, as it would have in the past (therapy!)." I wrote back, "I'm already hours away, sad and angry. I'm sorry to Brett and Bubbe but I just can't see or talk to you until I have a long, handwritten letter itemizing your lies and only then asking for forgiveness."

It's hard to say what that fight had even been about, specifically, especially because my anger was so old—it wasn't anger at the father who was actually there in front of me, who might have seemed a little sedated but whose life did seem a good deal more together and responsible than it had been in some time. I was angry at the father of my youth, the father who'd lied for so long and so often, it was impossible to know when you could feel safe trusting him or needing him.

That old anger had boiled up in what felt like a final way, and I'd been sullen for the few days he'd been in Berlin. He'd wanted to take Brett to see the Jewish Museum, but I'd said it was boring and stupid and that they ought to skip it, that there were better things to do. He said I was being difficult, always his favorite term of disapproval, that it was out of line for me to criticize one of the things that all visitors to Berlin are expected to go do. I told him I couldn't understand why it was so important that he do what *everybody* did and was unable to do even the smallest thing *I* might want him to do. He hadn't even acknowledged a magazine article of mine that had gotten some attention. He had excuses for everything, but there was nothing I could do with the excuses. I told him that, more than anything, the problem was that even if he wasn't lying anymore, I had no idea how to know that.

He said that he and Brett and Bubbe had had a conference about how difficult I'd been, what a "petulant brat," how I was ruining a trip they'd spent a lot of time planning, and that they had been forced to conclude that I was clearly crazy and should move back to New York to go into serious treatment. He'd been trying, he said, to stand up for me as my father, but now was distressed to admit that maybe the two of them were right, and maybe I should be heavily medicated. He said he could barely recognize me anymore. He talked to me the way he'd talked to me at seventeen, fourteen, ten, in his studied tone of profound disappointment.

On our way to grab some *bocadillos*, Tom asks me why I seem so upset.

"I got this email from my dad, and it was the same old bullshit, an attempt at reconciliation of the mistakes-were-made variety, no specifics, no acknowledgments of what the issues have been, no admission of past lies he'd rather forget about, just the hope that we can once more start over and pretend everything has always been fine."

"You wanted him to mention your fight in Berlin, or what?"

"Yeah, or if not the fight itself, then at least what was behind it."

"Which was what?"

"It's hard to say now. Part of it was that I'd been in New York the week before, to moderate this panel, and it seemed like sort of a big deal to me, and my dad skipped it because he had to go to some boozy birthday brunch in Chelsea that he claimed was a work obligation, and it felt like one more example of his having something more important to do. And the thing is that maybe it was a legitimate work obligation, but he's been dishonest about so many things for so long that I never know what I can trust."

"But you'd made it clear to him that you'd wanted him there?"

"He knew it was important."

"You'd told him that?"

I can't say I know what being on the Camino alone is like, but one of the weird things about being on it with a friend is that, due to the difficulty of coming up with twelve straight hours of ambulatory conversation each day, you end up repeating stories ad nauseam. (I am already someone who repeats stories ad nauseam.) And something about the repetition and the heat and the pain in your feet makes you notice the cracks in the story.

"Well, no, not explicitly."

"What did you tell him?"

"I sent him an email that said it wasn't a big deal, that I didn't mind if he had something else to do."

"But it was a big deal?"

"I don't know, yes and no." I hadn't entirely wanted him there because my mom was going to be there and I always try to avoid putting her through that. And I'd also told him it wasn't a big deal because I wanted him to decide that it was important enough to him to see me that he'd cancel his other plans and come anyway. And probably I said it also because I knew I'd have been so much more disappointed if I'd made a big deal out of it and he hadn't come. And maybe I'd wanted to have an excuse to keep being pissed off at him. "Of course, ultimately I did want him to be there and to be proud of me. But I was also so mad at him about this big magazine article I'd written that he'd ignored."

Tom knew the article I was talking about, which was for a magazine we'd both written for. "I was a little pissed off they didn't send me to write that story. Not that you didn't do a good job."

"We've talked about this before." We'd had a long conversation on the second or third day about how he'd replaced one of his mentors on the masthead of the same magazine. He'd had a dream in the last boutique hotel that I'd then replaced him. "They knew you had a book to finish and thought you didn't have time. But can we talk about that later?"

"Yeah, anyway, your dad, this article: Did he ignore it for any reason?"

"Well, one of the characters I wrote about is a stepbrother of his, who happened to be relevant to the story, and whom he's always been jealous of in the context of these unresolved divorce issues he pretends he doesn't have. I guess I could have predicted that would make him unhappy, but for what I thought were illegitimate reasons." I'd gotten a really angry email from his mother about it, about how she'd been so dismayed by my step-uncle's inappropriate presence that she refused to finish the article. "It was a piece of journalism," she wrote, "not a memoir."

"So it sounds like you just want excuses to be mad at him."

"Yeah, I think so. The thing that's so strange to me is that there's so much stuff I don't remember, you know?"

As an adolescent I often felt as though I were being punished for reasons I couldn't comprehend. But when people ask me why I felt so angry or rejected, I can rarely remember what the fights were about or what terrible things he'd done to provoke them. What I remember most was the pound of his heavy Doc Martens on the steps up from the garage late at night, on his way home from God knows where, knowing that soon I'd hear him call from his study "Can I see you in here for a minute?" and that I'd be expected to drop whatever I was doing right away—usually reading—to complete some absurd task that instant, like put together a grill or mow the lawn at night. It was always obvious that he was furious about something but he never conceded that, never allowed that what he was doing was punitive. He always just said that whatever it was simply had to be done that minute or there would be *severe repercussions*. But no matter what he did do, I think I've long felt angrier with him for the things he *didn't* do, the secrets he kept, the deceptions I know I still don't know about.

"Maybe you just need to be okay with having forgotten the details, and maybe you also need to understand that you will never get any redress from the father he was then. Being mad at the father he is now is never going to get you anywhere. Think about your vengeful, capricious god and how you still like your mom's seder despite the drowned Egyptians."

"Huh? What do you mean?"

"I don't know, I'm sorta just riffing, but I think you need to admit that sometimes you feel like a drowned Egyptian, but that there's no use dwelling on it. For now, just write your fucking dad back," Tom says. "It's fucking Father's Day." Tom had written a whole book about his relationship with his father, so I figured he had some idea what he was talking about, and, besides, I liked these moments when Tom told me what to do.

But it's also annoying to be told what to do, especially in a pat way, and especially when other people don't know your father. At an internet kiosk in a bar in some dingy town, I forwarded my dad's email to Micah with a short gloss: "Yet another contentless apology, but I don't think I can ignore it. My away message buys me a few days, at least."

Micah wrote back right away from his phone. "I'm not sure you should care about the content. I think that this is as sincere as it's going to get (no matter how sincere you think or don't think this is). Maybe it's worth another shot? Or maybe not. I dunno. I'm all out of advice. I'd give it another shot."

I wrote to my dad. I told my dad I loved him and was glad to hear from him but was still angry. My note was stiff. I wanted to have a relationship with him again, but it was "important for me to note that our previous models of reconciliation—a theatrical fight, some time apart, and ultimately a kind of nonspecific apology and the expectation of immediate normalcy—have only left me disappointed and hurt, and I do not want to feel that way again. There are fewer desiderata in my life as central and pressing as the ability to trust you again, the pleasure and solace of knowing I can trust you again, but it will not happen overnight." I told him I was walking across Spain

and didn't have a cell phone or frequent internet access, but that I
would write again when I could. I told Tom what I'd written. He said
he was proud.

B UT THE CONVERSATION about our fathers and my article acti-
vates some generational rivalry, and for two days we snipe at
each other about money and assignments and why were you included
in that anthology and not me and why did my piece get killed and
yours didn't. Though we're equally ambitious, professional competi-
tion has never been a part of our relationship before; now we can't
stop pushing each other's buttons. On the second day we decide to
take a half day—which is to say we stop walking after about two
hours—and leave each other alone for the afternoon and evening.

Both of us have ideas about the nonfiction writer as someone
who needs to get it right, set a particular record straight, but from
there we diverge. Part of Tom's writerly ambition—especially
in light of his profoundly beautiful book about his own father, or in
light of his idea that he can save Christian legend by decoupling it
from Christian doctrine—strikes me as being about the power to
vindicate, about being able to use his talents to redeem. He's managed to tell a story about his father's life in a way his father might not
be able to do himself. My own ambition seems almost the opposite:
it's often felt designed to force my father to pay any attention at all
and, beyond that, to force him to pay attention to my definitive version of events—the more public, the better. I remember that the first
thing I ever wrote for myself and not for a school assignment was a
very detailed record of a fight we'd had, and an indictment of what I
saw as his deceit and hypocrisy. I'd left copies under his door for him
and my mom as they slept. I can't remember how he reacted to it, if
he did at all.

. . .

IN THE EARLY MORNING after our afternoon off, Tom and I wake up feeling restored, the old easy camaraderie regained, the trail soft. We walk more quickly than we have in some time, through chunked-dirt fields that line an approach to ten or twelve kilometers of hills. For a short stretch we're on a road and the traffic is terrible. Tom starts singing into the traffic as Brierley advises, classic rock standards with their words replaced by the repeated phrase "pilgrim song." Soon he moves into pilgrim tunes of his own soulful improvisation. I try to harmonize and we almost fall into a ditch laughing. Tom insists I try. Mine is set to the tune of "Take Me Home, Country Roads":

> Pilgrim song!
> The trucks steal
> the energyyyyyy of our zeal.
> Pilgrim voices,
> sing our choices—
> old and young,
> Pilgrim song!

Tom asks me to stop singing, but he's pretty nice about it. We charge up the hills, the Montes de Oca, and there's nothing to talk about but how strong our legs feel and how we're finally used to this, and how slender we must look. It's hot and we're passing people without a glance back. We stop for tangerines by a Spanish Civil War memorial obelisk, then resume walking with a young woman on her own. She's Anya, a Polish student.

"I'm here in Spain with two friends, a boy and a girl, but today we decided we go at our own pace. Things are now little bit, um—"

"Tense?" Tom asks.

"Yes, tense with the boy, and because tense with the boy, tense also with the girl."

We nod and ask her why she's doing this and what she thinks so far.

"I am religious person. I am Catholic person. I try to go to the pilgrims' Mass every day, and I am disappointed when there is not one. These parishes in Spain, sometimes they only have priest one time in two weeks, so there are few blessings for pilgrim."

"Are your friends in Kraków all religious?" I ask.

"Some religious, many not. But I think religion offer young people way of life that's different from other option we have in Poland."

"What's the other option?"

"Being alcoholic."

"You mean the only two options for a young person in Poland today are being religious or being an alcoholic?"

"That is what I mean, yes."

"Oh."

Anya changes the subject. "Who are weirdest people you see on Camino?"

"That's easy," I say. "There are those two Asian women, the ones with the broad welding visors and the all-white outfits with the chef aprons. They walk single file and they never eat or drink water during the day, we heard."

Tom jumps in. "We've seen them up before dawn in the *albergues*. They each have one plate of white rice, and that's it. They sleep on their backs with their hands folded on their chests. They don't talk all day, and they don't stop. I think they're cultists."

"Yeah, my guess is like Aum Shinrikyo or something, those guys that spread the nerve gas in the Tokyo Metro."

Anya says, "You mean the two Korean nuns?"

"Oh," we say.

"Buen Camino," she says.

Brierley's suggested end stage, a little forest hamlet with one monastery and one restaurant, looks like a refugee camp: pilgrims splay on their packs in the scant shade as they wait for the *albergue* to open. We're feeling so well reconstituted—by our fine pace and blood-sausage lunch and our ability to leave behind our short era of professional squabbling—we decide to push on, down the hill through a pine forest toward the central plains. I wonder aloud if we might be able to make Burgos today, a full additional stage, and Tom looks at me warily. He knows that I have a tendency to push too far, and he also knows that my obsessive fixations always begin as casual proposals. I've already told him about the time I got Micah and my dad to come with me to visit three Andean countries in six days, and about the time I convinced Micah and my mom to drive hundreds of kilometers out of our way to visit godforsaken Gibraltar, the worst place I've ever been. Micah's still constantly giving me shit about Gibraltar.

But the trail is empty and shaded and soft, and the conversation is so lively and fluid and intimate, that neither of us can imagine what the point of stopping might be. It brings to mind only the stink and forced conviviality of the *albergue*, the deadening routine of arriving and registering and deciding if one has the energy to shower and stomp on one's dirty clothes in an attempt to clean them, knowing full well that despite the heat they'll still be clammy in the morning. So we keep going.

We pass what Brierley indicates is our last chance to stop before Burgos itself, which is still ten or twelve miles distant. It's only at this point that the dirt track becomes a road, and the shade disappears, and the landscape changes from idyllic pine forest to squalid suburb patrolled by slavering dogs. We've been wondering when we might have to take part in the ancient Camino tradition of beating a dog to death with a stick, and we think it might be now. In the industrial outskirts of Burgos the strange sidewalk tile slams into our feet like porcelain mallets.

We stop speaking; there's nothing to say. Six p.m., seven p.m., hours later than pretty much any day we've walked, auto body shops, furniture outlets, gas stations. Our bodies are beginning to break down. Brierley says this is the single most unpleasant stretch of the whole Camino. We speak through set jaws and only when absolutely necessary; we don't look at each other. A man is reslabbing a granite side street, his sledgehammer coming down on a block of wood, and my neck and upper back stab sympathetically. Pain flashes up in long flares from my feet to my hips.

How far to the cathedral, we ask a stranger, and he says fifteen minutes on foot. We've walked thirty-two miles today, and Tom begs to take a cab. I won't consider it, even though it's almost dark. I begin to dissociate, to find the pain in my body aloofly interesting, as if I'm examining it from some height. Tom is all howling animal, his jaw in a grudgy lock. We'd felt so good such a short time before, and now this. It would be a welcome relief, I think, to sit in the street and be run over by a bus.

At the hotel the receptionist tells us that to walk from Belorado to Burgos in one day is *demasiado*, too much. Tom is in bed in his clothes within a minute. I unpack some of my things and Tom demands to know why I'm still up walking around. We writhe between the sheets on our narrow beds, each in our own awful waking dream, the pain unwilling to quiet. When we finally sleep for real, we both dream about walking.

. . .

W E SPEND TWO DAYS obsessively refreshing our email at the boutique hotel in Burgos before we feel whole enough to keep going. I have an email exchange with my mom in which she is, as usual, almost maddeningly reasonable. "As a general position, I think it is always better to be talking than not talking. As a specific position regarding Dad, I never know what is best. On the one hand, you want to be open to forgiveness; on the other, you don't want to get wounded again and again. It is good that you are having all that walking time to meditate and mull over your blisters. Tell me if you really meditate (or do you just fantasize about finding a 7-11?)."

When we leave Burgos the streets are dark, jagged with glass and stained with urine and vomit; it's the last late hour of the city's annual festival. We pass the cathedral, a Gothic pile floating in a nimbus of yellow streetlight, and a gang of fourteen-year-olds yells *Buen Camino* and throws some beer on us.

Neither of us has slept well. Our bodies are used to the end-day exhaustion of walking, and the nights of our days off are tetchy and uncomfortable. It grows light as we hit the industrial meadowlands on the city's western fringe, where the Camino files by weedy rubbish heaps and under concrete overpasses.

We stop for *bocadillos* in the last town before the Meseta, the high, hot, featureless plain that takes up the middle two weeks of the Camino. I figure we're about a third of the way to Santiago. A sign over a bar advertises a ham raffle, which adds to the Lynchian frontier aspect of this town on the fringe of the Meseta. Tom doesn't feel like talking, so I repeat this to myself: *Ham raffle on the Meseta's fringe. Meseta-fringe ham raffle.*

The land resembles a vast sea of grain, the sky a basic blue potted with clouds. Brierley loves it, calls it not only "sacred" but "other-worldly," "sublime" for spiritual contemplation. The Camino appears as a narrow bridge of white gravel to the desolate horizon. Distance is impossible to gauge, and our bodies feel tiny. Colors are pale, drained. Giant cairns of rough white stone are the only built things.

We move quickly and see almost no one. "There's this Ashbery poem I really like," I tell Tom, "where one line goes something like 'To step free at last, minuscule on the gigantic plateau— / This was our ambition: to be small and clear and free.' That's sort of how I feel right now—small and clear and free."

"You're really getting something out of this, aren't you?" Tom teases, though there's an edge. "Maybe you should do more pilgrim-ages," he says. "Maybe you should fake-convert to Islam and go on the Hajj!"

"No, I can't do that. My mom would be worried, and you prob-ably can't email from the Hajj. And I wouldn't be interested, really. What I like about this experience so much is that the question of belief is absent. The ritual has remained close to unchanged even though the content has been mostly drained off. The Hajj isn't like that—that's still very much about the *content* of belief. What I need is to find another pilgrimage like this one, where belief is a nonis-sue and you can just walk with direction, and feel good while walk-ing with direction, and I want to do it alone, and I want it to be even farther away than Spain, and I want it to be even longer, and harder, and I want to do it in the springtime, not in the heat of the summer."

"Well, good luck with that, my man. If you're feeling so good about all this, maybe you should take it as your mission to recom-mend it to others. You'll have to look into the international pilgrim-age circuit, see what else is out there." What I vaguely wish he'd said then: *Be careful what you wish for.*

· · ·

F OR MOST OF THE CAMINO, you amble through a village every
few hours, but on the Meseta the towns are spaced out. They
sit in depressed basins with steep sides, huddled atop themselves.
They're set in clay and hay-specked mud brick, singed bronze by the
white sun. Nothing so far has felt quite so medieval, so much like
what the route must have looked like when Ferdinand and Isabella
traveled it. You can't help but feel as though you've graduated to
Camino Level II: there's less to look at, fewer places to stop, little to
no shade. The novelty's worn off and it's begun to feel more serious,
somehow, though of course it's exactly the same.

We relax in the plaza outside the *albergue* as the other pilgrims
file in. An older man sits down next to us, takes a cigarillo out of a
tissue-lined engraved silver box, and asks for a light. He introduces
himself as Román. He's nearing seventy and has done the Camino,
in sections, at least five times.

"I was just telling Tom," I say, "that I'm positive I want to do
this again."

"And I was just telling Gideon," Tom says, "that he's completely
out of his mind."

Román usually walks two or three weeks each summer. "I like
the villages, places like here, Hontanas, famous for its local water.
The cities, the cities are bullshit. I take buses through them." He's
got thin, muscular arms, strong legs, and a tremendous paunch. His
right calf is tattooed with a bull silhouetted against a roseate sunset. He wears a light graphite brush of a mustache and thinned-out
gray curls and projects an air of refined corruption, or corrupt wisdom. Tom tells him he looks like Gabriel García Márquez. He looks
a little bashful, opens his mouth to demur. "Sometimes García
Márquez, sometimes Al Pacino," he says.

By now he's gotten a light for his cigarillo, and he talks through his pluming exhales. "There's one thing you can't miss on the Camino: the *pulpo a la gallega* in Melide." He flutters his fingers like an octopus.

In the morning we sleep in past six, and by the time we get going we're right in the thick of the morning exodus. For the first time the Camino is almost crowded; all along the empty Meseta we can see a drift of pilgrims in either direction. We pass a sign to the historic Castrillo Matajudíos. "I think I better avoid that place," I say.

Tom doesn't laugh, doesn't even look over.

"Jew-Murder Castle?"

Still nothing.

"What's going on?" I ask as we begin to climb the only hill we'll see for days.

"Oh, nothing. I'm fine," Tom says.

"No, really. What's up? You seem so distant this morning."

"It's fine, I'm here. You know how it is, just thinking about stuff at home, settling down, all this crap I need to deal with when I get back."

"You want this walk to be over, don't you? I know you do."

"Don't be silly, this is great. I mean, I'm miserable and I hate every minute of it, but I'm still glad we're doing it. So, yes, I do want it to be over. But you shouldn't take that personally."

"You just seem somewhere else sometimes. I hate the feeling that the person I'm with would rather be anywhere but here."

I don't talk for a while. Tom looks over. "You're being a little oversensitive. It's this fucking Meseta, man. It messes with your mind. You're worried to distraction that I'm distracted. But what is this walk for if not to give me time to think about the rest of my life? What do you think it'd even mean for me to be less distracted? Just to think about *you* all the time?"

"That's not what I'm saying."

"Well, what, then?"

"I guess I just feel like if I can't have your attention when we're at the end of the earth as the only people around, then, well, I don't know."

"Gideon, you have my attention, like, ten hours a day. Where'd this needy petulance come from all of a sudden? Jesus. For a guy who's mostly a giant, arrogant dick who thinks he knows what's always best for everybody else, you can act like a real child sometimes."

"So do you."

"Well, then, I guess we both do."

"Sorry."

IF THE FIRST DAY of the Meseta was featureless, the second makes the first look like a mescaline stroll through Euro Disney. I've never seen less in the way of spectacle. Windmills turn like metronomes in the distance, reminding us that the only thing happening is time. It's tempting to call it lunar, but that would be an insult to the moon. The day's only event is a brief interim along a river, where we stretch out on the banks and wish we could just stop. The villages are portcullised against the heat. For what seems like hours, all that breaks the silence is the shuffle of our shoes in the gravel and the hollow plonk of our walking sticks. Tom's right about our dynamic. But he participates in it too. We've spent ten days, about a third of the Camino already, alternating roles. First it's my turn to be the adult: Why didn't you break your boots in, Tom? Why is your pack so heavy, Tom? Here, let me carry it. Why do you make us stop so often, Tom? If you really want to lose weight you shouldn't eat that ice cream, Tom. Then it's his turn: Forgive your dad, Gideon. Andy needs my attention now, Gideon. Go talk to the Québecoise, Gideon, she likes you. Get over your one stupid blister, Gideon. Don't mock the people who started in Burgos, Gideon. Grow up, Gideon.

The *albergue* at day's end has a pool, though, and a lively Australian is sunning herself in a bikini. We'd seen her with her brother during the day and right off the bat they told us they took a bus for eighteen kilometers into Burgos and didn't feel at all bad about it. We liked the two of them immediately, and Tom says he thinks she was flirting with me, but I doubt it, especially considering what I have come to look like after ten days of walking. Tom says it's something akin to an outré tennis-playing terrorist. I have a big black beard that prompts Tom to ask, rather unkindly, if it's going to grow up and cover my eyes. I've also got on an old pink Ocean Pacific tank top, an inheritance from my dad, which I use for even tanning purposes, and a sporty white tennis headband Tom bought me as a present on our day off in Pamplona. Tom and I had made an agreement not to shave, but when I got back from the internet café in Burgos he'd cleaned himself up. I'm keeping the beard until we reach the end of the world and I emerge a new man.

At dinner we decide to take a break from our unprecedentedly constant companionship and sit at opposite ends of the room. "You should sit by that Australian chick," Tom says. "I think she likes your tank top."

"Nah, I don't much feel like it." I haven't felt even the remotest sexual twinge since I began the Camino, I realize. It just seems sort of pointless, somehow.

"Oh, come on, man! She's cute. Go hit on her so you can tell me about it. Or I will."

"I'm not going to be press-ganged into the vicarious service of your monogamy."

He goes to sit next to her himself and I push him out of the way. Unfortunately some Japanese people sit next to her before I can get to the table, and I end up sitting next to them. This proves vastly, unimaginably consequential.

"Why are you doing the Camino?" I ask the Japanese guy.

"Fourteen years ago, my wife and I drove this road together for a tourist vacation. In Santiago we stood at the cathedral and watched pilgrim arrive. Pilgrim looked"—he consults his wife—"impressive. No. Inspiring. I wanted to look like that pilgrim one day. Now we retire, come back to Spain to walk like real pilgrim."

"Do you think that when you get to Santiago you'll feel like that guy did?"

"Don't know. I'm in now much pain. But hope so!"

"Do people in Japan know about the Camino? Everyone in Europe knows about it, and now more people in the U.S., but what about Japan?"

"Japanese people very drawn to pilgrimage travel. More pilgrimage trips in Japan than maybe anywhere except India! Part of Japan heritage. Many people have heard of Spanish Camino."

"What's the most famous pilgrimage in Japan?"

"Oh, very easy! Shikoku *o-henro*. *Hachijūhakkasho*. Eighty-eight temples of island of Shikoku."

What I know about Shikoku is that it is the smallest and least developed of Japan's four main islands, and that the latter part of Murakami's *Kafka on the Shore* takes place there. I look over at Tom, who's at the head of the table, seducing everybody with hilarious anecdotes of apostolic misadventure, and here I am at the far corner plodding through a pidgin conversation with two reticent retirees. I am going to walk the eighty-eight temples, and I am going to do it as soon as possible, and I am going to do it by myself.

"I am going to do that. I am going to walk the eighty-eight temples of Shikoku. Wait—can you walk it or no?"

The Japanese couple starts laughing. "In old times walk. Now

take bus, maybe taxi. Rich people helicopter! Mostly old people, retire people. Twelve hundred kilometers! Very small people walk,
small *number* of people, but no *albergue* like Camino, no many other
people like Camino, no international like Camino. Very long, very
difficult, very lonely. But rural peoples kind to pilgrim, they give you
osettai, gift."

"I'm doing it."

The Japanese couple continues to giggle. "Very hard but maybe
you try someday."

IN THE MORNING we wake very early and Tom accidentally sees
an elderly German lady's breasts. We're chained into the *albergue*
and have to sit and kill twenty minutes before they unlock the gate.
As the sun rises at our calves, we follow a rocky towpath along a swift
forsythia-lined canal.

At about eight I wait at the bar in the day's first village for our
bocadillos. On television is *El coche Fantástico*, the new European *Knight
Rider* series. Standing next to me is a young Hungarian guy, David
(pronounced *DAH-veed*), whom we've seen on and off for a few stages.
I'd had a brief skirmish with him the previous evening over his mo-
nopolizing of the *albergue* computer; I'd wanted to do some prelimi-
nary research on this Shikoku business and he'd been on Facebook
forever. But this morning he's chatty.

"Character development on this show is very strong," he says. "I
write Hungarian subtitles for internet episodes of *Scrubs*."

"Come sit with us," I say.

At the tables in the sun-flooded plaza outside, Tom is writing
furiously in his notebook, nods his head in the direction of a hale,
sunburnt, amateur-tattooed Australian in scuffed desert boots.

"I'm done," the guy rants to his one-armed friend. "Finished. I've done damage." He pronounces the word like *demmij.* "The tendons are inflamed. They won't let me walk anymore. I was in the army and I used to do a lot of pack marching"—*peck mahching*—"but I ain't never done anything like *this*. The insurance company, they said, 'You're done. You're finished. You've done damage.'" David can't stand to listen any longer and heads off with some Germans we're vaguely acquainted with. Tom and I have taken to him, and we tell him we'll catch up by lunchtime.

After breakfast Tom and I fall into a good walking rhythm and talk about the *albergues.* "What I hate about them," Tom says, "is their soft despotism. I hate the soft despotism of the *albergues.*"

"Yeah, I know what you mean: you're never really alone and at the same time never really with other people."

"You have to have those constant conversations about which town you started in and how long you're planning to spend here and are you going to go past Santiago to the ocean blah blah blah. It's just numbing."

"Oddly, though," I say, "I feel really placid in the afternoons." We ordinarily stop walking by about three; if you get to an *albergue* after five, you can have trouble finding a bed. I never feel bored in the *albergues.* I'm content just to sit and enjoy the sense of end-of-day accomplishment. And I've noticed that I'm especially able to focus on work despite the noise and my physical exhaustion. I can spend two hours writing up my notes from the day—in anticipation, of course, of the next email dispatch—without looking up once; I'm more productive in the two hours between four and six p.m. on the Camino than I ever was in an entire week in Berlin. I don't really feel like reading, though I've made it through about half of *Don Quixote*— which is, I'm given to understand via consistent Spanish eye roll, like reading *War and Peace* on the Trans-Siberian—and I definitely don't feel like drinking or smoking. Even when I can't fall asleep right away, I don't mind just lying there. There are so many things I find I don't think about, like what's going on at that moment anywhere else. All we're doing is walking and then stopping, but somehow that sense of structure and organization affords me so much productivity and calm.

Tom looks at me and squints. "Is this walk *changing* you?"

WE STAY IN A TENTH-CENTURY monastery converted into a luxury hotel, and we're sluggish in the morning. Tom bought us our first fancy dinner of the walk, put it on his room tab, and we'd lingered in the vast, empty dining room past our usual bedtime. When we get up there's no breakfast, no town, no nothing at all for the first seventeen kilometers, the longest such stretch on the Camino save the first day.

The path rises slowly through fields of bland grain. Cylinders of hay loll around like scattered game pieces. There's a thick cloak of gray cloud cover overhead and nothing to look at but the old Roman road ahead, a pebbly mosaic set into hardpan.

My right pinkie toe is mangled. Tom's heels are coming apart. Clouds of insects swarm at our heads and knees. For the last few days we've been shadowing, or being shadowed by, the young Irishman who'd asked us, at the end of that first day, what had taken us so long. He's all soft Trinity College lilt, and he waves his twinky little tush as he passes us now. "Fucking Lucky Charms," Tom says, and we smile at each other weakly.

After what feels like about forever on the old Roman road, we arrive at a café and drop our stuff. The place looks like a Gypsy caravansary, backpacks in the dust and greasy plates stacked in heaps on the tables. The scene has a coarse, snappy, appealing disarray.

Román is reclining with a cigarillo, his faded Dewar's cap in his lap and his curls matted to his forehead in the heat as he surveys the table—the Australian siblings, Lucky Charms, David the duck-gaited Hungarian, the usual assortment of fungible Germans.

"The best thing about the Camino," he says quietly, and we all lean forward, waiting for him to tell us something that explains this experience, "is the stopping. The walking is fucking bullshit. But the stopping is so great! The drinks, the chatting, the sitting, the smoking. Like this, now! I can't say I care much for the walking anymore, and I'm not sure I ever did." It's not the walking, we all think, it's the *stopping*. It seems so obvious now. What's been great about this is the stopping.

But there's always an end to the stopping. Back on the road, we hang back with Román, who says he knows a really nice family-run *albergue* in the next village. A few minutes after we arrive we hear a loud yell in Spanish, then in English. Tom jumps up and says he thinks it was Román. We rush to the bathroom, where the old man is contorted on the tile. He slipped in the shower and fell on his back.

"My *camino* is over," he says.

Román invites me to sit outside with him after dinner while he ices his back and smokes. "The thing that has brought me back to the Camino so many times," he says, "is the solidarity of affliction. In everyday life we know, you know, if only on some abstract plane, that everybody everywhere is suffering. But we're so caught up in the gift of our special, *personal* misery that it's hard to keep that in mind in any real way. But on the Camino all of us are in such pain, all the time, that it's impossible to forget." Everybody is hurting in the same dull, stupid way, so you can't feel too sorry for yourself, or maybe you feel sorry for yourself but you feel sorry for everybody else too. There's a real community in that shared suffering. "That's why people go to Lourdes, too, though they don't fucking walk there. The Virgin doesn't heal you, it's just that the crowds there remind you that pain isn't unusual, and that most people suffer worse, all the time."

We all sleep fitfully. I have a dream in which a couple I'm friends with in Berlin, a gorgeous, immensely talented painter and a brilliant novelist whose relationship I envy more than anybody's, invite me to a sex/dinner club, where you make a reservation for a nice dinner and then have group sex afterward. I am late for the reservation and afraid I'll miss it. But the woman at the door looks down at me and says, "You can't come in here like that." I am surprised to discover I am wearing my unwashed Camino clothes, the pink tank top and the dusty zip-off pants. In the morning Tom's patient or bored enough to listen to me analyze my dream. "I think that the significance of the sex/dinner club was that it was for couples who were both husbands *and* lovers, so to speak. I'd always thought of myself as a husband who wanted to be a lover, and then I thought of myself as a lover who wanted to be a husband, and now it seems"—I gesture at the dusty zip-off pants that barred me in the dream—"that I'm afraid I've become suitable for neither role."

We've reached about the halfway point on the pilgrimage, and we're seeing a first wave of pilgrims fall out. It's a more emotional experience than we thought it would be, especially considering how standoffish we've been, and it gives the walk a different sort of charge. Karo, a twenty-something Serbo-Bavarian with a soft, mercenary look, sits down with us at a café in Sahagún, where Román will depart for Madrid. She tells us that she started with the wrong kind of shoes and walked through three days of rain and pushed on to do too much too quickly at the beginning and now thinks she can't continue on foot. We watch her say good-bye to a German guy she's been walking with for a few days; he wants to wait for her to heal but he's got a plane to catch in Santiago. They hold each other for a long time and tear up and we look elsewhere. He pulls himself away and walks off and doesn't look back.

Román goes to check the train schedule. "I know the Camino is trying to teach me something," Karo says, "but I don't know what it is. Everybody in my family thinks I'm crazy for doing this—my boyfriend can't understand it at all, and keeps yelling at me for leaving him alone—but I needed to do it. I lost my father two years ago, and my sport is to ignore things. I've been ignoring his death for so long, I thought the Camino might give me a chance to think about it and accept it."

She stops, seems a little abashed. "I've only known you two an hour and I'm treating you like old friends!"

Tom eases her embarrassment. "It's okay, we're just doing it for weight loss."

She lights up. "Me too! I think that's everybody's secret reason."

She says she's going to write a book about the Camino. "There are so many books in Germany on this, but nobody mentions the pain! Maybe it is because afterward, when you get back to your real life, you remember only the good parts."

THE PROBLEM WITH the Camino memoir, of which the last millennium has produced hundreds, in dozens of languages, is the finale. I didn't actually read any of them until long after I finished the Camino, but it was clear even before we ourselves had reached Santiago that we were apprehensive not only about what we'd find there but how we'd manage to describe it later. Or, rather, we knew all along, no matter what our expectations for the trip, that Santiago was just going to be an arbitrary place, which is to say that both of us were well aware that nothing at all was going to *happen* there.

This was less of a problem in medieval accounts, where the adventure itself was presumed sufficient to sustain reader interest. But the contemporary genre demands either fulfillment or disillusion. Anticlimax is generally more honest, but it's a crappy, unsatisfying way to end a quest. Climax is either a lie or practically impossible to cash out successfully. Even if your audience is rooting for you, even if they believe you're right on the brink of becoming the person you always thought you could be, it's a hard thing to bring off in a convincing way; it's like the attempt to describe a full solar eclipse. And then, even worse, the consequences of epiphany have to be taken on faith. Very few Camino books bother to cull evidence from the return to the practice of everyday life. Even the Church won't call this a final redemption but, instead, a remission of temporal punishment for the sins committed thus far. This is perhaps what we lose in the absence of calendrical rite: We lean too heavily on the fantasy of one salvific ordeal, just like we lean too heavily on the fantasy that the right person will finally make us happy or whole. (This is the problem with, and the appeal of, the end of *Wings of Desire*: Who gives up the immortality of an angel to sleep with a trapeze artist? Is that really a justifiable sacrifice?)

If an ending is going to be successful, it can't turn on arrival itself. Instead, it has to refer both back to the single-minded motion of the route itself, to motes of silt setting out of a swift current, and at the same time forward to the kinds of alternative lives the future might now hold. The end can't be the terminus of a line. It has to be a point on a circumference. A circle seems like a far more reasonable way to go about the whole thing.

THE WAY OUT OF SAHAGÚN is along a *senda*, which just means path; these white gravel sidewalks have been built over the last two decades by the regional tourism councils, to get the Camino off of the roads. They're perfectly nondescript, planted with new oaks too young to provide much shade, and Brierley despises them. He calls them "soulless errors of national development agencies," bold-facing the initials in case you weren't previously familiar with acronyms. You can tell he fears that they will make the Camino too easy or too widely accessible.

It's our twentieth day, the first day we mostly walk with a group, and thus the beginning of our social epoch. There's Lucky Charms, whom for reasons of increasing trust and affection I'm afraid I've got to start calling Tim, and his confraternity: a near-incomprehensible Welshman named Lee; the young and bandy-legged Hungarian David; and Wiebke, an indefatigable German-Danish Valkyrie. The company prevents us from complaining as much as we usually do, but it also implicates us for the first time in idle and occasionally vicious Camino gossip. Most of it is relayed by Wiebke but sourced to a middle-aged German woman we've been calling, for purely descriptive reasons, Birdface.

Allegedly Tom snores, which isn't true; Lee the Welshman's urine is brown, which he doesn't bother to refute; and that one efflorescent woman from Grand Canary has left her own Canarian party to walk with the one-armed Australian who met his last wife on the Camino, which is such an uncontroversial and widely reported piece of gossip that it hardly bears repeating. When we have to start walking again I scowl—my feet are killing me today—and Wiebke lends me her Nordic walking poles, the sort of ski poles Tom and I have been mocking all along.

Camino graffiti covers the whitewashed façade of the bar on the main square of Reliegos, where we all stop to rest in the shade. It's all watery page-a-day-calendar observations, oleaginous bombast about paths and ways and journeys dripped in twelve or fourteen languages. Tom grabs a black marker at the cute waitress's urging and writes "GLK+TCB: THE CARAVAN INTO NOTHINGNESS . . ." and we think of Andy.

Tim and David and the others are ready to call it a day, but Tom and I decide we feel good enough to try for another six kilometers, and after a day of walking in a crowd we feel like debriefing alone. It's late in the afternoon and we're buoyant on the *senda*; we come to a rock-mosaic ichthys and race to kick it apart.

"You know, it's funny," I say as we push on, "this is about the time of day when we tend to wonder why we're doing this, but today I have no urge to ask that at all."

"Well, I was about to, but I do know what you mean," Tom says.

"I think it's got to have something to do with two days of watching people drop out. There's so much anguish and so much grief, and so much sympathy, even for people we barely knew. It's funny. I guess the reason that I no longer wonder why I'm doing this is because I know now that I'd be really upset if I had to stop." I no longer need to know *why* we're doing it; it's become enough to me *that* we're doing it.

"I also think it has to do with the fact that we've come to share this experience with all these other people—Tim and David and everybody—that I think we're sorta happily stuck with from here on out. They might be a bunch of crackpots and buffoons, but so are we, and I feel some new sense of belonging, of responsibility."

It's been our second-longest day, but we decide to stop into the church on the way to the *albergue*. Tom wets his fingers in the holy water as we enter and flicks some on me. "I just wanted to see if it would burn your Jewish skin."

At the *albergue* there's a very old man we've seen here and there. Somebody tells us he's eighty-three, that his name is Santiago, and that this is his tenth Camino.

"No way it's his tenth." I shake my head.

"Yeah," Tom agrees. "It's probably just his sixth or something."
He pauses for a moment. "Sixth *tops*."

WE TAKE A LISTLESS DAY off in León, in part because David
and Tim want to, in part because there's a five-star hotel
we've heard wonderful things about, and in part because we never
skip an opportunity to take a day off. We spend twelve minutes in the
famous Gothic cathedral, ten minutes buying me Nordic walking
poles, and the rest of the day in an internet café. Micah writes and
tells me that he spent the majority of a Shanghai typhoon reading my
last dispatch out loud to his girlfriend in the pauses of a Pixar movie
marathon. He couldn't possibly have been gladder, he says, to be
doing that instead of walking across Spain.

In the morning we rise early, cross the river, and trudge through
the seedier districts toward the ring of industrial suburbs, the auto
talleres and *ferreterías*. We're reminded it's a weekend by the presence
of drunk people at breakfast. We cross a busy road and come to a
fork, where there's a waymarker that seems to indicate contrary
routes for the next stretch. We're apparently hashing this decision
out too loudly for seven a.m. on a Saturday: a woman rolls up her
window's portcullis, leans out over her balcony, and gestures angrily
to the left. Behind us are David, walking his ducky hip-splayed sa-
shay, and Rachel, another opaline-eyed Québecoise. We wave them
in the right direction but leave them alone to flirt. We both get the
sense that David came on the Camino to find a girlfriend, which
seems a little crazy but appears to be not uncommon.

"I feel like their parents," Tom says.

"Agreed," I say, and somehow this shared feeling allows us to
stop parenting each other for our longest stretch so far.

After an hour or two we stop in a shabby village slithery with leprous cats for a coffee and fruit, and a few minutes later David arrives, now without Rachel but with a lanky dude named Martin. Martin has stringy shoulder-length hair matted under a wide-brimmed gardening hat, filthy sandals, and a shirt with a hip recycling slogan in Norwegian. The four of us head out together.

A butterfly loops into Tom's face and Tom jumps as though dodging a flaming brick. Martin leaps to help, unaware that Tom has a hard time distinguishing between bugs that can and can't hurt you. The road ahead of us is flat and straight and uninteresting, and we pass the time in idle cultural exchange. David likes English language very much and he repeats that he's subtitled several episodes of *Scrubs* on the internet. His English is heavily accented and he has a tendency to forget articles, but his phraseology is unusually elegant, and he has a magisterial but contextless command of outdated American idioms. He's constantly exclaiming "Goody gumdrops!" at quasi-opportune moments. He has a dark side, though, and soon begins to list in the direction of the sort of crypto-hardline nationalist sentiment that so often mars otherwise likable Europeans. We cut him off mid-Gypsy-derision, before he can move on to the Jews.

Martin admits he started in Roncesvalles. The rest of us, I tell him, are forever bonded by that miserable viewless climb of the first day, which means he's not a true pilgrim. He looks hurt and Tom tells him I'm kidding.

Someone realizes it's the Fourth of July. Tom sings "The Star-Spangled Banner," making a mere two errors and needing only three prompts. A round of national anthems ensues. The Norwegian one is a killer track, rousing and catchy, and Martin sings it in a classy baritone as we march along. David sings Hungary's with a toneless solemnity, and when Tom punctuates the finale with an imaginary cymbal clash David rebukes him, saying the anthem deserves no cymbals; it is neither joyous nor triumphant. It is, rather, about how the Hungarian people have been repeatedly fucked for more than a thousand years and please God can they have just one break. He says it's the world's only whiny national anthem.

Later on, the four of us abreast on the same hot, straight, boring road, I ask Martin and David if they ever wonder, in a late-afternoon hour like this, the sun unrelenting in our eyes, why they're walking across Spain. Martin says he never wonders at all—it's clear he's the sort of person William James was talking about in *The Varieties of Religious Experience* when he described the "healthy-minded"—but David doesn't hesitate at all before he says yes.

"Now and then I think," David says, "this used to be punishment, and now is voluntary thing we maybe think is fun for no reason."

Tom asks David how he'll feel when he gets to Santiago.

David responds slowly, reminds us he's not religious. "When you arrive at Santiago," he finally says, "you are supposed to ask God to forgive you, but I am thinking maybe it is I who will forgive God."

The *albergue* the four of us choose is clean and homelike, but it's now me, not Tom, who finds its atmosphere despotic. There's too much ambient New Age talk of healing energies and how a person walks the Camino so he can just get away from restraints and back to the freedom of the road. A young American with vacated eyes tells us that when he hit puberty he shifted from being predominantly left-brained to being predominantly right-brained, and in recent years he's been discovering Hemi-Syncing—he cups his hands over his brow as though checking to make sure he hasn't been shot in the forehead—and is certain that soon he'll be living a life of balance. He's in an open marriage and his wife is walking with somebody else and he took a bus today from León, his first bus of the Camino, and then he says that he really needed to take a day off because he has crotch rot. To the non-native English speakers he carefully explains that this means he has a foot fungus on his genitals. He performs the syncing gesture once more, this time over his groin.

I find all of this much more annoying than the usual *albergue* banter, and it makes me feel brash and combative. Some older Canadian women say they started out this morning in Mazarife, the town where we had a late lunch, and I say out loud, "That's a pretty short day." Tom gets up and moves to a different table. The women look back at me and huff that it's not a race. "When did you start in St. Jean?" I ask. "February?" Tom goes inside.

When everybody else leaves, I end up talking to a phlegmatic Belgian with gray eyes and a netherworldly aspect malingering in the kitchen. I ask if he's Flemish or Walloon, ordinarily a question that leaves Belgians thrilled with recognition. He looks at me with a pointed calm and says that he doesn't understand why the world is so quick to draw borders and boundaries. The idea of the Camino, he explains with acid gentility, is that we are all one. Nobody needs to be Flemish *or* Walloon.

All of this talk of freedom seems wholly wrongheaded and makes me even grumpier. The Camino isn't at all about freedom from restraint but about freedom *via* restraint. You've subordinated all other desires to the big aim of getting to Santiago on foot. Following the rules, which are meager but inflexible, liberates you from having to figure out what to do next. Total freedom doesn't feel like real freedom; real freedom requires the contrast of necessity. What can this walk mean to you if you haven't figured that out?

THE PATH TOWARD Astorga runs shady and ochre through hops and over hillocks. By a mud hut on a long straightaway there's an open-hatched Subaru with some volunteers handing out free drinks and snacks. A young Japanese woman is taking rapid notes, and I walk over to introduce myself. She's Kiyomi, she's thirty, and she's doing her fieldwork for a dissertation in cultural anthropology at the University of Tokyo. She's writing about how the *hospitaleros*— the volunteer wardens who, for the most part, are as obscenely kind as they are utterly useless; I mean, what are they going to do, point west?—mediate the relationship between pilgrims and locals. She did the Camino once last year, and this year has done one long stretch of the Camino Francés and a long stretch of the Camino del Norte.

We all set off, and Kiyomi and I walk alone up ahead.

I tell her I'm very interested in the eighty-eight temples of Shikoku.

She's surprised I've heard of the circuit, and wants to know how. I tell her all about the Japanese pilgrims back at the *albergue* in Boadilla, about how they laughed at me when I said I wanted to do it. I say I want to do it solo.

"You don't like your friend Tom?"

"No, no, of course I like my friend Tom. I love my friend Tom. It's just that I want to see what it's like to do something like this alone. I want to see if I can handle it. Have you done the temple circuit?"

"Oh, no, is only for retired people, old people in buses, and to go by foot takes a long time and it is very difficult."

"Do foreigners or young people ever do it?"

"Young people maybe sometimes, after university and before job, or maybe they do it in parts, one week now, one week next year. Foreign people not too much, but maybe more now. First English-language guidebook by David Moreton-san was publish one year ago, so maybe foreign *o-henro-san* come to do."

What does it mean, if anything, that the Camino is a line and the Shikoku pilgrimage is a circle? Does that change your expectations?

Or is this just a bad Western caricature of cyclical ideas in Buddhism? Tom and I have avoided any images of what Santiago looks like with the vain hope that maybe when we get there we'll be surprised. So what does it feel like to start at Temple 1 and know that, in six or eight weeks, you'll end right back there at Temple 1? Does that help you focus on the step-by-step journey? Does it help you remember that what is happening right now is real? Does it help wean you from the suspicion that the real is something imminent, something around the next bend?

Kiyomi goes on to introduce me to the academic discourse on pilgrimage, which unsurprisingly seeks to ruin any of the joy or longing associated with actually having the experience. The exception to this is the Scottish anthropologist Victor Turner and his wife, Edith, who developed the first big, coherent theory of pilgrimage. As practicing Catholics, the couple spent many years joining pilgrimage routes, primarily Marian ones—pilgrimages related to apparitions of the Virgin Mary in a wet dishtowel or whatever—and primarily in Latin America. Turner followed the early-twentieth-century French ethnographer Arnold van Gennep (who, not incidentally, coined the term "rite of passage") in describing pilgrimage in terms of what he called "liminality." The word "liminal" comes from the Latin *limen*, or threshold, and characterizes transitional milieux. Turner used the concept as part of a constellation of ideas relating to ritual experiences that represent breaks from the ordered configurations of everyday life, or what he often called "anti-structures."

The chief characteristic of the anti-structure, and the idea for which Turner would become best known, is what he called "communitas"—a spontaneous, rich, classless, nonhierarchical association of people who have stepped out of their routine lives and into a liminal passage like a pilgrimage. If the sociologist Erving Goffman, a considerable influence on Turner, described our daily lives as a series of performances—now as a father, now as a rabbi, now as a homosexual—all variously rehearsed and directed, so to speak, according to different rules and different standards, then Turner's idea was that pilgrimage was possibly the one place in modern life where one had the opportunity to tear oneself away from one's familiar environments and its tribal divisions. The pilgrim could step outside of *all* roles and just *be a person*, someone without responsibilities or expectations or any constraint besides continuous forward movement to a distant goal.

W E SLEPT POORLY in a room with an unwashed saint/murderer type whom Tom christened JBap, after the standard academic notation for John the Baptist. JBap has the stench of the abattoir, a bushel of beard, and a small gym bag presumably stuffed with unmatched body parts. He perfectly fits the role of the pilgrim/ beggar we encountered at the *albergue* back in Nájera. Kiyomi has told me that what was true in medieval Europe is even more true in Japan, where the line between pilgrim and indigent is always blurry. For a few hundred years, in fact, the *o-henro-san*s of Shikoku were pressed into service as standard childhood bugbears—as in *Eat your vegetables or a pilgrim is going to come get you*. We're so used to thinking of pilgrims as morally upright, it's odd to think that historically they were considered dubious. It's one of the realizations that makes you question your own motives for being here. Is this just a parasitic vacation? Is the difference between us and tourists that tourists at least help out the local economies?

Today is the climb to the Camino's highest point. We've been anxious about this day for weeks, and are now anxious about what it will feel like to have it behind us, knowing it's more or less all down-hill from here (except for the remaining steep uphills). We're on the trail by five, moving quickly in the dark, and the six or seven kilome-ters of ascent are at such a mild gradient that we barely notice the exertion. The landscape is low purple shrubbery, wildflowers of yel-low and amethyst in a thicket of groundcover, shelves of thin shale. The mountains round out just below the heavy ceiling of mist. This is a popular place for those of unrigorous disposition—or, I suppose, of delicate constitution—to begin, just before the Cruz de Ferro, an iron cross set into a little pile of devotional rocks at about fifteen hundred meters. Pilgrims are huddled around it taking pictures as we walk by, indifferent.

On the far side of the Camino's highest point are some scattered villages wedged into the incline. Gone are the mud huts of the Me-seta; these small mountain outposts are built of neatly placed flat stones. Some of them, apparently, were completely abandoned until the Camino's surge in popularity fifteen or twenty years ago; this makes me feel a little better about our glorified indigence. In one of these villages Tom orders the local specialty, *botilla de Bierzo*, for lunch. It's a sclerotic heart of cured pork plated with some beans.

"I think it's a pig heart stuffed with pig anus that's been digested by a third pig and served in the cloacal sac of a fourth," Tom says. I have the salad. The novelty of trying new, disgusting foods has never been part of this for me.

We push fifty clicks in an effort to reach the presumed Chinese restaurants of Ponferrada—we'll do anything at this point to avoid *bocadillos*—where we're planning another day off. The last bit, as all entrances to cities are, is hot and unpleasant on the asphalt, but we do our favorite Camino personality impressions for each other until we feel as though we can continue. On our way to our boutique hotel we drop by the *albergue* to find David and coordinate dinner. A German asks me to photograph him and his two sons in front of the *albergue* waymark, 202 kilometers to Santiago.

"We just started today, we were in Dortmund zis very morning!"

"How nice! But maybe you should think about doing the Camino de Santiago sometime, yes?"

He looks at me quizzically, doesn't understand.

"That's just fucking rude," Tom says. "I'm sorry for my friend," he tells the German.

"What's actually rude is starting in Ponferrada and fronting like you did the Camino," I say.

We'll see the German on and off for a few days, and it turns out he did the Camino alone—the whole thing, from St. Jean—after his divorce, and has dragged his sons here to share an experience that had been very meaningful to him. But whenever I see them, the sons are wearing headphones and walking half a kilometer ahead of him, and each time I want to smack them and tell them they'll regret having squandered this time with their father, who looks at the ground as he walks along.

A T BREAKFAST WE'RE ABSORBED by the brutal live coverage of Pamplona's festival of San Fermín, which begins today. It's hard to imagine what the five or six color commentators can possibly be saying about the strategies involved, but presumably it's an insistent reminder that you and the bulls are most definitely in a race.

On our way out of town, David, whom we've really become attached to, tells a joke involving the classic brainteaser of the Jew who finds a big pile of money on the Sabbath. Does he take it? The joke turns on the well-known facts that the Jew loves money but, infuriatingly, is prohibited from carrying it on his Sabbath. We're given to understand it's a tough call for the Jew. David tells the joke in such a rote way, so roboto-boyishly, and he seems to have such genuine sympathy for the plight of the tortured Jew, that it's hard to be annoyed with him.

We pass a standard poured-concrete scallop-shell waymarker and there are, as usual, a few rocks placed on top. David asks if we know why pilgrims do this, and of course we don't.

"Idea is," he says, "that you pick up rock like somebody else's sin, then you carry this sin for someone for little while, it is a burden, and you know somewhere else someone carries *your* burden for you." Tom and David make fun of this spiritual calculus, or rather, simple arithmetic, but I think it's actually one of the nicer Camino traditions I've heard about.

Pilgrimage, in the case of most historical religions, and certainly in the case of the Camino, has almost always been understood in terms of sin, penance, and redemption. The three of us do not believe in the possibility of divine absolution, but even the secular ritual this has largely become retains some promise of forgiveness. These rituals of travel seem to retain their power even when they're no longer about belief.

There are two ways to look at the contemporary Camino. The first is that it represents a historical break, which is to say that in its true, original form it was about bark crosses and now it's about yellow arrows. This is the view of those who say that this was once a matter of serious religious commitment and is now a cheap backpacker jaunt. It's an argument from belief, and it holds that the experience of the nonbeliever along the Camino is inauthentic. This is an ahistorical view. Pilgrimage has always been a pretext, a religiously sanctioned excuse to go have an experience of elsewhere, and it's always been taken up out of mixed motives. For medieval pilgrims this sort of trip was almost certainly the *only* opportunity an ordi-

nary person would have to leave his home village and have an encounter with the wider world.

The more interesting way to interpret the modern appeal of the
Camino is to propose its ritual continuity. The argument for continuity is an argument not from belief but from action: it claims that
there is something in the form of the ritual itself, and in the stories
that have accreted to that ritual, that leaves the pilgrim feeling somehow renovated, even if he's hard-pressed to articulate why. Part of it,
in fact, is probably just that: it's an exercise in freedom from the necessity of articulating your motives with too much exactness, an opportunity to be broad-brush about why you're doing what you're
doing, to just do what you're doing without worrying that maybe
your reasons aren't good ones, that maybe you should be feeling bad
about your decision.

On the divine model, *sin* is a bad decision in the eyes of God.
Penance is the expiation of sin through suffering in the service of
God, or the mortification of the worldly desires that put us in conflict
with God's plan. *Redemption*, the goal of penance, is forgiveness in the
eyes of God—God's acceptance of our sins.

In a secular vocabulary, these concepts might look something
like this: *anxiety* is regret over a past bad decision, or of a future bad
one, either in the eyes of our future selves or in the eyes of our community. *Austerity*—which can take the form of practicing yoga, or
running marathons, or even strenuously gardening—is the expiation
of anxiety through suffering in the service of simplicity. It is the mortification of the human desires that put us in conflict with ourselves,
the world, and the people we love. It is to admit that to try to spend
all of your time doing no more and no less than exactly what *I* want
tends to cause a lot of conflict—not only externally, but internally—
so here is an opportunity to escape the tyranny of desire and just

follow some arrows. *Forgiveness* is an acceptance of the inevitability of conflict, of the costs of our decisions. To forgive yourself or another is to acknowledge that we have a multiplicity of obscure motives and desires and obligations and we are all doing our best to muddle through and make the best decisions we can. On pilgrimage, privation is endured, shared, and collectively encouraged as part of the aspiration to *want less*, at least for the moment—and not only to *want less* for ourselves but, perhaps even more important, to *need less* from others and, at the same time, to be able to recognize their suffering and give them more. The experiences of wanting less, needing less, and giving more allow us to withdraw from the psychic conflicts that cause so much pain for ourselves and those around us. After all, we're just shipwrecked here together on this island, each of us doing our best to survive.

I pick up one small sin from the cairn, but it's a little heavier than I expected and I put it down. I figure I'll find some peccadillo somewhere.

T HE CAMINO is positively crowded with people; we've never seen anything like it, and we know it'll only get worse as we get closer to the end. We rail against the latecomers, but then David points out two Belgian guys who've been walking since Antwerp.

"Maybe we ought to try doing the Camino de Santiago sometime," David says to me, and Tom laughs.

We run into Tim and Wiebke and David goes off on his own a bit ahead, which he does sometimes. We can't tell if he's moody or if he just likes to be alone or if maybe he doesn't like Tim and Wiebke or doesn't like sharing us with them. We stop by an orchard off the path and help ourselves to some large ripe cherries. Wiebke, who's at least eight feet tall, climbs the tree and shakes the high cherries loose; we reach up from underneath, our eyes blinded by the sun, and the freed cherries pelt us, reddish and glowing.

"That was by far the best Camino cliché I've experienced," Tom says, smiling, cherry pulp on his eyebrows. Tom looks at the Brierley and tells us that there are two routes out of the next town, a difficult one up along the ridge and an easy one that follows the road.

"I'm sick of the road," I say, "and it's so nice out today. I vote for the hard one."

"I'm in a lot of pain and I don't want to do anything harder than necessary," Tom says.

"Oh, come on, you're fine," I say.

"No, man," Tom says. "In the past I've consistently done what you wanted in this sort of case, gone the extra ten or twenty or seventy-five kilometers at the end of the day or whatever you always make us do."

"I think we've been totally accommodating of each other, and I bet that there are just as many times that I've stopped before I wanted to, just to suit you."

"You think every time we stop we're stopping too soon or for too long."

"Well, we've been meaning to try taking some time apart, see what it's like, so maybe I'll just do the hard route by myself now and meet you later on, or tomorrow."

Tom looks hurt and says so.

"Fine," I say, "I'll do the easy route, whatever, I don't care." But when we start I march off ahead in a huff. Tom lets me go for a while but then catches up to apologize. I apologize, too, and we both feel better for the moment.

The content of our actual fight the next morning is immaterial—

only the form matters—but for the sake of discussion, let's say it is about money. Money works, as it usually does, as a good placeholder for other things.

Both of us feel anxious about money. Each of us feels, furthermore, that the anxiety of the other is silly.

"Your anxiety about money is ridiculous, Tom, compared to mine. You've got nothing to worry about! You're established and settled and have a job and get paid a lot for your books and magazine articles, whereas I don't even know how I'm going to pay my minuscule rent back in Berlin in August, and even if I wanted to move to New York right now, there's no way I could afford it."

"No, *your* anxiety about money is ridiculous, Gideon, compared to mine. You've got nothing to worry about! Your expenses are practically nil, your rent is a matter of a few hundred dollars, you're young and everybody's struggling and it doesn't matter. Whereas I've got a girlfriend whom, at least at first, I'll have to support, since she's moving for me to a city where she doesn't know anybody and where there's no work in her field, and we're about to start a new life together so I want to have a nice place and eat nice food and live comfortably. I'm old enough that I can't live in squalor anymore like you can."

We're assaulting a hard asphalt road; some traffic cones separate us from the speeding traffic. High above our heads is the concrete ribbon of new road, built to replace this dangerous one. A few hours ahead is the steepest climb of the whole Camino.

Each of us feels that the mere existence of the other's anxiety, the other's *trivial* anxiety, is demeaning to our own legitimate worry. All of a sudden our retorts are clipped.

"I'm going to drop back for a little while," Tom says.

"Fine." I don't look back, just speed up and pass two other pilgrims taking their time.

The Camino's lack of much in the way of diversion, which is to say anything but fucking *walking*, can allow you to dwell on minor irritants, but, especially compared to the major irritant that is *being on the Camino in the first place*, they feel exhausting pretty quickly. Thus not out of any virtue, really, but out of the pure blank stillness of moments like this, I start to think that Tom must actually be convinced that his financial problems are worse than mine, indeed orders of magnitude worse, and that I probably don't need to take his private anxieties as a personal affront. And then—not out of any introspective exertion or sympathetic imagination but one hundred percent because *I have nothing better to do than entertain myself by mulling it all over from his side*, nothing more to wish for than to stop being bothered by this so I can go back to just being bothered by the Camino, and, besides, it's sorta boring walking alone, despite the great time I'm making, my long unfettered strides—I begin to think that maybe he's actually *right*, maybe his problems are worse, and that maybe all of this stuff about money isn't actually about money at all but about his anxieties about settling down, his fears of adult responsibilities, and that maybe we're not arguing about money but about youth and the future.

And then I think—more bored now, a little frightened, actually, with the cars buzzing by—that Tom really was pretty upstanding in coming up to apologize to me the day before, especially since I was being a jerk. And this is the thing, I realize: I *was* being a jerk. I was definitely being a jerk. We're not in any rush, there's no reason to take a superfluously difficult path just for the hell of it, Tom's feet are much worse than mine are, so why was I being so difficult?

The one time I've proposed being alone was right when Tom was criticizing me, accurately, for being unsympathetic to his needs and his pain. All along I'd had such a romantic idea of what it would mean to be alone—how heroic it would be to do this without any diversion or any support from anybody at all—but now I see it as the desire to be able to walk away, to *Buen Camino*. As an evasion. As an attempt to get away from my close friend right when he's called me out for being selfish and stubborn and uncaring. An opportunity to meet some strangers, people who won't know that I'm selfish and stubborn and uncaring. Maybe my desire to be alone is my desire to preserve some image of myself that I know won't stand up to Tom's sustained attention.

So now, after ten or twenty or thirty minutes, I decide I'm going to rise to the occasion and apologize. I stop and wait. I've been moving pretty quickly, despite the brutal asphalt, and when I look back I can barely see Tom below me. It takes him a long time to catch up. Before he can say anything, I blurt out, "This is really stupid and petty and I've been selfish and unsympathetic and I'm really sorry."

"I'm sorry too." We hug in the road and continue on.

"You know, that was a pretty quick reconciliation we had," Tom observes.

"Yes, I know! It might've taken lesser people hours, or days, to do that. We've heard all the stories of how the Camino breaks up friendships, all the people who come with pals and within forty kilometers are walking alone or with other people. I think that just now we both really acted like adults."

"I agree. And I'd say our friendship has a great tensile strength," he says.

"Hold on," I say. "I want to write that down."

As we enter the last village before the great climb to O Cebreiro—the steepest section of the Camino, comparable in grade if not duration to that first day over the Pyrenees—we look back downhill into the narrow-walled valley and recognize the

ducky gait of young David. We sit and wait for him to catch up, both
of us figuring that in the wake of the last hour's intensity it'll be nice
to have a buffer.

As we start to climb, David tells us about his parents' divorce,
about how rarely he sees his dad, and about his mom's new husband,
not only their former cable guy but a Chippendales dancer, and the
subsequent baby that displaced him from his own room. I tell him
that a big part of the experience of this walk for me thus far has been
the start of a reconciliation with my dad, that something about the
relative safety of being a moving target has afforded me the courage
to be in touch with him again. On the Camino there's no reason not
to tell some intimate version of the story of your life; who knows if
you'll ever see this person again after today—though the fact that
we've known David for a week now makes him, in Camino terms, a
friend from way back and always—and the pain makes the bullshit
threshold pretty low. It's the sense that this is all taking place on
some distant shore and that, because nothing matters, you can get
away with complete exposure. You can see what that feels like, see
how people react.

At the top of the grueling hill there's a waymarker that introduces us to Galicia. Galicia, upon initial investigation later exhaus-
tively confirmed, is a province of desperate dogs, thatched-roof
rondavels, deep manure, and slanted hayfields in mid-thresh. Somebody's always threshing or baling on a slope that looks unsafe.

At the top of the hill we run into Tim and Wiebke, who've just
arrived, even though, we note out loud, they left two hours earlier
than we did. Two girls walk by and wave shyly at David.

"Who're they?"

"Two Germans, Alina and Nora. I met them in the *albergue* last
night when you abandoned me."

Brierley suggests stopping here, and the fact that these two German girls seem to be doing just that provides some incentive; but we're all feeling good, so we set off in a staggered group of seven or eight to do another ten kilometers downhill. Tom and I drop back with Tim.

"Where'd David go?" Tom asks.

"He ran ahead again for some reason. He can be so volatile; I don't really get it," I say, "but it seems possible that he, uh, doesn't like Tim's, er, lifestyle very much."

"Yeah, I was wondering that," Tom says. "Like, you mean that maybe David feels about gays the way he might also feel about Jews and Gypsies?"

"That had occurred to me," Tim says.

"Why don't you two say anything to him?"

"Sometimes you like someone enough that you don't really want to rule them out so quickly. Otherwise," Tim says, "you end up having to rule out a lot of people. So you just ignore, ignore and forget, and try not to take it personally."

It's more or less how I feel about David's Jewish jokes, which don't seem to bother me at all. One of the things you're reminded of in this sort of transient community is that there's rarely a reason to take much personally. So David gets mysteriously sullen and walks off; we've only known the guy for a week, so even though we feel close to him in this strange suspended world, we know that his moods can't possibly have anything to do with us. With so much displacement and projection thus laid bare, with on the one hand the awareness of ambient powerful emotion and on the other the knowledge that whatever is going on must be almost entirely internally generated, it becomes much easier to try to understand somebody else's behavior than be provoked by it. You're just less inclined to be defensive. With your defenses down, you start to see that the beginning of forgiveness is the intuition, a liberating one, that not everything is about you all of the time. David's never been out of Hungary before, he was raised in the Eastern Bloc until he was seven, and it makes sense that he'd have moments here of feeling threatened or overwhelmed. But we can already tell that some of these attitudes he brought with him are withering. I figure it makes more sense to mention that I'm Jewish in a casual moment than in a tense one.

"This has been an important lesson in Camino forgiveness," Tom says in all seriousness, "about how it's not necessarily a matter of specifics or apology."

"And," Tim adds, "how it's probably even more important for us to forgive than for him."

"Remember when David said, on that day when we sang the national anthems, that he thinks the Camino is not about God forgiving us but about us forgiving God?" I say.

Later we will conclude that all of our speculation was nonsense, that David has no problem at all with gays or Jews—Gypsies are maybe more complicated—and that he was just chasing after yet another Québecoise.

A YOUNG PRIEST PASSIVE-AGGRESSIVELY manipulates Tom into giving up our places at the small *albergue* in Alto do Poio, so Tom and I sleep in a hotel across the street. As the alarm goes off in the morning, Tom says, "I absolutely do not feel like walking today."

"Neither do I. I can't believe we're only six days from Santiago."

We walk along a hillside above a sink of endless fog; occasional summits form barren islands in the infinite frothy white. After lunch we take the less-traveled of the two possible routes forward, up a small river valley and over a steep ridge. The sun is strong today and the hills a wild bosky green. Flat slate roofs make the villages below us look like sparse associations of unfurnished patios. On our descent the path is a narrow channel between stone walls, and we get caught behind a woman with fourteen cows and four large dogs, all of which have diarrhea. We see a small snake dead in the path and Tom jettisons his pack and starts to climb the nearest tree, hyperventilating and hollering gibberish.

"I think you can come down from that tree," I say.

"You told me there weren't any snakes in Spain!"

It's true. On the first day, when Tom told me about his snake phobia, I'd reported to him that the entire Iberian peninsula was snake-free. I'd said all the snakes died trying to cross the Pyrenees.

"I lied to you, Tom. I'm sorry. Don't be mad at me."

"It's okay," he says, and comes down from the tree. "I understand why you lied."

We have dinner with Tim in a *pulperia* where a TV loops snuff-film footage of the morning's death by goring of a twenty-seven-year-old runner, Pamplona's first fatality in fourteen years. We'd all enjoyed watching the coverage of the event over breakfast each day. Now we feel guilty.

We're planning another day off and Tim isn't, so we're sad we might not see him again. "There are these traditional tales," he says, "of devils who try to distract pilgrims from reaching Santiago. I started the Camino with a bunch of wholesome goal seekers and look where I ended up, with a couple of cynical devils like you two."

"Cynical?" we both protest at once. "We're not cynical!"

"You are, but you're not, and either way it's okay. I'm just trying to tell you guys it's been fun to walk with you, and I hope we keep in touch."

. . .

F OR ONCE WE DON'T NEED a day off for physical reasons. But Tom checks his email and discovers his dad is in the hospital for minor surgery, so he wants to be near a phone. And I get an email from my grandfather, Max, letting me know that my dad is also in the hospital and that he'd like me to call.

Tom looks concerned. "What's wrong with him?"

"Oh, nothing's wrong with him, I'm sure, but Max's email wasn't that clear. He seems to have some sort of staph infection. But this is just a gambit to get me to call him." I haven't been in touch with my dad since I sent him that half-forgiving email, but I did add him to my (admittedly extensive) email update list. He's been responding occasionally, but I can tell from the responses that he isn't reading my missives.

"That's a genuinely shitty thing to say," Tom says.

"You don't know my dad. He's happy to go to emergency lengths to make everybody else drop everything and feel obligated to attend to him, and in a way that doesn't require him to take any personal responsibility for it."

"I don't have to know your dad to know that somebody does not put himself in the hospital to get his son to call him. Or let me put it this way: if he had to put himself in the hospital as an excuse to get in touch with you again, it means it's really important to him. Your grandfather said he was really sick. My dad could die today, man— you never know. Get over yourself."

"How about instead of saying 'Quit complaining, this could be worse,' you say, 'Hey, man, that sounds like it really sucks'?"

"How about I say, 'Hey, man, this whole situation sounds like it really sucks and I'm sorry to hear it, and now get over yourself and fucking call him and I think you'll find you feel a lot better'? What happened to everything you were saying yesterday in our conversation with Tim about David? About the forgiveness that can come from recognizing that not everything is about you?"

I stalk off to mull this over and end up distracting myself at an internet café. Facebook has created a strange record of our long drift. Andy's status update says he's within fifty kilometers. Martin's says he's closing in on Santiago. Karo's most recent note says she's had to take a bus but plans to wait around in front of the cathedral to see all of her friends arrive. It's a funny thing to imagine all these people finishing, as just a few days or weeks ago we were walking alongside them, listening to the stories of their parents' extramarital affairs, and now they're about to reach Santiago and disappear into the ether like Mayans. We might be in Santiago as soon as Wednesday, and then we, too, I guess, will disappear.

I'm prepared to be distant, but my dad's voice is weak and scratchy, and he sounds so excited to hear from me, I can't help but be glad to be in touch again. It's been eighteen months since I've heard his voice, save on the few voice mails he's left me, and I realize how much I'd missed it. It also reminds me, hearing his voice this way, how much older he is than the person I'm mad at. I say, "I'm sorry, Dad, for everything. I've been walking across Spain and it's been really hard to stay in touch."

"It's okay," he says, and coughs, and proceeds to chat away as though we'd never been out of touch. He tells me that he thinks he got this infection from cleaning out the attic without a mask on, and then goes on about the hospital, and what the doctors have been saying, and how Brett brings Yoshi, their shih tzu, to visit every day. He doesn't ask anything about the Camino. I realize I don't mind. He pauses at the end. "I'm just so happy to hear from you," he says.

"Me, too, Dad. I'll call you in a few days, when we get to Santiago, to see how you're doing."

On my way back to the hotel, I stop and sit on a bench and weep. Like poor Brierley.

W̲E̲ ̲C̲A̲N̲ ̲S̲E̲N̲S̲E̲ the new density of pilgrims even before dawn; they're spectral in the path. Sarria is the last institutionally legitimate place to begin and still get a *compostela*, and we're resenting the crowds in advance.

Over breakfast we watch a little of the old trample-and-gore with some posh British schoolboys on bikes, and we meet outdoorsy Bill from Chicago, who, like me, is about to turn thirty. He's headed to graduate school in the fall, and just quit a job working for a magazine called *Backpacking Light*, out of Bozeman. It's published for a semi-fanatical fringe hiking subculture whose members calculate weight-to-calorie ratios and then cross the Yukon with nothing but a groundsheet and a bottle of olive oil.

"That's somewhat different from your school of thought," I say to Tom.

"Oh, you mean *Backpacking Heavy*?"

Bill laughs and joins us. The trail this morning is probably the loveliest of the whole trip, with mossy dilapidated stone walls running alongside the lane, and overhead a canopy of chestnut and oak. Run-down fences in the fields mark off forgotten property lines; there's a lush, relaxed sense of overgrowth and decay. It has not occurred to them here, Bill notices, to plant corn in rows.

We sit against a wall with Bill while he begins a complicated procedure to repair his feet, which are the only feet I've seen worse than Tom's. As he cuts little strips of padding and gauze, he tells us the story of how he walked for a while with a Swiss girl, Chantal, and then somehow lost her, and how he can't think about anything but her. As we're sitting there a large, combat-vested German—whom

David calls, with some justification, "the least popular man on the Camino"—comes over and hands Bill a note. It's from Chantal, with her phone number and email. Bill texts her and she writes back that she'll wait for him in the town of Melide.

As we start up again, Bill's spirits now almost intolerably high, he waves at some people coming up behind us: Thomas, a French-Canadian actor, and Nico, a German. Bill's been walking with them on and off, and we're delighted to continue on as six. We decide as a group to stop after just over thirty kilometers. We all probably could keep going, but we're anxious to secure beds for the night, and besides, entering the *albergue* just before us are the two German girls David waved to at O Cebreiro.

Nora and Alina are nineteen and from Frankfurt. They've just finished school and are out in the world for the first time alone. They join us for dinner, and the pleasant anxiety of the occasion merits my first beer of the Camino. Alina, who has dreadlocks and baggy low-slung shorts and a lot of defiant poise, is about to start an internship as a baker; Nora is a redhead with a luminous, bashful smile, and she plans to spend next year as an au pair in Ireland. Nico takes one look at Nora and says that in two years she's going to be really dangerous. By the time we all hit our bunks, we've decided to continue along together in the morning, and if all goes well to remain together through the end.

D AVID SAYS EVERYBODY CALLS this part the "Galician gallop," but we suspect he made that up. In the *albergue* people begin to rustle their fabric at four fifteen, four thirty. Now that we're eight people, it takes us half an hour to coordinate, so we're not out walking until after five. We fumble along in the crowded dark. We use a few weak flashlights to find the yellow arrows on trees and rocks.

The two hours on either side of dawn this morning are charged with a special intensity. We're eight former strangers moving forward at a brash clip in the smazy blue of night, the light rain not so much falling as distilling itself from the mist. We're too tired to talk, too alone with our slow morning thoughts, and the only sounds are the plink and short drag of our worn sticks in the soft dirt. Alina and I keep perfect pace with each other, not talking, not looking over, but matching light footfalls in the damp earth, here and there speeding up or slowing down in uncoordinated unison. It feels even more intimate than holding hands.

Figures gain clarity in the first dawn to blaze through the fog behind us. We've all come together so effortlessly, and we all seem to feel so fit and so vital, so warm with roaring blood, so similar in stride and gentle in conversation. We pause for a moment, and when we continue we do it wordlessly. It's cool but it's not raining, much, and when it does, it's already stopped by the time we've put our jackets on. The day passes in euphoric canopied-lane muffle.

When it gets warm enough, I take off my sweatshirt and walk along in my pink tank top and white tennis headband and sunglasses. "I wouldn't wear that outfit sitting at home alone on my own sofa," Nico tells Tom behind me. I hear it and laugh; all I can think about is how much I'm enjoying this, how close I feel to these weird people, how sad it will be when this is over. We stop to share a Galician almond cake—a *tarta de Santiago*—and agree that we will arrive at the cathedral together.

After thirty-two easy kilometers we arrive in Melide, and as we approach the *albergue*, Bill sees Chantal leaning with rehearsed ease against a lamppost. She's been waiting here a day, maybe two; he looks over at us demurely, embarrassed to break the promise we've all just made, but we wave him off, and they go to find a hotel.

. . .

At four forty-five we sit in the *albergue* kitchen waiting for Thomas and Nico, who has a blister on his foot the size and perfect burnish of a new pinball. We're quiet in the invisible forest. At forks in the path a sudden battery of flashlights sweeps for arrows. Nobody says anything at all until it's light. It's our penultimate day.

Over breakfast we linger and watch the last day at San Fermín. One bull lifts a running man up, almost gently, and tosses him face-first into a brick wall. Another guy trips and is trampled in the narrow street by five bulls in a row. On the way out of the café we agree that they should combine the running of the bulls with the Tour de France, but there's no consensus on how. Tom thinks the bulls should chase the cyclists, Nico thinks the cyclists should take up lances and chase the bulls, and David thinks the two groups should start at a distance and bolt toward each other.

We're walking quickly but time has begun to lengthen. Time has acquired a strange and spacious irrelevance, as if we could turn around in it. As long as we keep moving, time is kept at bay; when we stop, it catches up in a rush.

Alina and I pull ahead to escape everybody else and talk about her inability to communicate what this has been like to her boyfriend at home, the looming end of her relationship. Neither of us has any desire to stop in Arco do Pino, where we've all agreed to spend the night. It's only twenty more kilometers on to Santiago, and we know excitement will prevent us from sleeping; our feet feel fine and our bodies are buzzing. We also know that everybody else tends to leave the navigational decisions—insofar as there are any—to the two of us, and by the time the rest of them realize that we've passed the *albergue*, we'll be halfway to the end. But we know we shouldn't try. Alina neither wants to nor can abandon shy Nora, whom she's protective of, and I neither want to nor can leave Tom, who would take the bus.

We've had almost no rain the entire walk, but this late afternoon sees intermittent downpours. They last three or four minutes and we don't bother with our jackets. At the very end of the day, a few hundred meters from the *albergue*, it starts to come down in torrents, but all it seems to do is expand our reckless end-times sense of election. We run along the road in the driving rain holding hands and can't stop smiling through the deluge.

IN THE STILL HOUR before dawn on our last day, I drop back with Sebastian, a friend of Nico's who'd found us at the *albergue* the night before. They'd walked together some weeks back. Sebastian has everything in his life—a flight attendant for a girlfriend, a good job with the local radio station, all the weed he can smoke—but isn't happy, and he came on the Camino to find out why.

"Maybe I smoke too much pot," he says.

In his first week on the Camino, he fell in love.

"Katy and I met and walked together for two weeks. We were never apart. We knew we were in love right away. One day I told her I could not walk with her anymore. It was not fair to my girlfriend, and not fair to Katy. We needed to stop, I said, before it got even more difficult." Katy agreed and they cried together in the middle of the path. They parted, kept walking at the same pace for another ten or twenty meters, and then Sebastian just started to walk faster, and then even faster. He walked faster and cried, never turning around, not even one time, and he neither stopped nor looked back for hours. He kept going past the usual end stage and walked deep into the night.

"I haven't seen Katy since, but I can't stop thinking about her. I thought about emailing her." As it gets light out he begins to poke around off the trail for medium-sized rocks. "We started a Camino gang called the White Snails." This is because they were both pale and slow. "Now every three or four kilometers I find a rock and draw a white snail on it with this paint pen. I leave them by the side of the trail where she'll see them." He stops to draw one, places it atop a boulder. I wonder how this feels to Katy. Does it make her feel good, or does it make her feel terrible? Does she want to remember or would she rather forget?

"Nico said to me once, if you are in a time of need you should ask the universe for something. Yesterday I begged the universe not to let me arrive in Santiago alone. And then yesterday I walked fifty kilometers and finally found Nico again, and all of you guys."

Over breakfast the café is showing the closing festivities of San Fermín, a greatest-gorings montage. It's been a nice final element of continuity, the breakfast snuff films, and we're teary as we watch the dignified mayor of Pamplona invite everybody back next year.

It's raining and we linger a little longer than we usually do. Just around the corner is Monte do Gozo, the first view of Santiago, and we want to see if the skies will clear. Sebastian takes out his ukulele and sings Jason Mraz's "I'm Yours." I ordinarily dislike both of these things, ukuleles and Jason Mraz, but there's something so tender about the way he plays that Alina and Nora and David and Tom and I can barely look at each other. Alina reaches over and takes my hand. David takes Nora's and Tom's.

This final stretch is an emotional welter and nobody can settle on how to describe what we're feeling. Alina says she has an odd sensation in her gut, a warm comic tumbling. We're all shot through with sad, nervous exhilaration. We fussily reconfigure: sometimes we walk alone, in a long defile, a narrow bridge connecting us to those who have gone before and those who will come after; and sometimes we walk in pairs, each of us making time to walk with each of the others for a while.

A lot of the conversations are inane. It's difficult to say anything serious that doesn't feel trivial or overwrought. We recollect into a single group and talk about the comic detritus of the internet. We're two Americans, a Hungarian, four Germans, and a French Canadian, and everyone but Tom has seen "Chuck Norris Facts" and many of the same dumb, hilarious YouTube videos.

"I don't get the metric system," Tom says. "It doesn't sound right to me. It sounds, like, I don't know, really *clinical*. How, for example"— and this comes out as an almost angry demand—"does one talk about dick size? Do you just say, like, I have a half-meter dick?"

"That would be a very big dick," says Thomas.

We cross the city limits into Santiago, take group pictures at the sign, and make our way through the usual car-dealership suburbs. Our pace slows and we find ourselves touching incidentally, casually, holding one another's glances. Now the yellow arrows spray-painted at our feet are captioned with the scrawled word *casi*, "almost." We see Martin, rushing from the cathedral directly to his return flight to Oslo, and we all hug him, even those of us who never walked with him. "That was a killer track," Tom says with a slow smile as Martin rushes east.

The old city's alleys are lined with tourist schlock—souvenir walking sticks, T-shirts with yellow arrows on them. We arrive at the little plaza around the corner from the cathedral. Two sets of stone stairs run beneath a broad arch to the main square. We stop to make sure we all go through the arch together.

Tom and I stand close. "Tom," I say. "It wasn't a race."

"It's okay. It was a little bit of a race. How are you doing?"

"I was just thinking about Alina and Nora, and how they only started in Burgos, and Martin only started in Roncesvalles, and Karo maybe did take a bus from Sahagún to Sarria, and maybe we did start hundreds and hundreds of kilometers earlier, weeks more of hard walking, all of it on foot; but as I stand here right before we turn the corner and see that cathedral, I know that no matter where you started, right now, just as you're about to finish, you're feeling the same dislocation, the same peculiar coil of wonder and dread, the same anxiety about what this has meant and who you were and who you now might be and what comes next, what life will be like at home without the yellow arrows, and it really doesn't matter where you started. You still did the Camino. We did the Camino and so did they, so did everybody."

Tom nods and hugs me. "I know, Gideon." He's as proud of me as I am of him.

He looks toward the rear of the cathedral and looks back at me and asks, "Even the people who started in Sarria?"

"No," I say. "Not them."

We descend the steps past a man playing a Galician-bagpipe dirge and come through the arch and into the square and stand before the cathedral, a looming godly parliament. Paned windows on its block-length facade, all lit in soft patina, give it the look of a baroque train station. Other pilgrims file in around us, their heads craned, their pace slow and unsteady. There are, most bafflingly, a great many people milling about who did not arrive on foot. We drop our bags from our backs, let them fall behind us where they may, and embrace. We're dumbstruck and we hold fast to each other. David is crying, and now Alina, and Tom, and now everyone. We sit down on the cool stone and lean against our heaps of battered bags and look up at the wide cathedral and around at the group and exhale. We swivel around, dazed, overwhelmed, unsure. Five hundred miles, and now what.

Interlude

BERLIN/
SHANGHAI

TOM AND I HUGGED TIM and then each other, repeatedly, said good-bye at the Gare du Nord after a few post-Camino Paris days that remain about as blank as the weekend in Estonia does. My train arrived at Berlin's Hauptbahnhof at nine in the evening at the end of the first stalled week in August, and there didn't seem to be a point in going home just to drop off a bag I'd been carrying for six weeks, so I went right to Bar Drei to meet David Levine. We embraced and he lit a cigarette for me, the first I'd even wanted since I'd left town, and we counted off the three or four competing things we might do later on in the evening if we felt like it. Immediately it seemed as though the Camino had been a dream. All that lingered was an evaporating memory of equanimity.

"What was it like to finish?" David asked. In my last email dispatch, from Santiago, I'd promised a coda about the few days on to the sea at Finisterre. I'd never sent it.

"Well, Tom marked 'weight loss' on his *compostela* and it looked just as nice as ours, even without the fake Latin. Then we got ridiculously drunk with David and Alina and Nora and everybody under the moon in front of the cathedral, and then everybody but Tom and me got on with the business of fanatical coupling."

In Santiago we met an attractive and articulate Italian named Lisa who once worked on the Channel Island of Sark, about which

I happen to know a great deal. At first Tom encouraged me to hit on her—for, as with the Australian girl, the vicarious thrills—but then he did an about-face and said she was too young and I should back off. It's not like it mattered to me, though. I'd never felt less sexually game than I did on the Camino. It's not that I didn't experience desire, it's that I felt no compulsion to act on it, to extend myself in its pursuit. This seemed somehow related to the lack of other desires: the lack of a desire to eat much, the lack of a desire to drink or smoke. I'd funneled my energies into wanting one thing; so much else had fallen away. But it occurred to me that perhaps I'd been maintaining some sense of solidarity with Tom—as if I could somehow shore up his new commitment to monogamy by staying celibate myself. As if by refusing to indulge my own desire, I could help reduce the damage desire does in the world.

"After a day of rest," I told David, "we continued on." Three days later, on the thirty-ninth day after we'd started—beating, by one day, both Moses on the mountain and Jesus in the wilderness—we came over a rise and saw the sea for the first time. We expected something emotional, but it mostly just meant there was no way to keep walking. We thought about turning around and doing the Camino backward to St. Jean, but Tom had to get home to his girlfriend and his new job.

Finisterre, I went on, had been a fucking drag. Most pilgrims who make it to the sea burn a piece of clothing in a beach bonfire to show that some part of them has been transformed, and for five consecutive nights we sat and watched the same stupid neo-pagan ritual performed again and again, both by new arrivals and—more irritatingly—by those who'd been there for days or weeks and couldn't bring themselves to leave the Camino. We met one guy who'd been there since February. And despite the boredom, I couldn't bring myself to send the promised last dispatch. I couldn't think of what else there was to say. I couldn't bring myself to do anything, in fact, but read Stieg Larsson's trilogy in the UK edition, the only English-language books to be found at the end of the world. We sat on the beach and felt the Camino experience slipping through our fingers. We could sense the dull pulse of routine worry like some far-off war drum.

"And now here I am, back at Bar Drei. Give me another cigarette, would you?"

"Yeah," David said, "but did you expect anything different? Did you expect yourself to come back in full control of your life and your time in a new way? I never got that impression from you."

I hadn't expected that, no, although after a few weeks back in Berlin it became clear that the enduring recollection of the Camino had, in fact, changed something: it made me recognize that Berlin, at least for now, wasn't a good place for me to be. I still couldn't come up with any one place that would be better. But what I knew was that, on a daily basis, I'd felt better on the Camino than I had in some time, and, furthermore, had been more productive in a month in Spain than I'd been in nearly two years in Berlin. It had felt so good to assume the purpose of pointless austere motion. Further pilgrimages, further exercises in pointless austere motion, struck me as a way to haul myself out of the near-irresistible entropy that Berlin had encouraged. Part of the problem with Berlin had been that it was so easy to kill time that you never really had to become interested in anything in particular, and now I was really interested in something: pilgrimage. I wanted to take up Tom's suggestion and write something big—a book, maybe—about pilgrimage, about what I'd felt while on the Camino, something at once intimate and theoretical, something about restlessness and purpose and what it means to travel with an expectation of change. I wanted it to be a grand exhortation to everybody I knew! I wanted it to convince everybody that they should run off right now to walk the Camino. I wanted the chance to figure out more definitively what was so powerful about it. And, perhaps more than anything, I wanted to go *do* more of these things. And if I told myself and others that I was writing a book, I'd have the license to go do it without feeling guilty or conflicted about not settling down someplace.

I'd kept my Berlin apartment while on the Camino because I'd assumed I'd go back and resume living there, but by the end of my first month back I knew I needed to leave as soon as I could. While I was thinking about what was next, I went to New Jersey to be with my mom for Rosh Hashanah and Yom Kippur for the first time in a few years. Not that I cared about the High Holidays themselves, really—they mostly evoked childhood synagogue memories of being just as listless and disengaged as anybody else but having, as the rabbi's son, to pretend I really cared—but it made my mom happy to have me around, and, after so many years, I had, despite myself, grown attached to this listless annual synagogue attendance. While I was in the States I even managed to spend a few uneventfully pleasant evenings with my dad for the first time in a long while. "You look so thin!" he said as he picked me up at the South Orange train station, which had long been his way of saying he was happy to see me.

When I needed to get away from New Jersey, I spent hours in the New York Public Library becoming increasingly enthusiastic about a variety of distant pilgrimages culled from exotic traditions I'd never heard of—to Mount Kailash, Lalibela, Mount Athos, the Kumbh Mela at Haridwar, Kataragama, Uman. Mount Kailash was presumed to be the world's tallest unclimbed peak—out of respect for the four traditions that hold it holy—and some of its circumambulants go all out and kowtow their way around the path. It takes them three weeks. Lalibela was a reconstructed Jerusalem in Ethiopia, a proxy built by a Christian emperor after the 1187 occupation of Jerusalem by Muslims made proper pilgrimage impossible. Mount Athos, the sovereign monastic peninsula in Greece, was practically *made* for travel writers; Robert Byron and Bruce Chatwin had both spent time there between wider peregrinations. The Kumbh Mela was the world's single biggest gathering. In Uman, forty thousand Orthodox Jews spent Rosh Hashanah saying psalms at the Ukrainian grave of a Hasidic sage and mystic. There were a lot of interesting places in the world, and here was a whole self-justifying subset of them. You weren't just bumming around planlessly, you were going *on pilgrimage.*

As appealing as all of these journeys sounded, none gripped my imagination the way the eighty-eight temples of Shikoku already had, mostly, I think, because the *o-henro,* as it's ordinarily called, seemed to offer the right sort of complement to the Camino. Like the Camino, it dated back about a thousand years, but had only recently experienced a surge in popularity. Like the Camino, it was nominally religious, but was now taken up in a largely secular mode (though these categories are a little less stable in Japan). And like the Camino, the path was fashioned after a compelling historical itinerant. Kūkai, or Kōbō Daishi, the Saint James of Shikoku, is one of the most revered figures in Japanese history. He was born into minor nobility in northern Shikoku in 774, near Temple 75, Zentsūji, and in the early ninth century brought Shingon, or Esoteric, Buddhism from China to Japan, where he became renowned as a holy man, scholar, calligrapher, and engineer. The idea of the pilgrimage is that it's a tour of the places Kūkai practiced austerities on his path to enlightenment, which he achieved at the precocious age of nineteen in a cave beneath Temple 24.

Unlike the Camino, though, the *o-henro* is a circle, not a line. Instead of descending from the mountains and approaching the distant sea, the route follows the shoreline, the sea on your constant left, the mountainous interior on your constant right. Expectations must be different, I thought. You end where you began, back at T1. The experience is one of both straying and returning. For the Japanese, this is particularly acute. Shikoku is the most rural and the least populated of Japan's four main islands. It wasn't even connected by bridge to Honshu, the main island, until the late 1980s, and a Japanese person is far more likely to have seen Paris than Shikoku. The island is idealized as a connection to Japan's mythic preindustrial past, where Japanese heritage hasn't been spoiled by modern efficiency. It's also long been associated with exile, and with the symbolic death that exile from an island nation means. All of these things make it both a sacred place, a different place, as well as a place that's traditional and familiar in its otherness. It's an experience of elsewhere that's also a deep experience of home. This is vastly different than the Camino, which if anything celebrates the beginnings of continental cosmopolitanism; it was one of the few avenues for cultural exchange before the modern era.

On the day I made my decision I called Micah, whose Shanghai apartment was a vast corporate-underwritten sky palace. I'd spent the previous winter there, working on the article that had gotten me into trouble with my dad. "How's your extra bedroom?"

"It's fine," he said. "I'm wary of you."

"Oh, come on! There's no reason to be wary."

"How long are you coming for?" I could hear him gesturing to his girlfriend in the background.

"Well, you know, it's just that the winter in Berlin is so dark and terrible, and David and Alix won't even be there, and I figured that if I'm going to do this Shikoku thing, it'll be a lot more convenient to leave from Shanghai, which is practically right there, only a two-day boat ride away—"

"How long are you coming for?"

"—and I don't have a home anymore, really, and there's nowhere in the world that feels more like home than being wherever you are—"

"For the love of God, Gid, just tell me how long you're coming for."

"Just three months."

"Ten weeks."

"Deal. I arrive into Hongqiao Airport on a Hainan Airlines flight at about five p.m. on December fifteenth."

There was a long pause. "You bought a ticket already?"

"Maybe. I had to figure out all the logistics. My boat for Japan leaves at the end of February, so I can start the temple circuit on the first of March."

"Why can't you just fly like a normal person?"

"Taking a boat seemed more in the pilgrimage spirit, and it's much cheaper. Besides, the boat sounds fun. The website has a picture of the karaoke room."

"Whatever. You're paying rent."

"But you don't even pay rent!"

"You're doing our laundry."

"Fine."

"And picking up our dry cleaning."

I went back to Berlin to get rid of my apartment and store my books at David's. In the first week in December—knowing, now, that I had found a way out, that I was about to embark on a series of purposive trips, and that all I had to do in the meantime was enjoy the time I had to spend with my friends (which is to say, to do exactly what I'd been doing before, but without worrying if I ought to be feeling bad about it)—I had more fun than I'd had since the night, two years before, that Emilie led us past the votive candles to the rave hidden in the woods.

Which meant that, by the time I got to Shanghai, I was exhausted. But it wasn't as though Micah and his girlfriend were all that energetic, either. The previous winter I'd spent there hadn't been quite like living with Micah in San Francisco—there were orange-vested men jackhammering in the elevator, for one, and legions of children singing patriotic exercise hymns twenty-one floors below us at the crack of dawn each morning—but we'd managed to cobble together a version of our old fraternal routine. Now, though, his girlfriend had moved in with him, and what they mostly did was nuzzle. Nuzzling complete, they fell asleep in front of the television. They were almost painfully adorable, and I felt both excluded and envious.

I also felt extraordinarily anxious. Maybe their future was up in the air—they were China-fatigued, ready to live in a place where people were roughly familiar with the concept of standing in line—but they knew that they'd face whatever came next together. Not only was my future up in the air, my present was as well. Restlessness was starting to seem less like an attempt to stave off crisis than a manifestation of one. I hadn't been in the same place for more than two consecutive months in a year, and in two more months I was embarking on a solitary twelve-hundred-kilometer walk in the most rural corner of a country whose language I wasn't the faintest bit acquainted with. And then who knew? I was pretty sure I didn't want to go back to Berlin, but I was equally sure I didn't want to be in New York or San Francisco. I still hadn't remembered to look into Kiev. In my terror of stasis I had chosen motion; in my total absence of stability or routine I felt both electrified and panicked.

In this electric panic I met yet another unavailable woman, a friend of friends in New York, and was instantly smitten. On a Tuesday at seven p.m. I met her for one drink at Yin Yang, a darkly wainscoted French Concession institution that played on Shanghai's prewar cosmopolitanism the way Berlin played on its Weimar decadence, and by the time we'd finished the red pack of Double Happiness cigarettes on the wooden table in front of us I was ready to follow her anywhere, by which I mostly mean I was ready for her to follow me anywhere. She took me to see her favorite Filipina cover band in the revolving restaurant bar at the top of the Radisson overlooking People's Park, which perched on the hotel's spire like a gentle glass UFO. She was in China, at least in part, for the same reasons I had been in Berlin, fretted similarly about where she was and where she might end up and why. She wrote—extremely well, I'd later find—about art and memory since the Cultural Revolution, and had also tried to read *Middlemarch*. China spent so much time proclaiming its emergence, she said as the savvy Filipinas played the opening bars of "Livin' on a Prayer," and she spent so much time feeling the same way about her own life, it was hard to keep her feelings about the country and her feelings about herself straight.

And then there were her feelings about her relationship. Her workaholic boyfriend was away on business for the week, somewhere up in the Chinese rust belt, in Changchun or Shenyang. She could never remember where he went. He was trained as an architect but here he worked as an urban planner. The Chinese would bring him to a city of five hundred thousand and ask how it would accommodate a population of twelve million in five years. He didn't speak much Mandarin, though, and resented the fact that he was often in the room just to serve as a white guy in a suit. In any case, he wasn't in the room then, and there was no reason to talk about him. We leaned back into the couches and peered up through the glass dome toward where some stars should have been. The band moved into "Don't Stop Believin'," and she moved her face-up palm in a slow, wide arc that included the band, the rotating domed craft of bar, and all of China. "I often feel like I'm living in an extended metaphor," she said, her fingers finally alighting on my shoulder.

Then she up and rolled around on the carpeted floor of the bar, impersonating in adorably muddled English-Mandarin the three-year-old child she liked to babysit. She had such tenderness for a world defined by absurdity and loss, and I wanted to spend the rest of my life watching her tuck her hair behind her ear. I realized, even in the moment, that this was all a cliché, that *of course* this felt like finding the person I'd always been looking for—that everything was setting me up for this, and that, after all, I hadn't known her nearly long enough to rule her out—but this did nothing to dim my affection: she was exactly the person I'd been looking for, this girl who went from quoting Perec to imitating a three-year-old imitating a triceratops attempting its first somersault. Or she was, at the very least, someone I'd be glad to sit still for, and that really was something.

By the time the Chinese sun, that largely abstract source of warmth and light, was theoretically rising over Tomorrow Square, I'd proposed she leave everything behind and come with me to circumambulate Shikoku. She laughed but didn't immediately say no. She was at loose ends and some part of her, I could tell, was thinking seriously about joining me. Neither one of us wanted to go home, neither of us were ready to be apart yet, so we walked along the Nanjing Road toward the Bund in the dawn quiet and I spun out whole vistas: we'd walk the route in Japan and then, once we'd finished the circuit, we'd hold hands the entire length of the Trans-Siberian from Beijing to Moscow, read *War and Peace* out loud to each other, then move to some pleasant city, San Francisco, maybe, where she'd never been but had long fantasized about and where I'd had the only thing that had ever felt like a real, settled life. She seemed, I thought, the adventure worth the lot of all possible adventures. The person with whom life would never grow fusty and calcific, with whom we would be damned always to become and never to be. Come with me on this last silly jaunt, I said, and then let's find a place to be still together. Needless to say, she said no. On our last night in Shang-hai I told her that if she ever became available she should let me know, and I would fly her the next day to wherever I was.

I went home and wrote a dejected email to Alix about how I'd met the woman of my dreams and that it was doomed for now but that I wasn't going to let go. It was Christmas and I didn't know if Alix was in Berlin or New York or her dad's place in the south of France, but she operates in her own time zone anyway, and she wrote me right back. "What is this girl going to do, leave her life behind? And isn't there a chance you'd freak out if she did? You set these things up so you can only be betrayed. You know what you should do? Try *actually dating someone*. You'll probably have to break up with them at some point but at least you'll get your pathos on the back end rather than the front, and presumably there'll be *something* in between."

Until the last possible hour I scrambled to convince people to come along with me. There were friends—David Levine, Tom, even David the Hungarian—before whom I nearly prostrated myself in the hopes they might join up, if only for a week here or there, but it turns out that for some reason it's not easy to convince people with actual lives to fly to Japan for a week of comfortless walking through nondescript rural areas on asphalt roads. Micah's girlfriend said the two of them would come if we carried her on a palanquin.

Part of me wanted to go to Japan alone, especially after I'd given Tom such a hard time for never letting us split up, but I mostly just *wanted to want* to go to Japan alone. Maybe the experience would be more powerful, or more lasting, if I endured it by myself. People were always telling other people to go off and do things alone, that it was good to get away from the crowd and find yourself. These were the romantic ideas about heroic solitude I'd entertained along the Camino, which ultimately seemed less about actually wanting to be alone than wanting to be able to more easily meet strangers, people I could be new for. But the more I thought about it, the clearer it was that I'd never had a hard time being alone. I spend huge amounts of time alone, in fact, and had rarely spent as much time alone as I did in Shanghai that winter. I'd never felt lonely sitting by myself— or with Micah's six-day-a-week maid service—in his apartment when he was off at the factory and his girlfriend was at work, though I'd often felt lonely when it was the three of us in a room together and they were off in their own world. It wasn't so much that I was afraid that I'd be lonely on Shikoku, it was that I was afraid I'd be bored. I was afraid I'd rush through it. Nobody to talk to, nobody to process the experience with. Nobody to give me a hard time, no-body's feet to tend to. Nobody to make me stop.

Part III

SHIKOKU

I N THE END, I managed to arrange company for the first five days of my second walk. Max, my dad's father, was the only person besides Micah who'd actually read all the email dispatches I sent from Spain. He'd just turned eighty-two and wanted once more to see Japan, where he'd traveled frequently on business before he retired. Max is the busiest retiree anybody's ever heard of. When I visit him and my grandmother, Lois, in Vermont, I have to call months in advance to make sure I won't conflict with their various obligations: they host book clubs, they volunteer for Meals on Wheels, they take photographs for the local newspapers. So Max could accompany me only as far as Temple 11 (T11 in the circuit lingo), and then from T12 to T88 I'd be on my own. He's practiced for months, walking each day the six or eight kilometers into downtown Middlebury with a loaded rucksack, waiting there for Lois to come drive him home. He'd read my dispatches about Tom, didn't want to hold me back.

Max is a retired engineer; he brought cable television to New Zealand, worked on UNIVAC, helped hollow out one of those mountains where the rich and good-looking survivors of the nuclear holocaust will go to start the rabbity business of high-pressure re-population, and owned a little three-seater airplane for a long time. For the last few decades of his career he ran a company that made thermocouples, a little widget used to make steel, and he traveled to Japan half a dozen times a year to work with companies here. It makes him almost giddy to be back, and he's uncharacteristically epigrammatic and wry. He met me at the boat from Shanghai and we took a bus to Tokushima, one of Shikoku's three cities, which he deemed "not exactly a wonderland." In Tokushima we met David Moreton, the John Brierley of the Eighty-eight Temples, who picked us up and drove us to T1. Moreton and I had emailed when I ordered his guidebook, and he'd kindly offered us an initial lift.

Moreton takes us around the pilgrim shop at T1: Ryōzenji. He helps us overpay for our *osamefuda*, the little name-slips one leaves at the worship halls and gives out as a receipt for *osettai*, gifts to pilgrims; our calligraphy books, for the proof-of-temple-visit stamps, like Camino *credenciales*; our matching white *hakui*, the vests the *o-henro-sans*, or Mr. Pilgrims, wear, with a line from the Heart Sutra inked on the back; some matching felty eggshell boating caps, the usual wide-brimmed sedge hats being too oblong for our Western heads; and finally our *kongō tsue*, walking sticks.

I'd expected Moreton, having written the lone English guide-book and everything, to take the temple rites seriously, but he's pretty breezy and peremptory about it, indicating with a few gestures where you're supposed to bow, when you're supposed to ring the gong, where to burn the incense, say the Heart Sutra, light a candle, etc. He advises against performing the whole schmear at each site. "It would take you a full *half hour* at each temple," he says. We barely have time to poke around at the temple before he suggests we get going; it's late in the day and he's booked us a room in a *ryokan*, a traditional Japanese inn, a few kilometers down the road, near T3.

We hurry off, glad to be under way at last. The route from T1 to T2 runs along a muddy shoulder behind a guardrail, past some florists and auto body shops and a few dozen convenience stores.

There's a light rain. It's the first of March and feels wintry still. The path from one temple to the next is marked not with the spray-painted yellow darts of the Camino but with discreet red pointer stickers and hand-carved marble bollards, some of which date back centuries, and cute decals of rutilant staff-holding potatoheads in kimonos. It feels so nicely familiar to fall into the old rhythm of just following the arrows and letting the nondescript landscape recede.

"This is like doing a pilgrimage along the side of Route 17 in Paramus, New Jersey," Max says.

"It is pretty drab, yeah." I feel like I should apologize. Moreton had said that most of this first walk would be on paved roads—he'd pointed to the road we were driving on for effect—but I hadn't quite imagined this. The houses we pass are a bland assortment of off-white stacked boxes with weather-beaten linoleum siding, the wealthier ones with gray pagoda-style roof tiles and ornamental koi frozen mid-spring from the eaves. The neighborhoods are choppy latticeworks of irregular smallholdings, crisscrossed by narrow irrigation channels with grooves for flow diversion (Max points this out), and tiny avenues patrolled by elderly farming couples in gigantic toy trucks. On every patch of ten square meters there's something growing: bushy purple cabbage leaves, roots fussily tucked under plastic, enormous waxy yellowish tubers.

"This isn't quite what I expected Japan to look like, Max."

"Well, imagine if, on your first trip to the States, you skipped New York and the Grand Canyon and went straight to the suburbs of Kansas City. That's more or less what you did."

"Or like going to Spain and skipping Madrid and Barcelona and going straight to Burgos or León, which is just what Tom did!"

"Well, I'm sure it'll be nicer when you get into the mountains," Max says, always the careful optimist. We're in a long, narrow valley, headed away from Tokushima and toward the center of the island.

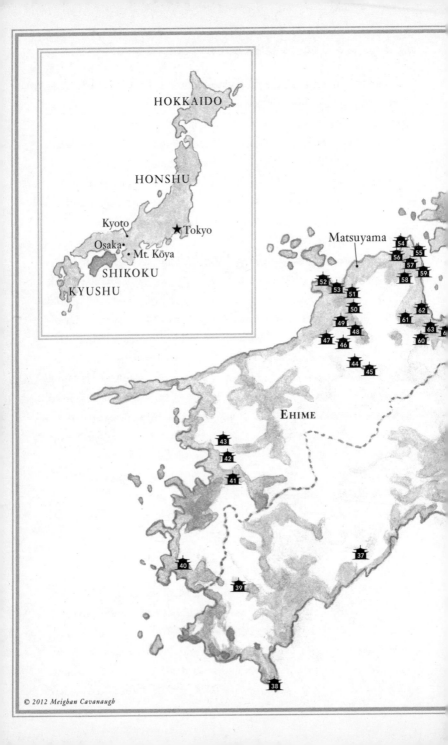

HOKKAIDO

HONSHU

Kyoto

Osaka

Mt. Kōya

★ Tokyo

SHIKOKU

KYUSHU

Matsuyama

EHIME

© 2012 Meighan Cavanaugh

EIGHTY-EIGHT TEMPLES *of* SHIKOKU

Most of the temples lie more or less along the island's shore, but these first ten are close together, running in a row up the Yoshino River. After T11, Max will leave and the trail will track up into the mountains and then back toward the coast. I lift my eyes to the peaks ahead of us, trying to figure out which hide that first real challenge. We almost walk by T2, concealed behind a parking lot and some trees off the road. We stop at the main gate, which is festooned with heavy coils of rough rope, symbols of the simple sandals Kōbō Daishi wore in his ascetic wanderings. On each side of the gate is a large belligerent sub-deity held in a cage (though sometimes the cages are occupied by storks or ostriches); these flaming Gargantuas are supposed to scare visitors into dutiful practice. We bow as we've been instructed.

Beyond the gate, there's a little spring under a roof, with long-handled tin ladles for ritual hand washing. Two large halls front onto a tidy courtyard flanked by a number of smaller outbuildings, offices and the like. The central buildings are a main hall, with a statue of the presiding deity, and a Daishi hall, dedicated to Kōbō Daishi. The temples, I'll find, are in varying states of repair—most of them are privately operated, often by just one family, and some are clearly better kept than others—but they tend to be built of wood long gone gray velour. Outside the main hall there's a pair of posts connected by wires, and tied in ribbons to the wires are pieces of green paper. These are fortunes, which cost one hundred yen apiece, a little more than a dollar. Sometimes they're good and sometimes they're bad, but, from what I can tell, either way you tie them up to the rail before you make your offering. I watch one of the bus pilgrims, who opens a hip pouch and withdraws two white candles the size of golf pencils, with notches in the bottoms. There's a glass box at the base of the stairs with iron spikes inside, and he lights the candles from those already burning, then fits their notches over empty spikes. The pilgrim takes three sticks of incense, lights them on the candles, blows them out, and plants them in the sand basin at the foot of the altar.

The pilgrim then climbs steps to the altar, where small rectangles of thin calligraphed wood, like decorated paint stirrers, are tacked to the wall. They're wishes, someone at the temple shop tells me, for good health or good fortune. The pilgrims on the altar begin to chant what I think is the Heart Sutra in an airless staccato, reading off of laminated cards. I glance down at the Moreton, which has a transliteration, but I haven't yet read his gloss on the meaning of the prayer.

"We'd better go," I say. Moreton has warned me that it's rude to show up at the *ryokan* after four or five o'clock, and this particular owner had to be convinced to allow foreigners to stay there.

We walk over a bridge, Max plinking away with his new stick.

"Oh, yeah, I meant to mention, you're not supposed to bonk your stick when you cross a bridge."

"Really? Why?"

"I read on some website that Kūkai, Kōbō Daishi, once had to sleep under a bridge when he was circling the island. It's near, uh, T43 or something, on the far side. And the stick is supposed to be the incarnation of Kukai, accompanying you along the route, sometimes performing miraculous intercessions. They have this saying about how the journey is two people but one practice, like that Jesus business with the footprints. In the evening you're supposed to wash the dirty end of the stick right away when you stop, and then put it in this little mihrab-ish nook where it sleeps."

"That's pretty demanding, for a stick," Max says, just as we're arriving at the *ryokan*. The proprietress pantomimes the slipper protocol—there are different pairs of slippers for pretty much each room in the little inn—and shows us to our room, a low-ceilinged tatami space with a shallow basin behind a rice-paper screen. She takes our walking sticks and rinses the ends, already nicked and splintered, in the basin, then sets them gently into their sleeping nook.

She shows us to the tiled bath, which she's already filled. We take turns sitting at the stool and washing with a bucket in the traditional Japanese style, then soaking in the tub. I come back from the bath and Max has already donned the traditional *yukata*, the light cotton evening robe, they've put out for us, and together we roll our futons out on the tatami mats. It's been years since Max has done this stuff, but he seems immediately oriented and comfortable. I sit on a meditation pillow at the low table, pour myself the toasted brown-rice tea they've left out for us, and begin to teach myself some rudimentary Japanese on my phone as Max futzes with chargers for his gadgets. At six thirty the proprietress fetches us for dinner. On our way past her office she indicates that she'd like us to sign her guestbook. She shows me the last English entry, from some eighteen months back, and seems to want to know if maybe I know this Ian, of Los Angeles.

The dining room is done up in a provincial catch-as-catch-can way: it's part rustic cabin, part hunting lodge, with kitschy ornamentation in a Renaissance-fair motif. It's dimly lit, and there are only two other people at dinner, both men in their late sixties or early seventies sitting a few tables away from each other and eating silently.

"Looks like you're the only young guy around," Max says.

"Yeah, most of the people who do this are apparently retirees. It's the only time in a Japanese person's life that he's got enough time for it. I gather it's something like three hundred thousand retirees a year." About one percent of the pilgrims, I've read, do the circuit on foot, of which maybe a dozen in any given year are foreigners. Moreton told us that there's a nineteen-year-old from Alaska a day or two ahead of us, Erik. I wonder if I'll catch him.

An old woman stoops to set fourteen tiny courses in front of us, each one intricate and fragile in its own lacquerware dish. She gestures for us to sit back as she lights the Sterno beneath individual cisterns of tofu and shiitake. As we wait for the broth to boil, Max asks me about the significance of the stuff we acquired at T1. "I know about the stick," he says. "That one's the Daishi guy."

"I've got to admit I know very little about all this stuff, Max. One nice thing about the Camino was that there wasn't anything like this. You just showed up and walked and occasionally you looked in at a church or ruined monastery and that was it. You didn't have to wear a special vest or not bonk a stick over bridges or make advance reservations at places where you had to know which pair of slippers to wear in which room." All I really know about any of this is what Moreton told us in the car, and what he wrote in the introduction to his map book. Japanese pilgrims apparently get really into the trappings of the journey. Some people are buried with their sticks. The white vests we're wearing resemble funeral shrouds, and are supposed to remind us that death can come at any time; while you're on the walk, the tradition goes, you're actually "dead to the world." This is similar to the Camino, where Catholics say that if you die en route to Santiago, you go straight to heaven. "Oh, and I read that many Japanese who have done the circuit are later cremated in their pilgrim regalia."

It occurs to me that I don't really want to be talking about death with my eighty-two-year-old grandfather, although he brings it up all the time, in his engineer's matter-of-fact manner: what will happen to Lois if he dies first, whether as they get older they'll have to give up their house in Vermont.

"You don't really seem too scared of death, Max."

"Well, I've been lucky enough to have had a very full and rich life, and I'm grateful for all I've had, for the good health that allows me to come on something like this, and for the fact that I've had so much time to spend with my family." He pauses for a moment, grasps at loose bracken with his chopsticks. "I guess before I die I'd like to make up with your dad, maybe, but I don't know if that's going to happen." It's never been clear to me what, exactly, has been at issue between them, and I'm not sure Max really knows, either; my dad finds the thinnest pretexts to decide they're not talking. They often have something to do with my dad's fear that Max—who didn't even get divorced from my grandmother until my dad was almost finished with college—loves his stepchildren more than him. As far as Max and I can remember now, the current issue has to do with Max's unwillingness to intervene with Brett. My dad and Brett had apparently been having a hard time for a while a year or two back, over what I don't know, and my dad wrote out a long email putatively from Max to Brett about how much my dad loved Brett, then asked Max to send the email as if he himself had written it. And if that hadn't been odd enough, there was a bizarre mid-email digression about how if Max had been as good at communicating and being affectionate thirty or forty years ago as my dad was now, he wouldn't have ruined his own marriage. It was as though my dad was demanding Max wield the special authority he had as a father first to fix his son's relationship and then to undermine his own special paternal authority. Max never sent the email, which struck him as evidence of "arrested development." Max doesn't seem angry, or even particularly hurt. "Whatever's going on with your dad, with these emails and everything, it's got nothing at all to do with me, and I know that now. For a long time I blamed myself, but now I can't see it that way anymore. And it definitely isn't all just because he's gay, though it seems he'd like to think that. It'd be nice if he wanted to be in touch again, but that'll be up to him.

"At any rate," Max says, "I'm so happy you two are in touch again, even if it doesn't feel normal or resolved. It probably won't ever, but from the little I've heard from him, I know he's so happy that he hears from you now, and got to see you."

"I'm sure he still won't read the emails I send out along the way." My father seems to have made a habit of not reading what I've written. He'll buy a copy of a magazine I've got something in, he'll put it out on the coffee table and show all his friends, and he still *won't read it*. It boggles my mind.

"Well, Gideon, you do write a lot sometimes. Those emails you send are pretty long." Max peers down at what looks like a raw quail egg, shrugs, and pours it over what's left of his rice. "Also, I've been meaning to ask you about those. Lois and I really liked all the dispatches you sent out from Spain, but you didn't do the walk *just* to send out emails, did you? And obviously it's a great adventure, but there are other adventures, so why pilgrimages?"

"Yes, I definitely did it just to send emails. Most of what I do is designed to generate material for indefensibly long emails."

"Really?"

"No. Well, yeah, but no. And as for why pilgrimages, isn't there something immediately appealing about following these red arrows? It's not just an adventure, it's a commitment, and it's not necessarily supposed to be fun or easy."

He nods, but he's never been somebody lacking in a sense of direction. "It sounds a little bit like marriage."

IN THE MORNING Max gives the proprietors Vermont key chains he's brought along as gifts. The old woman is tickled, but I tsk.

"No, Max. We're supposed to *get* gifts, not give them." It's the custom of the island, to give an orange or a liter of water or a bottle of Pocari Sweat ion renewal drink. It's called *osettai*. (When we get some Pocari Sweat as *osettai*, I make Max try it first because it looks gross. Max doesn't mind it, and I wonder if he's the source of my dad's and Micah's obsession with off-putting and unusual beverages.) Pilgrims are actually not even allowed to turn the gifts down, because they're also a gift for Kōbō Daishi, and there's karma at stake. Max looks skeptical of the whole thing but is as thrilled as I am when we get our first *osettai*, two heavy, dark, and pendulous apples an older couple gives us out of the back of a van near T4.

"You're right," he says. "I could really get into this gift thing."

T4 looks pretty much just like T2 and T3, but it's not really until around T8: Kumadaniji, a hillside joint spread out over a series of cascading terraces, that I realize, to my relief, that all of these things are going to look pretty much the same, so I won't have to worry too much about learning the differences in architectural styles. Or really pay very much attention to the temples at all. The University of Hawai'i professor Oliver Statler, who walked the pilgrimage in 1968 and was probably the first American to do so—the anthropologist and Japanophile Frederick Starr did it by coach and palanquin in 1921—has a famous line in his 1983 account, *Japanese Pilgrimage*, about how the temples "punctuate the pilgrimage but do not constitute it." I liked that insofar as I took it as license to ignore the temples completely, which I'd planned to do anyway. I dislike travel writing about temples, or churches, or mosques, or architecture in general, or, for that matter, trees, or trains, or roads, and especially the Khyber Pass; in fact I think I only like travel writing when it's not about travel at all but rather about friendship, lies, digression, amateurism, trains, and sex.

I'm perfectly happy to have a look-in at the temples and then resume following the arrows. Max, however, needs enough time to photograph each place such that he might reconstruct it to the last detail if he later needed to. He photographs the bus pilgrims with their full white costumes, their emerald and garnet sashes, their heavy wooden beads, sedge hats with the radii of lawn sprinklers, and observes that "there's an inverse relationship between pilgrim fashion and the likelihood the pilgrim is walking." He photographs the statues of Jizō, red-bibbed stone dudes who protect travelers and escort dead children to the afterlife. He discovers that his camera has a voice-recorder function that allows explanatory memos to himself: "Pilgrim getting into taxi"; "Pilgrim buying memento." I just sit in the wispy incensed silence and feel glad to be off the road for a minute.

Max and Lois have become perfervid gardeners in their busy Vermont retirement—they discovered, in their mid-sixties, all sorts of new interests—and he's fascinated by the small-bore agriculture along the river valley. "Are those onions?" Max asks as he looks out over a little field. "Gentlemen harvesting cabbages," he articulates into his camera. He takes out his little yellow notebook and writes something down. I notice that when I stop to write something down, he often does too. With Tom it was always clear what he was noting—mostly because he tended to announce it out loud as he wrote—but Max is inscrutable this way. Near T10 his notebook falls out of his pack and I steal a glance. "Cabbage planted early, alluvial plain must be frost-free zone," it says. Max knows so much about actual *things*. But most of the other notes are just details to report to Lois when he gets back. He doesn't want to forget a moment. I sympathize with the urge. A calendrical ritual doesn't require an additional memory aid; a calendrical ritual *is* a collection of memory aids. Every seder is supposed to recall the history of all seders, just like every Thanksgiving contains within it every previous Thanksgiving. But these one-off events we rush to record. The anxiety about excessive self-consciousness I experienced along the Camino was well worth the preservation of all the dumb moments I'd otherwise have instantly forgotten.

We don't see too many other pilgrims on foot, maybe three or four a day, and they're all recent retirees. None of them really speak English, but we have a nice kinetic chat with a man at T8 in which he tells us that until last month he worked as either a sashimi chef or a devil-may-care accountant; Max and I differ in our interpretations of his gestures. But Max has a kooky gestural lexicon himself. "Eat," for example, seems to involve using a two-by-four to stir a giant vat of congealed oatmeal, then raising a helmet-sized iron ladle not to your mouth but toward your hair.

Exaggerated mime vocabulary aside, though, it turns out that being with Max is surprisingly fun. The proprietor of our second *ryokan* drives us over to the nearby *onsen*, a traditional Japanese hot spring. We sit naked on the stools at adjoining wash cubicles and shave. (David Levine had warned me that if I didn't want to get odd looks in rural Japan, I should shave every day.) We float around in the hot pools and talk about the rigorous cross-country ski marches he and Lois took us on as little kids. Afterward we put on our robes and drink beers over another seventeen-course meal, and I even get him to gripe about Moreton with me. At a *henro*-bibelot shop near one of the temples we've discovered we could easily have kitted ourselves out for half of what we paid at T1, and I curse Moreton out loud.

"I can't believe that guy. I knew we shouldn't be trusting this stupid guidebook after he told us he hadn't even walked the whole route." Moreton had told us that he'd done *most of it by car*, which had been my first clue that my second guidebook relationship might be as antagonistic as my first.

"Yeah, I don't know about that guy," Max says, which is pretty much the worst thing Max will say about anyone.

Which I later, by the end of a relatively long day, feel just terrible about. Max would never have minded Moreton, would only ever have been delighted that an English survey existed, if I hadn't foisted upon him my bat-shit guidebook-author complex, my infantile rage against people who are only doing their best to get us from one place to another with minimal friction.

"I'm a terrible pilgrim, Max. All I do is complain, and I'm sorry. You haven't complained about a single thing."

"Well, I've got nothing to complain about. I'm just having such a good time being here with you."

Max is such a grateful and present guy, so different from the way my dad describes what he was like growing up. I wonder if Max has changed or if my dad's memory is faulty. I can't imagine what being here with my dad would be like; I'm sure he'd be asking around about the LGBT scene on Shikoku, making us stop to divert himself with hidden gay bars the way my mom always makes us stop to divert herself with hidden Jewish cemeteries. How would Micah complete that sentence if he added a clause about me? He'd say that I'd divert myself by refusing to stop at all.

"Oh, wait! You did complain, once. About having to change your slippers all the time in the *ryokan*."

"Those slippers drive me up a wall!"

WE MAKE QUICKER PROGRESS THAN we'd expected—Max's training has really paid off, and he has no trouble at all keeping up—so on his penultimate day we only have to walk for a few hours in the morning. It's still overcast and cold; we're both wearing fleece hats and gloves, and Max complains about the lack of good sunlight for pictures. We stay in another *onsen*, this one at the foot of the mountains, and once again spend an hour or two soaking quietly at the end of the walking day, talking about Micah and his girlfriend and how great they seem together. I tell him about the girl in Shanghai and he doesn't seem to know what to say except that he hopes it works out. He'd always really liked my San Francisco girlfriend, and I think he always hoped I'd marry her. I tell him I liked the girl in Shanghai so much, so quickly, and that I immediately felt as though I'd give up my plans—not that I really had any plans—to be with her. I can't help but think that maybe I should've canceled this trip and stayed in Shanghai, tried to make it work. As it is I can't stop thinking about her, and everything reminds me of her. There's a road sign, presumably warning contractors to call before they dig, which shows a mean cartoon backhoe making a buried rotary telephone cry; I can imagine her elfin mimicry of the weepy Japanese utility. On the side of a suburban greenhouse there's a poster of fifty varieties of Japanese eggplant that she would've delayed us for an hour looking at. I take pictures of all of this, spend our silent times composing interminable emails to her in my head.

"Maybe that's why you want to give up your plans, because you don't have any plans. Maybe you just want her to be your plans."

"Yeah, definitely. But the hard thing to figure out is whether this is just a crush or something, you know, *real*. I mean, we only did know each other for a week, and we didn't even kiss, much less sleep together."

"You never know that until time passes. The difference between an infatuation and something serious is just the fact of willingness to put in the time and the sacrifice it takes to find out."

We sleep in another tatami room with large windows fronting onto a swanned pond; it's the off-season and we're the only guests in the entire complex. Max reads a book about Japanese Buddhism as I write up my notes for my first dispatch. The rain falls lightly on the swans.

In the morning on the way to T11 we stop into one of the tchotchke shops that line the alley heading up to T10 so Max can buy some gifts. It's no exaggeration to say that Shikoku has a pilgrimage-based economy, and stores cluster around the larger temples. The woman in the gift shop tells me that two other foreigners have been in, a day or two earlier. "They spoke funny English," she said. Australians, I think grimly.

We walk over a dike and down through the sodden Yoshino River plain toward T11, which lies across the valley. We realize we're running out of time together and that if we're going to have any more serious conversations, we've got to have them now. I feel like there's some pressure on in general. On the Camino everything felt like a lark, but now that I've got the idea that this could all ultimately amount to some grand exhortation to pilgrimage, everything feels like it has to count. I ask Max what he regrets.

"I look back on my marriage to Bubbe and wonder if I couldn't have saved that. I did the best I could, but your dad is right that I didn't know very well then how to communicate in a relationship. I don't think the divorce was my fault, but I also don't think it was your Bubbe's. Maybe if I'd known how to talk better I could have understood what was making us both unhappy, and then maybe things might've been better for your dad. I don't really know. As I said, for the last decade or so he's imagined that the problems and frustrations he's had in life have to do with just being gay, but I doubt it's that simple, and I think he always had difficulty with the divorce.

"It wasn't until I was a bachelor for a few years that I got the chance to figure out what, exactly, I wanted out of life and relationships. It was also really the first time I learned anything about sex. And then, when I started to get together with Lois, right around the time you were born, I had some good counseling and learned how to have the kinds of hard conversations you need to have to make relationships work. And we've now had almost thirty years of marriage. For a long time I regretted how things had happened with my first marriage, but by now I've come to see that it took the failure of the first marriage to force me to figure a lot of stuff out, and then I ended up in something healthy and wonderful."

It's clear that Max has come to a point where he's got a story that makes everything make sense; he's connected the data points, as he might say, with a line that ties it all together in bringing him to where he is now. He knows he's hurt people along the way, as we all do, but he's tried to repair what he can. We all have regrets, but regrets don't have to undo you. His suggestion that my dad's issues have to do with a lot of things other than just being gay seems like a point he's making as much for my own sake as for his or my dad's. Max knows that I have this idea that if only my dad had made better decisions at age twenty-five, he would have avoided causing so much pain, for himself and for all of us. But Max is saying that he made a similar sort of bad decision at twenty-five—getting into a marriage for which he and my grandmother were equally unsuited—and that it led to some years of hardship and dislocation but that ultimately it was all necessary for him to end up where he's arrived.

Your forty-six-year-old self doesn't need parenting, and your thirty-year-old self doesn't need to be congratulated for being so considerate. Your forty-six-year-old self will be able to take care of himself, is I think what he's saying. You can acknowledge that things might have been different without feeling as though your life, or parts of your life, were wasted. There just isn't a point to that. Max and Micah are similar this way, oriented toward what might be better in the future instead of what ought to be regretted about the past.

"These are hard conversations, I know. I do wish that I could have some of these hard conversations with your dad, but I don't know if he's interested anymore, or maybe he's just so sure of his own version of every story that he doesn't want to allow anything to shake it."

"I mostly feel as though I don't even know what his story *is*," I say. "It's changed so many times. It's hard to keep track of what he regrets and what he doesn't, and who he was at any point and why."

"You could try asking him."

"I'm afraid to. And it's been awhile since I've let myself be in one place with him long enough to start. Maybe someday I'll take a trip with him, maybe for the sake of this book I want to write recommending pilgrimage, but it's hard to imagine having a conversation like this with him."

"I wouldn't be too hard on yourself. You'll have them when you're ready to have them."

We walk the old narrow bridge across the Yoshino. At T11, Max's last, there's an old woman outside, bowed over in a ratty apron, toothless, arranging oranges on a counter for sale as traditional temple offerings. How old is *ojīsan*? *Hachi-jū-ni*? She points at herself and smiles. *Hachi-jū-ni-sai!* She and Max are the same age, and she can barely walk the few steps from the temple office to this offering stand.

Over final beers at the hotel by the train station, Max and I are both a little solemn. We're primed for a sentimental good-bye and he pauses for a long time.

"There's only one thing I don't like about Japan," he says at last.

"The pillows?"

"No, but the pillows are terrible. They don't eat cookies here. The food is so good but they don't have cookies for dessert. I miss cookies."

"That's too adorable of a thing to say. You're just hamming this up now."

Max smiles. He's a canny guy, and I can't blame him for trumping up a good exit line.

"I figured it was a little less cheesy than my more serious possibility."

"Which would have been?"

"As my first boss used to say to me, 'Life isn't a dress rehearsal.'"

"Sometimes that's what these pilgrimages feel like: dress rehearsals."

In the morning we take some final pictures in front of the train station and hug for a long time. He knows everything there is to know about cameras, but still, somehow, the shots of me walking away toward the mountains turn out pretty blurry.

T12: SHŌZANJI IS ATOP a nine-hundred-meter mountain, the second-highest of the circuit. The book says it's the first of the eight *henro-korogashi*, literally "when a pilgrim falls down," and one of the six *nansho*, the officially inconvenient temples. This is presumably in comparison to the rest of the temples, which are unofficially inconvenient. The path runs at a harsh slant through beds of scruffy fern, bamboo columns, and towering Japanese cedars. This first difficulty is actually welcome; it makes it easier to stop thinking of Max's departure and of the long solitary weeks ahead. I pass three or four retirees as I climb but passing fellow pilgrims is hardly the thrill it was with Tom.

The path along the ridge is narrow, with steep drops on either side, an elevated walkway high above a forest floor littered with pine needles and ribbons of the first real sunlight in the five days I've been in Japan. It's steady for a kilometer before it climbs toward the first peak, where some deteriorating concrete steps lead to a massive Kōbō Daishi statue, dark iron blooming in rashes of mint green, a heavy sedge hat and rope sandals and an illegibly stony expression. He stands sentry beneath a vast cedar umbrella.

"Now it is long ago," Japanese myths begin, there was a rich man named Emon Saburō, who lived in Iyo province (now Ehime prefecture), the third of the four provinces of Shikoku. One day he turned away an old priest who sought alms at his door. The next day the priest returned and asked for rice. Emon Saburō ordered that feces be placed in the priest's begging bowl instead. This was repeated each day for a week, until on the final day Emon Saburō dashed the priest's begging bowl to the ground, where it broke into eight pieces "like a lotus flower." The priest departed. The next day the eldest of Emon Saburō's eight sons died, and one more each day until they were all dead. Emon Saburō understood that the old beggar had been Kōbō Daishi himself. He repented by giving away all his holdings to his peasants. He donned the sedge hat and cut a walking stick and went in search of the mendicant priest.

Emon Saburō hoped he would catch up with the old man in a few days, but he followed just behind him in continuous circuits around the island for four years without success. Finally it occurred to him to turn around and walk counterclockwise, and after some twenty thousand kilometers, on his twenty-second circuit, he finally met the Daishi-san, here on this ridge below T12. Exhausted and near death, he fell upon the Daishi-san's feet and begged forgiveness. The Daishi-san forgave him and asked if he had any final requests. Emon Saburō asked to be reborn as the lord of Iyo so he could treat its peasants with fairness and mercy. As he died, the Daishi-san placed in his palm an inscribed stone and planted Emon Saburō's staff in the ground, where it sprouted into this cedar.

A short time later, a baby was born in the castle of Matsuyama, the feudal seat of Iyo, his hand fixed in a fist that would not open. For three years this persisted until a priest coaxed open the child's fingers and found the Daishi-san's stone. The local temple, T51, was renamed Ishiteji, Stone Hand Temple, and is now one of the most famous of the whole circuit.

It's sort of a weird foundational myth. First of all, this great religious figure, a patriarch who's only ever praised for his wisdom and compassion, kills off this guy's eight sons, visiting the sins of the father upon an innocent generation. Then the route by which the guy *walks himself to death* seeking repentance becomes a popular thing for hundreds of thousands of people to do. And finally, as other commentators have pointed out, the guy is then rewarded by being reborn as the lord of his province? Why should the fact of his successful repentance mean that he's then allowed to correct for it as a generous aristocrat in the next life?

Just past Emon Saburō's grave the path drops three or four hundred meters over a series of mossy switchbacks, tiled in scatter with shards of wet slate, that lead to a clearing with a rest hut and a shrine. A young woman sits there waiting for her mother's slow descent, and I give her my last orange. In exchange she gives me a white *osamefuda*, which means this is also her first pilgrimage.

Off to the side of the trail there's a squat hut with a glass door and a stone figurine. Inside there's a tatami room, large enough for five or six people, piled with blankets. Guides and maps are stacked along a plywood ledge, and there's a guestbook where people have recorded greetings and the nightly temperatures. There's also a one-thousand-yen bill under a paperweight with a signed *osamefuda* beneath. I wonder how long the money's been sitting there. The walls are thickly insulated and there are tools, tissues, cigarettes, books, and a map. Unfortunately it's too early to stop for the day; I'm happy to be making my own time now, and want to feel the exhaustion of a long slog. I take off my pack and sit for a while, glad this hut exists.

Ever since I started out on the Camino people have frequently sent me this Mary Oliver poem called "Wild Geese." It begins by telling you to take a load off. "You do not have to walk on your knees for a hundred miles through the desert repenting." After that you've got some boilerplate nature description, shiny pebbles in rain, potted scenes of terrestrial greenery in all of its simple splendor, and then the poem ends with how some untamed, squawky birds are generally kind enough to swing by and remind you where you stand "in the family of things."

There are presumably many people who read this poem and stop for a moment and really *feel* it as an injunction: they remember the birds mid-flight and the soft love of your animal body, and they truly recall their place in the family of things. But for some people, for me, this is the kind of thing—this gratitude, this reverence, this sense of the world's invitation—that cannot be inspired by fiat. I wish I'd been able to articulate this better to Max before he left, when I was trying to tell him what differentiated this from a mere adventure. A pilgrimage like this is an old and corporeal kind of shock therapy, a structure that is maintained and promoted to help inspire an *embodied* sense of gratitude and wonder at the variety and generosity of the world, a world much bigger than our petty fears and desponds and regrets. It's gamed for you to have the experience, and then the memory, of finding an unclaimed one-thousand-yen note in an insulated shack in some middle of nowhere between remote mountain temples.

I BOW AT THE MAIN ARCHWAY to T12 and a retiree with a Hubble-lensed camera takes a picture and gives me a milk candy for my efforts. I sit and eat a seared rice ball—little triangles of rice with a filling, in this case pickled plum, they are the staple of my Shikoku diet—in the wide space between the imperial cedars while a monk leads a bus tour group in chanting the Heart Sutra. He keeps a wooden metronomic plock, which along with its rushed, breathless delivery and minor key makes it sound like a martial dirge. I still haven't spent much time looking at the sutra in Moreton's transliteration. He hasn't included a translation, but he has noted that "various English versions can be found on the internet." I'm not sure how much the translation really matters, though, since the Japanese is apparently only a transliteration of the original Sanskrit anyhow. Moreton writes that this makes it "an all-encompassing sutra that gives no regard to the religious affiliation of the person reciting it." Besides, he says it's okay to pray silently, which I take to mean it's okay to stand there silently for a moment amid the incense and occasional reverberation of the gong. I feel a little free and a little sad as I set off down the hill through groves of rotting early oranges and the first plum blossoms. I pass a young man practically running up the trail toward me, and he stops and says hello in English. It's not important to the Japanese what order you hit the temples in, and he's doing it backward, counterclockwise. It's considered three times as hard, because all of the signs face in the temple-ascending direction. He'll be back at T1 in a day or two, and I can't believe he's almost done. He seems unable to believe it, either.

In a small town below the next ridge, an old man and his pretty daughter invite me to sit in the street and have tea and a coconut biscuit. They ask if I'm going to stay in town, clearly implying they think it's the right time of day to stop, but I figure lodging will take care of itself later, as it always did on the Camino. Within twenty minutes of leaving town I'm miserable and I think I'm lost, and I'm someone who takes not inconsiderable pride in never, ever getting lost. The Moreton has abruptly switched to a much different scale, and by the time I make my descent from T12 to the valley floor I've been walking for nine hours, have seen no signs for kilometers, have had no food besides some unripe kiwis, am cold and tired and afraid and have absolutely no idea where I'm supposed to be. At last there's a single decal arrow pointing toward T13. Then it starts to rain and I find myself cowering in the dark along a guardrail, a river far below on the ravine floor to one side and speeding cars on the other.

At last I come to an intersection with a single streetlight. The convenience store is closing but they've still got a few cold potato croquettes, which I eat sitting on the parking-lot curb while I consider my options. It's very cold in the rain and my body is sore and scuffed from the mountain trails, but now that Max is gone I've sworn I'll sleep outside, in one of the huts Moreton mentions in the book. I spend an hour wandering around in the dark, looking for a hut marked on the map, but I can't find it and there's nobody anywhere to ask. I hunt around near a quarry and an antique tractor-repair shop looking for a dry place to bed down; there's an old shed with some stacked timber, but an invisible dog barks nearby and I'm afraid I'll be discovered there. It's too cold to sleep on the ground. Crouched in a bus stop, I start to unravel. At last I decide that tonight, and tonight only, I'll sleep in a hotel.

The room is big enough only for a twin bed—I can reach out and touch opposite walls with my elbows—but I'm asleep within ten seconds.

IN THE MORNING the hotel owner gives me a tiny banana as a junky *osettai* and says I should shoot to cover T13, the next temple, through T18, about twenty-five kilometers ahead, which is what most people achieve from here. For the next eight hours I navigate the run-down snarl of Tokushima's dreary suburbs, looking for the series of unremarkable teen temples; they're not arranged in a way that describes an arc or gives any sense of forward progress, they're just haphazardly distributed in a jagged hook across the outlying districts. By lunchtime I start to suspect that I'm miserable, but I decide to wait for the end of the day to pass definitive judgment. Tokushima itself looks as though it was built one state-of-the-art afternoon in 1968 and then left unattended in forty years of rain. The rain today doesn't let up and my feet are throbbing, but each time I see another retiree trussed in a flapping poncho I try to stop feeling so sorry for myself.

The highway out of dreary Tokushima is lined with car dealerships and cafeterias and *takoyaki*-takeout joints and DVD porn stores and twenty-four-hour fishing shops. For the last thirty-six hours there has been nothing but rain, asphalt, traffic, fear, despair, all through a landscape that makes the last ten kilometers into Burgos look like some mythical orchard. I can say now with utter certainty that I'm absolutely miserable, miserable in a way I never once was on the Camino. I sit on a curb outside a strip mall and write emails of distress, to Micah and David and Alix and Tom—I don't want to worry my mom—on an open wireless signal.

Four kilometers short of T18, there's a red banner with the ubiquitous characters for "pilgrim" and I infer an invitation to rest. This is one of the huts Moreton has marked in his book, though needless to say this particular one isn't noted. There's a guestbook inside with entries that run back about a year, two of them in English: one from a Belgian who passed through six months back, and one from the pair I suspected were Australians, who are only a day or two in front of me. On the wall there's a laminated newspaper spread about the pilgrim-hut project, with a key that locates the few dozen huts around the island's perimeter. This is the first one I've come across, though it's apparently number nineteen; number one is some eighty kilometers on, and it looks as though they've been numbered in construction order. They're of the fanciful school of contemporary hut design. The fancy, I realize as I try to set up camp, is a function of having to design a hut that's pleasant enough for a short rest but impossible to sleep comfortably in. There are no doors, and the entrances are located in such a way as to allow no draftless corner; the benches are too shallow to lie on, and a divider below prevents you from sheltering yourself underneath. The place is a masterpiece of understated passive-aggression, the crowning achievement of a thousand years of melancholy anti-utilitarian Japanese aesthetics.

As I'm fluffing my sleeping bag and wedging myself under the little coffee table, a man of about seventy jumps off an overloaded bike and joins me in the hut. He proceeds in gummy Japanese, of which I can understand exactly one word, *henro*, and some of the numbers. From what I can tell, he's saying that he's done the entire circuit, on foot and on his bike, fifty-five times. Japanese pilgrims don't seem hung up on authenticity the way Camino pilgrims are; there doesn't seem to be a difference between walking, biking, and riding, and in fact the walkers are as likely to be considered crazy as authentic. But a person who's done it fifty-five times is almost certainly regarded as both saintly and insane. I've read about guys like this, people who live out the remainder of their lives as perpetual pilgrims, living off *osettai*. There's even a Japanese word, *Shikoku byō*, or "Shikoku sick," for such pilgrimage addicts. They've got to be out of their minds. I'm less than a week into this and already unsure if I'll be able to finish it even once. He looks at me curled under the table and, before he hops back on his bike, hands me four cigarettes as *osettai*.

It's a Saturday night and the traffic never lets up, but I find a piece of plywood to block the door, and that keeps the worst of the rain out. I drift in and out of sleep, dreaming of the Camino. At first light I rise to look for an open convenience store for a rice ball and a can of coffee.

· · ·

IT'S A SUNDAY SO T19: Tatsueji has more visitors than the temples tend to have. A generation or two ago, I'm given to understand, temples still played an important role as community centers, but these days they're mostly visited on special occasions, or by tourists. Some of them have fallen into disrepair, though given the standards of Japanese aesthetics it's never easy to differentiate incidental disrepair from the purposeful varieties. I poke around for a bit while the other pilgrims and the locals busy themselves with their rites; from what I can tell, the locals do more or less the same routine the pilgrims do. I sit on a bench and have a second can of vending-machine coffee.

Moreton notes that this is the loop's first *sekisho*, which I think of as the *Four Elimination Temples!!!!!* The *Four Elimination Temples!!!!* are where, tradition has it, you discover whether you're pure enough of heart to continue. The idea was apparently a spiritualization of the military checkpoints at feudal borders, where medieval pilgrims had to produce religious permits in order to proceed, so now there's one for each of the four prefectures of the island. (The name "Shikoku" means "four lands," so named for its four prefectures.) If religious pilgrimage was one of the few excuses for travel in medieval Europe, it was pretty much the *only* legitimate reason to be away from home in medieval Japan. Myths have twisted up to cover the functional scaffolding, and the one here tells of an adulterer's hair becoming caught in the temple bell. Her only recourse was to take the tonsure as a nun. To the right of the main hall there's a little cabana with a relic of her hair. I make my way through the temple unpunished. My trial, it turns out, has simply been delayed until the evening.

On the way to T20, Kakurinji, I pass a tea house. A woman runs out and fishes me from the rain, asks if I'd like some tea and *mochi*. It's the first functional English I've heard in a week in rural Japan.

"Why are you doing *o-henro*? Something wrong in life, something bad?"

"Do people usually do it because something is wrong or bad?"

"Yes, either there is big change in life, like retire or finish university, or they need help, or are maybe just bored or want eternal life."

"Well, I did it because I did a similar walk with a friend, in Spain, and it felt so good while I was doing it—I felt so clear and present and content—but then I went back to my life and a lot of those good things went away so quickly."

"Oh, Camino de Santiago! We know this one. Is Spanish *o-henro*, very famous. Maybe one day Eighty-eight Temples of Shikoku also international famous, with more *gaijin* like you." She fills my pockets with *osettai* tangerines and pushes me back out into the rain.

Half an hour later, the red arrow decals swerve off the road and the path turns steep. There are help-yourself bins full of free shoddy staffs if you don't have one, or want a second. I help myself, trying to approximate the effect of the Nordic walking poles. The temple, T20, is another *nansho*, one of the seven or eight temples that are designated as particularly difficult to reach, usually because they're atop mountains. T12 was one, and T21 is, too, and then there are a bunch toward the end. This is pretty smart, I decide, from the perspective of pilgrimage design. You want your toughest days to be at the start and at the finish, so you spend the middle with the right ratio of pride to fear. The climb to the temple is slippery in the freezing, constant rain and I encounter nobody else at all, but the sense of progress makes me feel marginally less glum than I felt in the morning. At the temple the bus-tour pilgrims, at least a hundred of them, crowd the steps up to the main hall with their wide umbrellas. I wait until they get to the part of the Heart Sutra recitation that I've picked up, and join them for a line or two. I go to the stamp office and get my book calligraphed, a nonnegligible expense I've decided mostly to avoid, but the challenge of this temple seemed to make it worth the price of the record.

The next temple crowns the next mountain over, but there's a plunging valley between the two and I'm not sure I can make another big climb before nightfall. Moreton shows one of the free-accommodation huts—I've figured out that in the book these are marked with a little floor, whereas the icons for the basic rest huts are unfloored—along the river below, and I set off downhill into the rain and mist.

The descent is sharply pitched and I can barely see the towers of cedar through the motionless sulk of cloud, but I know I've got a place to stay ahead and I feel as though I've begun to get the hang of this. I pick my way with care between the slick rocks. Across the valley gray panes of mountain stack flat against the late horizon; a dense brume of smoky white gives depth to the ridges. Toward the bottom of the hill, after about an hour of descent, there are a few flights of steps that lead down to a little complex of three buildings, one of which I assume has to be the *zenkonyado*, the free sleeping hut. On the far left is a locked toolshed. In the center of the clearing is a tidy little temple with a basic wooden lattice at the front that looks through to a small, empty, well-swept hall; there's a step up behind the hall to a ritual promontory, like a *bimah* in a synagogue, and beyond that is a second lattice that faces a little Buddha statue a few feet up the hillside.

I try the door to the third building, assuming it's the *zenkonyado*, but it's locked too. There's no sign anybody's been around recently. Given that it's only the end of the first week in March, the very beginning of *henro* season, it seems possible that not all of the huts are open yet.

If only that asshole Moreton had bothered to do the pilgrimage himself, he might have known there was no accommodation here, and might not have stranded the good-faith users of his garbage guidebook at four p.m. in the rain in a remote river valley between two fucking mountains, with no time before nightfall to get back to the last temple or on to the next one. I stop for a moment, breathe, take stock, look over at the temple in the clearing.

The front lattice is chained and the side door is dead-bolted, but there's a little annex on the right wing with a barn-style door threaded shut with rusty wire. I unwind the wire, fetch a stick to lift the latch on the inside, and step in sideways. There's a giant wooden chest and a ceremonial drum in a room about eight feet by ten. I jimmy the handle on the door to the main hall and push my way inside, look around in the fading light. I remove my shoes out of respect and pace the cold slatted floor in my wet socks. Although the lattices are open to the rain and the wind, it seems the best option for suffering through the night. It seems to be the only option.

I splay my things around the raised pulpit area, hoping they'll dry despite the chill, and with my unpacking complete I type up my notes for a while before I lose the light completely. I sit and try to rest, which is to say I sit and work myself into a real lather over Moreton and his stupid book. Brierley might have been a weepy, sanctimonious bastard, but at least his maps managed to avoid major distortions and outright lies. I'm so pissed off, I take out my flashlight and open the Moreton right there and then to examine once more, with leisurely righteous indignation, the page where I've been betrayed.

There are, I discover, *two* hut icons on the map. One of them is where I'm standing. *That* one has no floor. The one with the floor icon looks to be about five hundred meters down the trail, just before the path crosses the shaky bridge over the river and climbs toward T21.

I look around the temple I've broken into and strewn with my wet pilgrim effects, take a moment to apologize for my trespasses to the decent, hardworking hill people of Shikoku; the industrious and quietly suffering citizens of the economically stagnant nation of Japan; and, furthermore, to anyone who has ever owned a Walkman or watched animated pornography.

I close the temple door gingerly behind me and rewrap the wire. It's almost six and has already gotten quite cold, so I hurry down the path toward the river, through a small orange grove, the early fruit hanging rotten on the tree, and then down to the main road. There's an open rest hut with a simple picnic table surrounded by a school of folding chairs emblazoned with vintage seventies American corporate iconography, Xerox and the like, and which immediately strikes me as some sort of art installation I might be ignoring right at this moment at an opening in Berlin. I hope this hut/installation isn't what Moreton meant. I continue to the bridge, trying to reconcile bad map and territory. Two peevish Shiba Inus follow me like slightly domesticated foxes. There's nothing anywhere.

A car fishtails around the bend and pulls into the driveway of one of the corrugated-tin shanties. I walk over and tap on the door. The driver is seventy years old, puttering around in paint-spattered pajamas. I point to the hut on the map but he doesn't seem to recognize his town or region. He talks at me in Japanese and I protest in Japanese that I can't speak Japanese, which of course only confirms his initial impression that of course I speak Japanese. I give up, shrug histrionically, bow histrionically, turn back into the street.

He rushes at me brandishing a piece of metal. I duck and start to run before I see it's just consumer electronics, a brand-new Casio electronic dictionary. It's totally unclear where this rural toothless wizened trash-car pajama man has come up with this, but soon enough I see that he doesn't know what the point of it is, and instead of entering Japanese text and having it translated, he just enters Japanese text and holds it up to my face. As if what I need are some pixilated characters to set things straight. I take the dictionary from him, input the English for "hut," and hold up the corresponding character. He shrieks with glee, jumps in the air, literally kicks his heels, and hurries me along. I realize right away he's bringing me to the open rest hut filled with folding chairs. I make a sleeping gesture. He smiles broadly and gestures back that I ought to go ahead and sleep on as many folding chairs as I like.

I retract all of the apologies I made earlier, especially the ones to the local hill people. I climb the hill in the dark, break into the Buddhist temple again, and make camp in the side storage room, where there's no open lattice. I search the cabinets for something warm, but there's not much I can use unless I want to start setting things on fire, and that's a level of sacrilege even I remain unprepared for. I square up a two-by-four in the paired grooves of the door to prevent anybody from coming in. By now it's seven p.m., pitch-dark, and silent.

I lay my sleeping bag on the floor against the wall and put on all my clothes. I get into the sleeping bag, zip it up over my head, and begin the process of lying there for eleven hours of frozen terror. I realize I would do anything not to be alone. If I weren't alone, this would be a funny story, an adventurous thing to do, something we would endure together now and laugh about later. I wrap my arms around myself and wonder what the girl in Shanghai is doing right now. Probably drinking a beer or going to yoga. I wonder what she'd be doing here. In her last email she said that if she were here alone she'd probably spend most of the time telling herself jokes, which, she says, is what she likes to do when she can't wake up in the morning. I wish I could wake up with her in the morning. What kind of weirdo tells herself jokes? How many jokes could she possibly know?

There's a sharp crack outside and I'm jolted from my reverie, my body rigid. I strain to hear what sounds like footsteps, but it's too hard to tell. It's near zero, sleeting and wind-lashed and sodden with thick forest black, and I can feel the icy pane of hard floor beneath my sleeping bag. Occasionally I find the comfort to doze off long enough to endure one of those dreams where my dad chases me with a gun through the alleys of a dark city before being awoken by a noise outside, always something that sounds like footsteps or a rap at the door.

B Y FIVE IN THE MORNING I'm back on the path over the narrow river bridge and up toward T21, which Moreton, in one of his more Brierleyish moments, has already warned me "has a mystical feel" to it. I'm shaken at first but quick up the mountain with the new vigor of somebody who's gotten away with something, who's emerged from some small rite of passage one increment more courageous.

After an exhausting two-hour climb, the temple unfolds in front of me in a series of wide terraces, the wet-dark cedars framing a cloudy sanctuary. The grounds are lit here and there with pendant gold lanterns burning a soft, damp yellow. The more challenging the approach, cheesy as it is to say, the grander the temple estate seems.

I bow at the gate and a college-age kid materializes next to me, introduces himself as Kintarō; he studies English literature in Kyoto and took his spring break to do the pilgrimage on bike. He skipped some of the mountain temples, mostly because they were on mountains, and is back in his car to get the last dozen stamps he'd missed. He says he's not religious but invites me to participate in his temple ritual.

Kintarō and I stroll along the path to the main hall, where he draws candles and incense from his hip pouch and we light them together. Fifty elderly pilgrims from a bus tour come around from the cable-car station (it's a six-minute ride) and begin to chant the Heart Sutra to the usual metronomic plock. Kintarō and I join in; he reads off of a laminated card and I consult Moreton's transliteration.

We repeat the whole ritual at the Daishi hall, which is around the corner and down a small path. On our way back to get our stamp books signed, a big man with a booming street-preacher voice calls us over and says something to Kintarō. He's a *sendatsu*, an official tour guide, and is leading the bus group. There are elaborate hierarchies for the *sendatsu*—it turns out there's a lot of politics and favor-currying involved—and Kintarō says this man is very distinguished. He wears snowy linen and his sedge hat is lacquered a deep chestnut brown. Kintarō tells him I'm American and this is my first pilgrimage, and that I'm on foot. He opens his white satchel and gives me, as *osettai*, three *osamefuda* slips. One is his own, a red one, which indicates he's done at least twenty complete circuits. The next is his friend's, a gold one for those who've been around more than fifty times. The third is a color photocopy of a brocaded *osamefuda* of a woman, Kintarō explains, who is the most famous living perpetual pilgrim; she's in her nineties and has done the route hundreds of times. The *sendatsu* takes a lot of pictures of all three of us and then gives me an additional *osettai* of half a roll of cough drops.

It's fourteen kilometers wending down out of the mountains and toward the coast, past quarries and enormous greenhouses full of dying peonies. There's not a single convenience store to be found, and I haven't eaten anything in twenty-four hours but four cans of vending-machine coffee and a two-day-old rice ball I found at the bottom of my pack. My feet have begun to hurt badly for the first time. It's only noon when I get to the next temple, but I know I'm done for the day. There's a *zenkonyado*, free lodging in a seedy tatami room that smells of crusty hot plates and old cigarettes. Naturally the hut isn't listed in the Moreton. I email Moreton to ask why this free hut by T22 isn't in the book and he says he thought it would be more satisfying for pilgrims to ask around and figure it out. I ask him what he thinks the purpose of a guidebook is, then, and he doesn't write back. I have walking dreams that meld the Camino and Shikoku in a hallucinogenic delirium. I wake up worrying that I missed a temple in Spain.

TODAY WILL SEE MY FIRST encounter with the sea, and I've very much been looking forward to it. On the Camino the sea was so freighted, the big final thing to look forward to. But the sea here isn't a finale, it's a hem.

In the morning it's pouring. I sit on the futon and watch from the window for half an hour, hoping it'll let up. It doesn't, but when two men in their seventies walk by, it's embarrassing to keep sitting around. It rains all day en route to the coast, and at first I tell myself to be glad it's not worse. It gets worse. It's in the mid-thirties and the rain is coming down in cataracts and the entire way is on the cramped graveled shoulders of heavily trucked roads, and anytime there's an option to go one of two alternate ways my guess is invariably the extra bonus mountain climb, and I can't even stop to rest because I get too cold. This continues for eight hours until I reach T23: Yakuoji, which looks like a delicate crimson-and-ecru bomb half sunk into the hillside overlooking a famous beach where giant sea turtles come to lay their eggs. Now that I've seen the gray sweep of sea for the first time, I will never be far from it.

The next morning it's hailing, and besides, I need to go to the hospital for my infected blister, so I decide I'll wait a day before I set out to walk the coast. As I'm sitting in the lounge of the regional hospital, waiting for them to fill my prescription for antibiotics, I finish typing up my notes for my second dispatch, then force myself to read some of Moreton's introductory material. He writes that the pilgrim is supposed to make three oaths before walking. The first is that the pilgrim believes that Kōbō Daishi will save all living beings, and will always be by the pilgrim's side. The third is that all can be saved in the present world, and the pilgrim promises to continually strive for enlightenment. The second, and most relevant, is that the pilgrim will not complain when things go wrong on the pilgrimage "but consider such experiences to be part of ascetic training." I delete from my notes the four pages I've written about the three hours of hospital-based ascetic training. Instead I write at length about my experience breaking into the temple, and I make fun of myself for how badly I wished a certain anonymous someone—someone who likes to tell herself jokes—had been with me. It occurs to me that perhaps I ought to feel bad about appropriating that longing for dispatch material, but transforming my actual misery into stylized self-deprecation seems to lighten my burden. It's also, I figure, an acceptably encrypted way of telling the woman in Shanghai that I miss her, that the only thing keeping me going is the thought of seeing her again.

Before sunrise I hobble off once again. Shikoku has a kind of sharpened-Australia/swollen-dumbbell shape, with pectoral swells on the north side and two long peninsular fangs dripping south into the Pacific. The two remotest temples, the two farthest from their preceding sites, are the fang points: T24, two days and about eighty kilometers ahead at Cape Muroto, and then T38, almost ninety kilometers south of T37, at Cape Ashizuri. Cape Muroto is known for being the place where most walking *henro* decide to take the bus. Cape Ashizuri is known for being the place where, at least in myth, most remaining *henro* kill themselves.

It's two long days with a seawall on my left, or rather a series of imbricated seawalls. Little claustrophobic anchorages of rusty bobbing boats are folded into the breaks between them. On my right are steep craggy hills brushy with dry chaparral. The seawalls protect villages whose only point seems to be the constant upkeep of the seawalls, like the trapped sand dwellers in *The Woman in the Dunes*. There are very few villages here—I go hours without seeing anything but a seawall and traffic—but there are occasional fringe surfing communities, flophouses and Day-Glo peace signs, and intermittent tsunami-evacuation billboards, which from what I can tell advise you in case of a tsunami to jump at least 4.1 meters into the air and wait there for the all-clear. I sleep in the cheapest business hotels I can find, unwilling to compound my misery by sleeping in bus stations or huts.

For two days what I mostly think about is the Camino. More specifically, I try to remember if it was ever this bad in Spain. I forget the plot of any given movie within hours of seeing it, but I can remember an almost alarming level of detail about the Camino, every village we passed through, how long we walked each day, where we stayed, where we met Tim and Román and Nora and Alina. I stop on a bus-stop bench to queue up an email to Tom.

"Was it ever this bad on the Camino? Did we ever wonder what the point was?" The next time I find an unencrypted signal, in an alley behind a cell phone outlet, I can almost see the glinting spittle on the screen in his reply.

"It was bad ALL THE TIME on the Camino! Jesus, man. I was miserable on the first day! And every day after that! And depressed the entire time! But I did love talking to you. That made it all worthwhile and endurable. Wait . . . I guess I shouldn't be bringing that up for you right now, huh? Sorry you're so lonely, buddy. Remember what this misery feels like, because it will be good material later. And just walk. It will get better. Enjoy how shitty it is right now, because you know, YOU KNOW, you'll look back at this, too, with fondness."

"Well, that's actually the weird thing—I'm not that lonely," I reply. "Loneliness is always relative to possibility, right?" Or it is for me. So when I'm at home in Berlin on a Wednesday and nobody has called to see what I'm up to, and I can imagine all those people out having fun without me at the abandoned U-Bahn stations, I feel lonely. But here on the margin of the end of the world, there's nothing I could possibly be doing and nobody I could be doing it with, so I don't feel lonely. What I mostly am is bored, and when I finish calculating for the fiftieth time how many clicks I've got to walk each day to finish this in time to meet a friend I've convinced to join me in Tokyo when I'm done, I spend hours reliving every step of the Camino.

I wait around outside some municipal office building for Tom to reply and instead I get a note from the woman in Shanghai.

"I am livid and sick to my stomach." She's enraged by my half-occluded reference to her in the last dispatch, in which I've made anecdotal grist of her. Worse, I've selfishly made our relationship, such as it is, public, have disrespected her and her privacy by suggesting, to my friends and family, that she might be available—even that there'd be some chance of her joining me on Shikoku. I've gone too far, she writes, and the whole situation is making a liar of her. She wants an end to the reckless invitations and coy references to the certainty of a shared future. It's not funny, and it has consequences. She makes it clear I shouldn't bother to write back.

This walk is no longer boring; it's terrible. I feel rejected and exposed. No matter my reservations and fears, I'd thought that doing this alone might be good for me, but it's clear now I didn't need to learn how to be by myself. Turns out I'm too good at being by myself, stringing up diverting little scenes of rural nutjobs and slapstick foibles for the entertainment of people on my email list. All that this vaunted solitude seems to have done is make other people seem unreal, bit players in my precious performance of self-discovery. I nauseate myself.

All of the pain in my feet and calves and shoulders feels like punishment for how cavalier I've been, but of course that makes sense too: here *I* am, preempting criticism by accepting the charity of the hard moments as they're doled out. Maybe I'd been able to treat her feelings so lightly because I'd been corroded by Berlin's experiment in unaccountability. Or maybe I'd just become so caught up in the story I was hoping to tell about myself—where I went from being resentfully accountable to gloriously unaccountable to healthily accountable—to notice that she wanted something different. I had announced to myself that I had found the person to whom I would commit and thus I *deserved* a serious relationship; it was still just a crush, sure, but the point was that I was willing to see it through. Her feelings of conflict and guilt and worry were frivolous, irrelevant, would pass in time. If this worked out, our relationship would redeem all the lazy cruelties that had come before: in the light of something that proved so right, I could look back and justify everything else as a necessary prelude, like Elizabeth Gilbert and the dashing Brazilian guy. But if there was no trusting rest to look forward to, no shelter to hope for, what were these years in the desert for?

THERE WASN'T A SINGLE DAY on the Camino, with the exception of the marathon into Burgos, that I couldn't have kept walking at least a little while longer, but over the next few days I find I've got to stop after my daily convenience-store lunch, never making it more than about halfway to the end I'd planned. It's pathetic, and it's hard to figure out how much is physical exhaustion and how much is the emotional effect of the girl's email. Micah says she's being a baby, that she's overreacting to one little email aside, but I think he's wrong. She wasn't reacting to the email. She was reacting to my tyrannical demand that she play the part in my story I'd wanted her to play. I sit down by the side of the road every twenty minutes and consider giving up, but I can't even stand to let myself rest very long. It only makes me feel worse.

I console myself by remembering that this is where everybody wants to give up. Kōchi prefecture, the *dōjō* of discipline, has only sixteen temples, but it takes up a third of the pilgrimage's length. It has the worst weather and the longest stretches of absolutely nothing. Even the convenience stores only pop up every three or four hours, and then they only have the less delicious varieties of rice balls. There are a handful of other walking pilgrims I've come to recognize, like the older woman in the floral pantsuit who sings to herself and gives me candy—she's sixty-nine years old—or the man in the spotless purple tracksuit who listens to his transistor radio and does push-ups at the huts. Ordinarily we nod and smile when we see each other, but for these two days I don't even run into them. I keep thinking maybe I've taken the wrong trail. Even two voluptuous hours bathing in the one *onsen* does little to raise my spirits.

Micah reminds me, "You are not doing this to have fun or not have fun, you are doing this to see why other people do it, and why most people, at least sane people, do not do it. Don't forget," he finishes, "you did, after all, choose to do this. And nobody is holding a gun to your head to keep going. Every time you don't stop and come home you're choosing to continue."

He's right, I am choosing to continue, and it does improve my spirits a little to feel so resolute. But right now being reminded that the pilgrimage experience is a choice only makes me feel even more deluded about what happened with the woman in Shanghai. I'd treated that as if it were a choice, too, a matter of resolve that could transform a passing fancy into a serious commitment. But that, of course, hadn't been anything like a choice, or at least it wasn't a choice that was mine alone to make. What Max said about pilgrimage being like marriage wasn't quite right. On pilgrimage there are all sorts of humbling obstacles, but none of them has a will of its own.

There's an entire day back along a seawall, this one stoppered with vault doors. When a vault is open, the sea to my left is scarred with revetments of boulders and interlocking concrete tetrapods. The sky is as gray and unruly as the sea, and the only person I interact with for twelve hours, besides convenience-store clerks, is a man on a scooter who stops short to deliver some urgent warning or offer or advice. I wish I had the faintest idea what he was trying to tell me.

I COLLAPSE INTO A DAY OFF IN KŌCHI, which is known for having played an important role in Japanese history—cynosure of revolutionarily energetic pro-Imperial sentiment during the late Edo period, birthplace of Sakamoto Ryōma, vanguard of modernization— which in another era I might've felt compelled to describe here. I stop at a commemorative plaque but all I can think to write in my notebook is that the avant-garde travel writing of the future, thanks to the internet, might successfully swing free of place entirely. I visit the mall—the comfort of generic experience Tom and I discovered on the Camino—and buy new shoes and some Nordic walking poles. Later, when people ask me what the big difference between the Camino and Shikoku was, I'll say that in Spain it took me twenty-two days to buy them, but in Japan it took me only sixteen, and that is proof enough that a person can change.

I stay at a hostel, figuring I'll be more likely to run into somebody I can talk to, but the half-dozen backpackers there spend the evening wondering why the hell they bothered to come to Shikoku, and they clearly think anyone who would walk the island is loony enough to be given a wide berth. Before I go to bed a German in his early twenties comes over and starts to talk to me in that international hostel ambient-*Legend* sort of way. He's a teacher, in Japan to visit two dudes he met traveling.

"I'm here, in Japan but especially on Shikoku, because this is a place where they really care about *tradition*. Here they live *authentic* lives, you know this? The States, they are okay, I spent one year on student exchange in Minnesota, but I know that the problem with the States is that it is becoming so *Westernized*. Going to the States, it is like going anywhere else in the world. Japan hasn't been as *Westernized* as the States."

This is a koan, I realize, and this German must be a Zen master. I experience for the first time *henro boke*, the blankness of the pilgrim mind.

I pull myself coherent. "Right, it's a traditional country, but doesn't it also seem like, er, one of the *rapiest* places you've ever been? In the sense of weird bottled-up sexual aggression. Like, there are flipsides to the picturesque traditional life. Have you seen all the porn in the convenience stores?" Costs to so much social organization. Psychological costs resulting from such a tight structure. Few remissive rituals. "This country is to porn what Germans are to beer."

He looks at me quizzically, though I can tell he liked it when I mentioned beer.

"And anyway, doesn't your presence seem contradictory, then? You say these people live *traditional* lives, which means mostly scripted, and what makes them *authentic* is that they're not self-conscious. They do what they do with a certain kind of wholeness you only get if you've got no choice in the matter, or *feel* as if you've got no choice in the matter." Either what they're doing is so necessary and unquestioned that there's no point to thinking too hard about the costs—that is, the other things they might be doing—or they've been so well socialized, it just doesn't occur to them. "Doesn't it seem slightly, well, fucked-up that your ability to indulge in an *authentic* experience here—customs, rhythms of unchanging life, et cetera—is a function of the fact that you *have* a choice, that you're aware of the costs and make decisions?" Isn't our freedom to be authentic purchased at the price of their inability to choose much at all?

The German looks at me as though I'm high.

I TAKE THE TRAM across town at dawn to the point where I left off, between T30 and T31. All of this morning's temples stake out the fringe of the city's alluvial plain. In an otherwise flat landscape, they sit astride the highest hills around. But the climbs usually aren't too steep or long, and I'm no more put out than usual. In fact, I realize that for the first time since Max left I feel terrific. Maybe it's the new shoes and the Nordic walking poles—not just having them but having made the decision to stop for a day and get them, taking care of myself. Or maybe it's just that I know I'm nearing the point where the pain won't be so consuming. By my Camino estimations, it's on the magic Day 22 that the foot misery wanes, and I've got that good independent feeling I associate with being happily alone at the end of the world. There's even something nice about not awaiting emails from the girl in Shanghai. Such good, moving, funny emails! But such anxiety, hoping each time I find a stray wireless network that I'll have some news from her. It's liberating to feel hopeless.

I take a little open ferry across an inlet and stop in at T33, Sekkeiji, long enough to buy fruit. The landscape on the way to T34, Tanemaji, is all extremes. Mountains irrupt without warning off of the horizontal, and what's not mountain is perfectly planar, the flat fields and flat flooded paddies flush. Near T35 it begins to rain. I check into a business hotel, drop off my things, pull on my poncho, and head out toward the temple, which is another "tag" temple—a temple that's off the circuit, one that requires you to retrace your steps. By the time I'm back outside, the streets are drying in radiant afternoon sunlight, and when I reach the top of the utterly superfluous hill to the temple I'm feeling downright charmed. The temple is in the Chinese style, with bright algae blooms of patina on the tin pagoda roof. Off to the left there's a *tsuyado*, a free room for pilgrims, and a white guy is hysterically waving from the window.

"You're Gideon, who did the Camino."

" . . ."

"You wrote it in the guestbook, at that *zenkonyado* near T22. I'm JR. I did the Camino, too, seven years ago, when it wasn't nearly as popular, and I did it in February, when it's cold and lonely and a lot of the *albergues* are closed." It's a strong opening, establishing his pilgrim credentials like this. He's in his late forties, grew up in Boston, but divides his time between an island in Maine and somewhere in southern Mexico. "I do a little landscaping and gardening, teach some classes and do some side catering, and of course I make my art, but I do most of that at my place in Mexico." He pronounces "Mexico" in the Spanish style. He teaches a slow mix of Feldenkrais and yoga, and found out about the Shikoku pilgrimage while searching the internet for "sacred walks." On the Camino he had many of the same visions that Paulo Coelho did.

"How's this been for you?" he asks.

"It's been pretty hard, actually, more or less until today, which was my first really good day. It's been a lot harder than the Camino was, with all this asphalt and everything. I'm about to lose a second toenail, and my right Achilles has pretty acute tendinitis, and my left knee hurts a lot, and I've been kinda bored sometimes by myself, though I'm really digging the *onsen*. They're the only things that make me happy. Well, that and email, I guess. You?"

"I haven't checked my email even once. I blew out my knee between T11 and T12, on that horrible six-kilometer climb to the first mountain temple. It was snowing the whole time"—he was a day or two behind me then, I figure, and what was snow in the mountains was hail on the coast—"and I slid in some mud and hurt myself. I was walking with two American girls around your age and they helped me out a little bit, but then they dropped out and went home back around that weird spring-training town past T27. My boots are killing me, so I'm wearing Tevas."

I look down. His feet look recently and repeatedly mangled, an uneven spectrum of bilgewater indigo, with Band-Aids on all but one of his toes and an array of missing toenails. I want to take a picture to send Tom but JR's feet smell so horrible I start to gag.

He notices. "Yeah, I've been leaking all my toxicity out through my feet. But other than that, it's been great. Much easier than the Camino, but on the Camino I was carrying sixty pounds. Some days I just feel like I'm getting up and going for a stroll, and then forty-two kilometers go by. Near T27 I was walking along and I just felt my heart breaking open, my whole chest opened to the world to allow a healed person to come forth."

"I would not describe my experience that way."

"My mom and my sister both passed away in the last year. My sister was only forty-two, in December, and then my mom, also unexpectedly, in February."

"Oh. I'm so sorry, JR."

"I needed to do something to get through my grief. So I searched for a sacred walk, and this has been just what I needed. Where have you been staying?"

"I had a few nights in huts and mountain temples but I decided that the anxiety about where to sleep was occupying too much of my experience, and I like to be somewhere I can write at night, and where I can relax and take a bath, so I've been staying in cheap business hotels, at a temple or two, and at the beginning I went to some *ryokan*. What about you?"

"I've been sleeping mostly in the pilgrim huts, sometimes out under the stars, and at the temples whenever there's a free room like this one." He looks out the window at the last bus of pilgrims leaving. "I was going to be really uptight about only walking the entire way, but after I blew my knee out it's been tough to go up or down too much, so I took a train for seven kilometers around T18, and I don't think I'll walk back the long way from Cape Ashizuri, where you've got to retread twenty or thirty kilometers you did in the other direction."

"I hate that! You should never have to walk back the way you came. It's just undignified. Any moment in which you've got to break from a fluid circle back to T1 is absurd and, furthermore, wrong."

"Yeah, okay," he says, clearly grappling, after weeks alone, with my disproportionate indignation. "I even accepted a ride down the hill at T27, where you had to go up and down the same steep trail to that mountain temple."

"Three kilometers," I say. "I got a lift too."

"You want to walk awhile together tomorrow?"

I take his Moreton and mark my business hotel. "I'm here, across from the Family Mart. Let's meet for rice balls there at six thirty. Family Mart has the best ones, I've found."

"Rice ball? What's a rice ball?"

"Oh, man, you've really been missing out."

JR is waiting when I arrive. "I got here a little early because I misapprehended the scale of the map, which seems to change from page to page."

"Yeah, there's this complicated color-coded system he uses about which map is to which scale, but it definitely sucks. I've been fuming about it for weeks."

"Yeah, I even got lost a few times. Once I went ten kilometers in the wrong direction."

That sounds like slightly more than a faulty-map issue, but I'm happy to have a *compañero* in my overheated rancor about guidebooks and their inaccuracies. "I spent most of my days on the Camino wanting to garrote John Brierley, and I spend most of my days in Shikoku wanting to defenestrate David Moreton."

JR is an almost disquietingly mild man, large and slow and lopsided and remonstratively childlike, and he looks at me with the sort of bedeviled tolerance you must pick up on the Maine/Mexico landscape-watercolor/Feldenkrais circuit. He doesn't only use the word "laxadaisical" but likes to describe himself that way. He doesn't walk laxadaisically, though, and we're setting a good pace.

"Each time there appears to be a discrepancy between the reality I'm experiencing and the reality of the guidebook, I take it as a lesson," he says. "I try not to focus on the quote-unquote error but on the immediate present. You might be better off if you relax your fixation on this."

But this fixation is the only way I get through my day. I can only endure any of this by dint of my own constant indignation, especially now that I no longer have recourse to the fantasy that at the end of this I'll end up with the girl from Shanghai. If I weren't pissed off at Moreton all the time, I'd have nothing to think about. "I spend at least an hour or two each day planning out exactly how many kilometers I have to do for how many hours a day to finish this."

"I do my best not to look ahead in the book at all. I just focus on each day as it comes. But, uh, do you have any sense how far along we are, now that we're talking about it?"

By my estimation—and with the help of Max, who emailed me a helpful spreadsheet of distances between temples—we're at about kilometer 375, which means that later this afternoon, along a long peninsula a little past T36, we'll be at a third of the way around. The quarter mark was just before Kōchi, and the halfway point is between T38 and T39, about ten clicks short of the latter. "So you see," I tell JR, "if we average thirty-three kilometers a day from here on out, we'll be back at T1 around the twelfth of April. That, incidentally, allows for two more days off, in Matsuyama and Takamatsu."

"How interesting," he says, as if he didn't just ask for this information. He's got to make a plane out of Osaka by April eighteenth, and he wants to make sure he has time to visit the temples in Kyoto first. I might stop through Kyoto if I have time, but frankly, there's almost nothing I'd be less enthusiastic about than visiting more temples—I have, after all, fifty left on this damn island. Anyway, I suspect I'll be in a rush to get to Tokyo, where I've planned to meet one of my oldest and best friends for a week of recovery. Peter's getting there on the nineteenth, so this plan gives me more than enough time.

"Oh, I wouldn't visit Tokyo if I were you," JR says. "That kind of place will just disrupt the equilibrium you've worked so hard to attain here. But, anyway, what was so wonderful about my experience on the Camino, and my experience here thus far, is that I meet all these wonderful teachers when I need them."

Hard to figure what he's getting at. But, okay, I'll take his lead on this. For the rest of the day, and maybe as long as he and I choose to keep walking together, I'm going to treat JR as my own teacher. After all, he's suffered far more than I have. I figure it can't hurt to try to see him as someone sent to help me be less of an angry, self-absorbed jerk. With Tom I could feel pretty good about myself in general just because, in comparison, I didn't complain much and because I got all those Jesus points for tending to his feet all the time. But here I've been thrown back upon myself in a way that disgusts me.

"Let me guess," he says, "you haven't really been doing much at the temples, right?"

"Well, I like to take a little break, sure. Sometimes they have a wireless connection."

So at T36, Shōryūji, we do the whole business, with the hand-washing and the bowing and the invocations of Kōbō Daishi and the sutras at the halls. We sit and share some fruit and continue uphill. T37 is fifty clicks on, so we know we won't get all the way there, but it's a beautiful day and we want to make as much progress as we can. JR pulls out his Moreton to check the trail.

He gets us a little lost but we find our way. The next twenty kilometers follow a serpentine road along a high, rolling, hillocked ridge of peninsula, and the air is warm and clear, and off to our right are glimpses of an emerald inlet, and to our left and a few hundred meters below, sharp crimped spines of steep jetty shear and buckle into the silver sea, their steeps felted in dark cedar, unruly lime feathers of bamboo, and the occasional pink burst of new-blossoming cherry. In the little bays the water pools in absinthe clouds, the beaches pebbled black.

"Now, *this* is what Moreton should've put on the cover of his book, instead of those ugly stairs."

"Actually," JR says, "those stone steps are a perfect image. They suggest ascent."

"Well, right, I'm not saying stairs per se are a bad image, but we've seen so many sets of nicer stairs! I liked those stairs back at, what was it, T31. Excellent stairs there. Just gorgeous stairs. But the stairs on the cover have that tacky metal banister that makes it look like a parking lot."

"Goodness, this is such an incredibly beautiful day. Let me stop a second to take a picture of those cherry trees."

I'm about to keep arguing with him when I think, *Teacher*, Gideon. He's your teacher today, remember? No more senseless arguing.

"Yeah," I say at last, "doesn't this sorta remind you of Big Sur?"

"No, it's more like the North Shore of Maui, or remote northern Vietnam."

We're poised on the brink of an idiotic competitive-travel argument—I'm about to play the old Madagascar trump card, forgetting once again that he's the teacher—when we come around a corner and see our first other pilgrim of the day. It's the sixty-nine-year-old woman in the flapping floral pantsuit who likes to give me candy.

"That's my friend!" I tell JR. "She trained to do this for five years." I call out to her, *"Kon-ni-chi-wa!"*

She turns around and lights up, grabs my raised hand in combination greeting and solidarity gesture, tries to throw her arm around my waist but misses and instead grabs my butt, seems briefly embarrassed, then grabs my butt again.

She's called Masako and we pass the first cherry trees in fragile bloom and she tries to teach me a Japanese song, something schmaltzy and nostalgic about the *sakura*, the cherry blossoms, but she croons too fast for me to keep up. She's delirious with good cheer and it's a pretty sharp reminder to me to suck up whatever pain and irritation I'm feeling. We stop at a viewpoint to take pictures of each other and then she gives us two milk candies apiece and sits to have her lunch. We head off in even better moods than we'd been in before.

JR talks about sleeping in huts and I can tell he really needs a night somewhere warm and dry, but he's just been too afraid to deal with a hotel or *ryokan*. I tell him it's not as hard to navigate the whole thing as he might think, and that sometimes they do speak a little English. "One night when I was back in Aki Town the girl at the receptionist's desk spoke amazing English, and she drew me a map to a place I could get a heel support for my Achilles." I pause. "And she was really cute."

"I got that impression," JR says. I don't totally understand the implications of this, but I definitely don't care for it. He's the teacher, though, and maybe his point is that such desires are the sort of distraction that makes it hard to feel as though my heart is breaking open. We return to the safe topic of how nice the day has been, the weather and the landscape, maybe my favorite of the whole trip. JR says he's had so many wonderful moments he can't choose just one. I suspect that what we're saying is that despite the mutual wariness, we're glad to have found each other.

We stop by the side of the road and lie in the sun reflecting off the inlet and rest. JR introduces me to roasted mung beans and I introduce him in turn to these things that look vaguely like rotini but taste like Bugles and we both feel idle and content. I tell him about meeting Román back on the Camino and how he used to say that the best part of the Camino was the breaks.

"All of it is the best part, Gideon."

IT'S AMAZING HOW QUICKLY, after a long spell of solitude, someone else can go from seeming like a cosmic blessing to being an enormous nuisance. With JR it takes the hour and a half we spend together, after a wonderful thirty-five-kilometer day, wandering around drab concrete Susaki City looking for a place to sleep. By the time I manage to find a *ryokan* that's okay with him, it's after six and I'm ready to crash standing up. The Moreton mentions that the local specialty is a soy-based chicken ramen with a raw egg, and I've been looking forward to it for weeks, but the only *ryokan* that has any availability—after we've spent such a long time, at JR's insistence, looking for a place to sleep outside—is just outside of town, and I no longer have the energy to walk back looking for food.

The sly red-faced proprietor asks if we'd like to sit and have a beer. All I want is a bath and bed but it seems impolite to refuse. JR is allergic to gluten so he can't drink beer, but the proprietor brings out a rare and very expensive chestnut-distilled *shōchū* for him. JR takes one sip and sets it aside; I finish it out of politeness. Initially the proprietor, whom I'll call Yukio-san, seems like a fascinating guy— he's got a master's in international relations from an American university and has written seven or eight books, including most recently a self-published effort about Japanese immigration and investment on a South Pacific island—but as he begins to properly tie one on he starts seeming a little odd.

"So you're an academic?"

"Hate teaching. Besides, I know too much greasy stuff. Too dangerous to have me as professor, so I mostly am just farmer. Some peaches, loquats, new summer oranges. *Biwa, buntan, mikan*." I believe these last few are varieties of the local citrus. "You are retire?"

I laugh and say no.

"Most pilgrims, they are retire. You finish working, dentist or lawyer, you think, What now? So you go on pilgrimage to figure out, you are used to live one way, and now to start new era of life not as profession but as man."

He asks JR what he does and JR goes into a long spiel about his artwork and his Feldenkrais and his Mexico/Maine lifestyle. Yukio-san pays no attention at all and pours several more large beers for the two of us. He insists I take one of his clove cigarettes.

and most legible ones—he could've taken the wrong forest trail and might be out there still. I feel terrible I left him; I should've just taken the goddamn train for twenty minutes instead of insisting I do the mountains on foot. I think of the time I frog-marched Tom into Burgos at the end of our fifty-two-kilometer day and all he wanted to do was take a taxi and I refused and now I feel awful about that too. I get off my greasy car cushion and queue up a quick email to Tom, apologizing for making him more miserable than he ever needed to be.

And the funny thing about all this is that I don't even really *like* JR much. He's *fine*, nice and genuine and very well-intentioned, if more judgmental than he thinks he is. But he's also obviously sad, and hurt, and I realize I do genuinely hope he's okay. This is one of those things that feels rare about meeting people in this context: you find yourself caring a great deal about the suffering of people you don't particularly like and whose suffering is neither crushingly obvious nor dire. Pilgrimage helps you pay attention to the low-level distress and indignity of people you're not all that keen on.

At six it's no longer raining and whatever sleep I might've had is long past and I know once I start walking I won't be too cold, so I stop congratulating myself for worrying about JR and get going. After an hour I hear a dog start to bark furiously and I turn around and it's charging. I square off and prepare to beat a Shiba Inu to death with a Nordic walking pole but then he hits the end of his tether. Another hour later I pass the hut where JR had planned to spend the night; I wander over to inspect it for blood and fibers and signs of struggle but find only a scrap of paper tucked between posts.

"HELLO GIDEON—HOPE YOU WAITED AND STAYED AT T37—LONGER WALK FROM THERE THAN I'D THOUGHT—HEADING ON—HOPE YOUR DAY HAS BEEN GOOD." The hand is loopy and the note is time-stamped ninety minutes ago.

The chase enlivens my day and now I'm practically running. By ten I've descended from the highlands and regained the coast; great floods of sunlight sweep off the rocks and the sea. A college-age kid in a pilgrim vest whizzes by on a bike, whizzes back to chat and practice his English.

"Can you do me a favor?" I take out an *osamefuda* and write, "JR— AM EIGHT TO TEN CLICKS BACK—MEET AT THE *ONSEN* BY THE WHALE- WATCHING BEACH ON MORETON P. 35?" I turn to the kid and say, very slowly, "In about twenty minutes you will pass another *gaijin*. He's tall and very, very white. He shaves unevenly." I mimic JR's loping limped gait, his loose pants and off-kilter pack. "Will you give him this note?" The kid nods excitedly and rushes off.

An hour and a half later there's another modish anti-sleeping hut, this one shaped like a pirate ship. I'm beginning to wilt from moving so quickly, and the sea is frantic with tiny whitecaps. An *osamefuda* sticks out from the guestbook pages. "GIDEON—THANKS FOR NOTE BUT HAD ALREADY PASSED *ONSEN*—WILL SEE YOU LATER TODAY OR AT CAPE—ON A ROLL AND WANT TO KEEP MOVING. CHEERS, JR 11:30A." My heart sinks a little bit. I can understand the desire to keep moving but I'd really hoped he'd wait. At the end of a forty-five-kilometer day I bed down at a business hotel with an ocean view from my tiny window, and prepare for another long day alone.

The next afternoon the peninsula proper begins. The trail crosses back and forth and sometimes along a road, with laborious stretches in and out of ravines, the path more or less entirely un-groomed, strewn with downed bamboo and upended cairns. There's no evidence of JR anywhere. For the last few kilometers the now tropical trees hang in a low canopy over the single-lane road, and after a long day of racing along I enjoy taking my time to enjoy the closing stretch of the first half of the island. Finally around the last corner there's T38: Kongōfukuji, a wealthy assembly of opulent pa-

godas staged coolly around a rippled pond and rock garden. Story
has it that Kōbō Daishi founded this temple himself, in 822. Cape
Ashizuri is a legendarily remote place in Japan, and its visitors are
almost exclusively pilgrims; there's no reason it would ever occur to
anyone else to come here. In the early days of the circuit, when tat-
tered, holy mendicants haunted these long coastal stretches with
only a weathered staff and a begging bowl, this craggy, exposed spit
was a mortal wharf. The ascetics would come to board small wooden
rowboats, pushing off toward the south seas, in search of the Pure
Land of Fudaruku, the arcadian dwelling place of the Buddhas of
compassion. Their pilgrim's stampbook was their passport to that
land beyond death.

I'm sitting on my pack outside the *ryokan* and up strolls JR from
the wrong direction, looking a little the worse for wear. I'm surprised
to feel so glad to see his familiar lope. He got lost and ended up taking the mountain route down the center of the peninsula rather than
the shorter, easier coastal route I took. He's on the brink of dissocia-
tion. I give him my last rice ball and an *osettai* grapefruit, given to me
by my purple-tracksuited geriatric friend, that I've lugged for hours.
We set off for the *onsen*, where we sit in the hot pool on the balcony
and look out over the darkening granite cliffs over an empty copper sea.

WE STAY IN THE SAME *ryokan*, meet at dawn on the way to the
bus stop. It's pouring, we've each done two successive forty-
five-kilometer days, and neither of us has the least interest in spending four or five hours retracing the route back up the cape we just
walked down. It's the sane thing to do and we don't feel apologetic
about it. The bus stops every twelve feet and we only save an hour or

two in the end, but it's nice just to sit and look out a window at the scenery for a while.

The cherry blossoms steep a subdued pink in the wet chill and the mountains look settled in the heavy mist, and despite the rain we're both in good moods. "I feel ten years younger than when I started," JR says as we start to walk again. "My body feels stronger. The bags under my eyes are gone. I feel whole again, healed."

"Yeah, that's how I felt on the Camino after life in Berlin, but this time around I don't feel the renewal as such a physical sensation—that sloughing off of old layers."

"You did the Camino, what, eight months ago? Ten? You've been recently purified. You don't have the same toxicity to get rid of. And this time you were coming from your brother's place, not from Berlin."

"That's true, but being in Shanghai wasn't particularly easy this time." I explain how, much as I adore Micah's girlfriend, I'd often felt like an intruder now that they were living together, and I hardly ever got Micah to myself. On my thirtieth birthday he'd spent the second half of dinner texting her, then got up from the table at nine thirty and announced that he had to head home. I'd felt really disappointed. Friends from home were emailing to say they'd spend their thirtieth birthdays renting taco trucks or camping in Big Sur and I'd spent an hour and a half walking home along Huaihai Lu by myself because my brother had gone three days without seeing his girlfriend. I'd stopped into one of the frowsy bars on Heng Shan Lu to have at least *one* celebratory drink by myself but the only other people there were bored prostitutes who wouldn't leave me alone. I gulped my drink and walked back out into the damp cold.

"And then, after a few years of making sure I never got myself into any real romantic commitments, I met this girl, a friend of friends in New York who is also living in Shanghai, and fell for her harder than I've fallen for anybody in as long as I can remember. Now she's not talking to me." I look over at JR, who is fiddling with his Moreton.

As we walk through the soft rain, we turn to what it feels like to become a lower priority in someone else's life. I say I can't figure out whether I'm jealous of Micah's reprioritized affections or just jealous of his relationship itself, which seems so idyllic.

"Get used to it," he says. "My brother is the only remaining member of my immediate family, and he has this habit of getting into relationships and ignoring me completely, for months and years at a time. He forgets plans we made, has no idea how to share his affection. It's been a long road to understanding that we're not as close as we once were." He pauses. "And as for me, I can't say I've ever really done the whole relationship thing."

It's a heartrending comment, delivered entirely without self-pity, and it makes me look at him with new tenderness. And I can't help but feel as though I don't look very good in contrast. My father might be difficult, but he's alive and healthy, and Micah might be obsessed with his girlfriend but he still let me lie around their apartment in my pajamas for almost three months. On pilgrimage, the fact that everybody's immediate suffering is so banal—blisters, foot pain—and so chosen (i.e., none of us have to be doing this) both eradicates and emphasizes the hierarchy of pain. On the one hand, the general level of discomfort allows you a break from comparative anguish. You don't have to ask whether it's okay for you to be suffering, whether you're suffering enough to justify the word; you just accept that you are. On the other hand, the company of those whose suffering is so much worse encourages you to get over yourself. This seems particularly true on Shikoku, where the pilgrims are a mix of mourners, like JR, and the just generally confused and disoriented, like the majority of the retirees. Confusion is its own form of suffering. Your sense of crisis or loss is legitimate, and, perhaps most important, you become no more compassionate if you deny the legitimacy of your own sense of crisis. It is only through the acknowledgment of your own pain, trivial as it may ultimately seem, that you can attend with real sympathy to the suffering of those around you.

WE STOP ON A BENCH under a little roof out of the rain. An old woman comes out of a nearby house and brings us hot tea and potpourri-flavored candies. We give her *osamefuda* and she returns with miso soup thick with *enoki* mushrooms and seaweed.

"This kind of thing is so humbling. It makes your day," JR says.

Most accounts I'll read talk about the *osettai* custom in terms of the pilgrim's experience: this walk is equal parts hardship and exactly what JR's referring to: the gracious, humbling acceptance of support. The one exception I'll come across is an academic study of the pilgrimage by a Manchester professor called Ian Reader, who writes, of *osettai*, that it's the patent neediness of pilgrims that allows the locals to rise to the occasion, to be their best, most generous selves.

We get back into our ponchos and walk.

"Back when I did the Camino it wasn't nearly as crowded as it must've been when you did it," JR says.

I hate this conversation already. "Yeah, probably."

"We're the only Westerners I've seen this whole time here. Do you think more will do it in the future?"

I can tell that the answer is supposed to be, No, JR, forever and ever it will just be special people like us. But that doesn't have to be the case, and if I were in charge I know what I'd suggest. The first thing they'd need to do is get it off this asphalt, and then they'd have to handle accommodations, and they'd need a more comprehensive guidebook. They'd need *albergue*-like *zenkonyado* all over the place, simple tatami rooms with futons and blankets where you could stay for free or a small donation. There seems to be such a network already, but you have to speak Japanese to find them. All it would take is a little money; the locals are already primed by the culture of *osettai*. All the hand-lettered signs we see along the trail are the work of a single individual, apparently.

"UNESCO wants to make this a world heritage site, but then you have people like fucking Moreton who say they don't want more money or more people. They want it exactly as it is. On the day he picked me up, he even went so far as to say that from what he'd heard, the UNESCO money had 'ruined the Camino.'"

"I have to say, Gideon, that I agree with David Moreton. This is perfect as it is. Look at what we just experienced with the tea and the miso soup. If you had tons of people going by like on the Camino, they'd just be, like, 'Oh, there goes yet another *o-henro-san*.'"

This is driving me bonkers. What about the people *here*? There's no economy here at all; the young people leave for the other islands the first chance they get. "It's utterly presumptuous for people like Moreton to tell them they're better off in their corrugated-tin shacks just as long as people like us get our fucking soup."

"It's presumptuous of *you* to come here for three weeks and talk about what the locals want."

This is coming from a guy whose Japanese consists of saying *Lo siento* in baby talk when he bumps into somebody by the rice-ball cooler. Though my Japanese is limited to ordering in restaurants and securing antibiotics, I've *been* talking to people every chance I get. There are places here, like Hiwasa Town by T23, where the population has been cut in half since 1960. "They built those three big bridges to Honshū and all it's done is made it easier for people to leave."

"That's not just Japan, Gideon. All over the world people move to cities."

"Yeah, uh, okay. But look at the Camino, where whole villages were *dead* in the seventies and now have come back to life in the last two decades."

"Maybe we should stop having this conversation."

"No. I don't think that the increased popularity of the Camino has in *any way* diminished the chances of interactions like the miso soup one we just had."

It's almost impossible to imagine this becoming as pedestrian, so to speak, a trip as JR fears. The sheer difficulty of walking twelve hundred kilometers in the rain to visit these eighty-eight idiotically indistinguishable temples on the seawalled periphery of an island associated with exile and death is going to prevent it from becoming one more cheap, prepackaged thing.

"This should be made available to anybody who wants to do it. The world would be better off for it. The last thing this should be about is the fragile egos of authenticity-hound Westerners."

"I'd like to talk about something else now, Gideon."

"Don't condescend to me, JR. This is important, and it cuts to the heart of this experience." People like JR get off on having done something that other people haven't done. He's afraid that the experience is only meaningful insofar as it's rare. In another age, he'd have souvenirs from the Eiffel Tower, but now that's no longer rarified enough. I think I felt that way when I began, that this would be like the Camino but *more special*. But—and maybe this was just the loneliness talking, or the fact that the experience with the girl in Shanghai had made me feel like a solipsist—it seems to me now that exclusivity isn't what makes a journey like this meaningful. What makes it meaningful is that it's really hard but it's something anybody could do if he or she made the commitment to do it. The possibilities of resonant human encounter aren't diminished by the simultaneous decision of others to make the same commitment.

"The thing is, JR," I conclude, "the absurdity and difficulty of this experience—the way it demands activity and participation, even if it's just walking in the fucking rain—allows it to scale, you know?"

JR finally says something. "Tomorrow I'm going to take a short day and stop at T40. There's a free place to spend the night there. But you should feel free to continue on."

LET'S DEFINE "MODERNITY," for the sake of discussion, as "the era in which you are not overwhelmingly expected to do with your days what your father did with his." Victor Turner once wrote that he was interested in pilgrimage because he sees it as the signal rite in a society in transition from premodern ("tribal" or "archaic") to modern organization. Tribal communities have initiation rites, where a young person is taught simply how things are done; from then on, he's expected to comport himself according to the rules. There are times—during annual festivals, say—when those rules are suspended and members of the community are allowed to let off some steam, but for the most part it's an initiation into a set of inflexible commitments to an unquestioned authority. Where initiation teaches you to function in a society with little in the way of individual choice, pilgrimage helps free individuals cope with the problems of relative autonomy. As Turner saw it, "initiation is an irreversible, one-way process, transforming the state and status of the initiand. Pilgrimage is part of a lifelong drama of salvation and damnation, hinging on individual choice, which itself involves acceptance or rejection by an individual of 'graces,' or freely volunteered gifts, from God."

But this distinction—between societies that are fixed and societies that are fluid—is a bit of a fiction; all societies, and all human lives, lie upon a spectrum between fixity and plasticity. What's so weird and interesting about pilgrimage, if you take Turner's argument a little further, is that on one end of the spectrum it can function as socialization and on the other it can function as therapy.

Pilgrimage for an early modern was probably the only chance you ever had to leave the insipid, stifling, monotonous routines of your tiny village and go "beyond the fields." It was a break from constraint, a little holiday of self-determination, and the genius of it was that it was at least putatively commanded. It was volition operating behind a front of obedience, a desire dressed up as an obligation, a want externalized as a must. And nobody could really predict the effect it would have. You might return from Santiago de Compostela and decide that your one experience of elsewhere has been quite enough, thank you, and has reconciled you to the constraints of your old preordained life. Or you might return from Mecca, as Malcolm X famously did, and decide to insist on some new measure of freedom from a scripted existence. Turner's point was that a process of initiation was designed to change you—from a child to an adult, say—but that pilgrimage's outcome is far less certain. It's part of the "lifelong drama" by which one works out his or her relationship to the manifold authorities and decisions of a modern existence.

So what Turner was just nibbling the edges of is that we modern individuals are burdened not by the monotony of routine, like our medieval predecessors were, but by the abundance of choice. A medieval pilgrimage meant an experiment in individual desire dressed up as religious necessity; a modern pilgrimage means an experiment in obligation dressed up as just another desire. Whether the pilgrim is a retiree, like the men Yukio-san described, who's unsure how to lead a life unstructured by a professional schedule; or a late adolescent, like Nora or Alina or David, who were all struggling with questions of relationships and jobs and how and where and why to settle; or somebody like me, whose experiment in recklessness highlighted my limitations rather than dismantling them, contemporary pilgrimage isn't the old push to escape the stultification of boredom with the novelty of travel, but the new desire to escape the anxiety of novelty with the guarantees of obligation. The medieval pilgrim longed, at least theoretically, for a chance to live a life other than the one he inherited. But we're like those actors whose headshots David Levine collected, auditioning for direction, ready to rehearse. We long to feel some sense of purpose that isn't necessarily of our own invention.

Except, of course, that it *is* of our own invention—or if not exactly of our own invention, then our own election: a free choice to feel obligated. And Shikoku is, for the most part, so difficult and lonely that, even now, every single day, I think about electing not to continue.

It's thus not a surprise that, as Turner writes, "scholars generally hold that after the Holy Places of the Holy Land, the tombs of the martyrs, scattered throughout the Roman Empire . . . became the first pilgrimage centers. They exemplified the supreme act of Christian free will, the choice of death for the salvific faith rather than life under the auspices of state religion." The pilgrim pays her due to men and women of rare conviction, visits the monuments to ultimate sacrifice, because she is working out her own relationship to desire. She weighs the worths of sacrifice.

This, I think, is part of what the German at the Kōchi hostel and JR mean when they say that this—Shikoku itself, or its circumambulation—feels authentic. When people talk about authenticity, they're usually talking about the fantasy of an unself-conscious life. This fantasy tends to take two forms. There is, on the one hand, a life where everything is inherited and nothing is decided, like Sartre's waiter or the ideal of the noble savage; this is behind the desire to visit pygmies or "eat where the locals eat." There is also, on the other hand, a life where all is unapologetically willed, like Nietzsche's Superman, or Gauguin. In the former case, everything is settled; in the latter, it's all up for grabs. The former has given up trying to think about the costs or consequences of his decisions; the latter affects not to care. What a pilgrimage does is stake out some middle ground. It's both sorta commanded and sorta voluntary. It's a dress rehearsal, and it's also real.

THE NEXT MORNING JR and I decide to stay together after all. We're both looking forward to crossing the high pass that forms the border between Kōchi and Ehime prefectures, the boundary between the *dōjō* of spiritual discipline and the *dōjō* of enlightenment. It's tough on JR's knees in the mud but he takes a spin with my Nordic walking poles and is, like everybody, pleasantly surprised. The rest of the day is rainy and cold but I think we're both so glad that we haven't—or, rather, that I haven't—totally wrecked our relationship, that it passes without incident. Near T40 JR sees me to my hotel. He's staying in the free room at the temple but I want to be by myself and get some work done. It's been a week since I've sent out a dispatch, not that anybody besides Max cares, and it's hard to get myself to care much, either, now that I'm not sending them to the girl in Shanghai.

"So, uh," he says, "what time do you want to meet in the morning?"

"Six thirty's fine, JR."

At six thirty I stand JR up. I'd told him that if it was still mon-sooning this might happen, and that he should then leave me notes in the guestbooks about his progress and where he planned to spend the night. I'm happy to be alone for the first time in two days. But I feel sort of bad about it, and I imagine there is probably something to be said for a commitment to the discomfort of unchosen company, especially when you're spending so much time thinking about your family. (For what unchosen and discomfiting company are we more involuntarily committed to?) Turner's idea of *communitas* holds up in a material way—this experience certainly does shear us of our eco-nomic, geographical, and professional affiliations in a way that allows for intimacies that everyday life rarely encourages—but I don't think that's the main draw. I think it's actually a psychological fantasy: the hope is that we might step out of a more profound level of role-playing and encounter other people in a way that's not structured by habitual dynamics. This is why those first moments with a stranger on the Camino or, less frequently, here can feel so intoxicating; they loosen the hold of our selves. But, as I've found with JR, the self is quick to reestablish the routines it's used to. JR treats me as Poor Volatile Gideon in a way that I've long grown accustomed to; I treat him as Flaky Naïve JR in a way he presumably recognizes as well. We were already treating each other like family insofar as we carried each other around even when we were apart. Whereas in a romantic relationship both people make the choice to be together, and they fear it will fall apart.

Beneath the low menace of storm clouds, islands tear shadows across the shallows of the Inland Sea to my left. I've got to lower my shoulder to the wind to keep moving. The trail diverges from the road and heads up and over a five-hundred-meter pass; for the first time in a while I'm forced to stop every few hundred yards to catch my breath. The physical exertion quiets my anxiety about having abandoned JR. On the far side the woods are quiet, wet and white with vapor, and the walking just feels simple and good.

In the next town, I see a familiar form bobbing awkwardly at a pace of frank bewilderment, gawking upward for some legible sign.

"JR!"

He looks over and comes toward me without seeming remotely surprised or delighted. He's wearing a rain suit I've not seen before. It must be new, and it's already torn. The pants are flapping at the seam as though he's been inexpertly half flayed. I wonder if the toxicity has finished with his feet and begun a new campaign of general savage exit.

I clap him warmly on his big stupid back. "What the hell happened to you?"

"My pants are coming apart."

"I noticed. What are you doing wandering around this godforsaken town?"

"I'm looking for a place to spend the night, maybe one of those cheap business hotels you're always recommending, but I can't read the signs." Helplessly he holds up the piece of paper on which I've written for him the Japanese characters for "hotel."

"Look, just come along with me, we'll go to Uwajima City, it's only fifteen kilometers up the road, and it'll go quick because we're together. We'll find a hotel together there, I promise." He agrees immediately.

We talk bullshit in good spirits. "Okay, so when it comes to the trail markers," I say, "this is my preference: first, the little potatoheaded kimono men. Then the little red-arrow decals. Then the handmade signs, and finally the tiny blue carrots, which are so hard to see!"

JR agrees. "The ones I don't like are the two little dancing cartoon characters."

"Oh, I find them charming."

"I trust the Moreton over the signs."

"That's why you get lost all the time."

"I do not get lost all the time!"

"Yes, JR, you do. But it's okay. It's Moreton's fault."

JR changes the subject before I can piss him off again. "I was moving so fast this morning! I passed so many people, it was great."

"Is that right, Mr. I Take Each Moment As It Comes?"

"Very funny. Yeah, I was hanging around that city where you saw me for, like, I dunno, an hour."

I realize he's embarrassed that I left two hours later and still caught up to him.

No, that's not it. He's embarrassed that he was *waiting* for me.

Was he lonely? Or did he also worry and hope that if we stuck together we might somehow turn our petulant dynamic into an adult one?

We both seem to put new effort into our conversations now. We spend a heartfelt and emotional four or five sodden hours asking each other about our families. We've both relaxed a bit, seem less wary of each other. He talks about his niece, the daughter of his recently deceased sister, and how close they had been for so long, and how they were originally supposed to go somewhere together during this month but she didn't feel up to it, in the end, so he came to Shikoku by himself. He tells me he'd always been so proud not to have a telephone in Mexico, so glad to be off the grid, but that when his mother died it took his family three days to reach him, how terribly he regrets it now. Eventually we get around to our fathers. He says the eight weeks before his father's death from cancer were magical, healing, special weeks, when after a lifetime of struggle the two of them managed to find each other. I tell him about my dad and the recent halting reconciliation we've had. At least we're talking now, even if there aren't any signs of real resolution. And he's still not reading my email dispatches. JR tells me that I should forgive him; it's that simple. The bottom line, he says, is that I either want a relationship with my dad or I don't. If I don't, I should just walk away. If I do, well, then I do.

My immediate response to this sort of thing—this too-pat chat of deathbed reconciliation, the suggestion that in the end you'll wish you'd just forgiven and moved on—is to dismiss it now as I dismissed it when I heard the same thing from Tom. But maybe this is exactly the hackneyed JR blather to pay attention to. Maybe all it ever can possibly come down to is a pat reconciliation, a resignation to the fact that, if the future is what's important, and if there seems to be a possibility, for the first time in a while, of a future we can both live with, there's little use in a full reckoning. We don't have to talk our extinction to death. What we do have to do, in the jargon that a damned pilgrimage like this can't help but make you vulnerable to, is recognize and accept our limitations—mine and his—and what the limitations on our relationship might be: how much honesty and expectation it can support without collapsing again.

We're late arriving in Uwajima City—we had to stop for JR to get some new rain gear—so it takes us a while to find a business hotel with vacancies. I throw a little fit because they won't give me the wireless password and JR hides behind a lobby pillar. Fine, I think, I'll drop it. Before we go to bed we exchange email addresses. His has the word *namaste* in it.

"I'll write you notes when I pass the huts. Take care of your-self, JR."

"You too."

A BLOCK FROM THE HOTEL I see two large cats leashed to a stoop with bungee cords, which seems odd, auspicious, like an early scene in a Murakami novel. I stop in a convenience store and do not have to wait twenty minutes for JR to decide between the one rice ball with the label he cannot read and the other rice ball with the label he cannot read.

The entire day is on an incline—I'm headed back into the mountains—and there are two high passes. In the first few hours I hit T41, Ryūkōji, and T42, Butsumokoji, neither of which has much to say for itself. On the five-hundred-and-fifty-meter pass over to T43, Meisekiji, there are panoramic views of the Inland Sea, the is-land of Kyūshū in the distance, and I feel exceptional again, able to meet with ease and dignity and humor the successive demands of the day. I've managed to think about the girl in Shanghai only once in a while, and I resolve never to bother her again, much as I miss her emails. I practically skip down the mountain (actual skipping being dangerous, ill-advised).

The afternoon is more difficult, as it always is, and there's a long stretch in the shoulder of a road that leaves me feeling jarred and nervous, but some retired civil engineers give me a tangerine and ask if I've ever had rice before, and then I get a soft grenade of energy glop as an *osettai*. I'm sitting on a curb and a woman rushes over and thrusts it into my hand, escaping back into her house before I can even thank her. I look up and catch her eye through the window and wave.

I've been turning over Ian Reader's idea that having the pilgrim-age route here does as much for the locals in some ways as it does for the pilgrims. I'd thought I was identifying with the porch and window-seat dwellers along the Camino because I, too, had a tendency to feel abandoned, but now it seems it might be the opposite. Berlin, in its way, expected and allowed for the worst in a person—or at least I often felt as though it had allowed for the worst in me—and I wanted to be in a place where I felt I had to rise to the occasion. Where at times along the Camino I had the odd unjustifiable sense that the locals had to be reassured—these were, after all, people who had to live in the wake of hourly announcements that their place wasn't enough, that it was a place to be merely passed through—I could now imagine seeing them as reassuring, as people who understood that all of this constant moving on passed no judgment on them, people who could say, "You are moving on because of some need of yours, and rather than take it as a judgment about myself and my home I will take it as a sign that you need help."

THE NEXT DAY follows a river upstream into the mountains toward T44 and T45, the farthest inland of all the temples. The *henro* path runs through a few towns known for their well-preserved nineteenth-century streets, which I observe desultorily without slowing down. Mountains loom serenely in the distance, and in the villages they're doing some sort of spring burning. The sunny air is acrid; blankets and futons wave from banisters. At a *henro* hut there's a canister of dried sweetened persimmons and I take more than I probably should. I walk slowly. The only imperative is to stay ahead of JR for the moment.

In the *ryokan* in the evening there are two older men smoking in one corner and two cute girls around my age in the other, sitting down to an obscenely large and complicated *kaiseki* meal, hautely enigmatic collections of tiny variegated repasts.

One of the men waves me over, introduces himself in good English as Mick, from Yokohama. "I retired this past year at sixty after I worked as an engineer at the same company for thirty-six years." I ask why he's doing the *o-henro*. "After I retired, I finally had the freedom to do whatever I wanted, not just what my company wanted. What I wanted to do was take this trip." He sips his beer. "Mostly because I did not know what else I wanted."

"What does your family think?"

"My wife and children think I'm crazy. I spent three years convincing my wife to let me come. I call her every morning before I walk and every night when I get to the *ryokan* to tell her I'm safe. Many people do *o-henro* because they are sick, or have a bad injury. Sometimes lepers. They used to say this was 'kill-or-cure' trip. Or maybe their friend or relative died. For me none of that is true. It is hard for me to say why I'm here."

These conversations always make me think of a line in Wittgenstein where he's talking about the chain of reasons we give for doing something. If you ask someone "Why?" enough times—if every time they provide a "Because . . ." you respond with another "But why?"—they get to a point where no further account is available, where they are doing something that seems to them self-evidently worthwhile. You must then simply say, "I have hit bedrock. My spade is turned [i.e., turned back on itself, can dig no more]. This is what I do."

People say, "I'm doing this because I'm in pain." But the more I heard that, the less sense it made: the causal connection isn't at all obvious. Nobody can say why *this* experience, rather than, say, a spa trip, or marathon training, ought to provide solace. I think Wittgenstein points in the direction of an answer. There's something satisfying about having to throw our hands up, acknowledge our final inscrutability to ourselves. It's a relief that there's only so far we can take an explanation, and a comfort to be thrown back upon the nontrivial fact that we have preferences—that custom and idiosyncrasy and accident have given us the desire to do something instead of some other thing, or instead of nothing. It short-circuits the usual chain of accounting and gets right to the part where you have to shrug and say, "This is what I do."

The girls walk by on the way to bed, bow at the men, and turn to me and smile and say, "Good night."

THE OTHERS TUCK INTO their tiered arrays of breakfast—they stir stringy pockets of *nattō*, gross fermented soybeans, into their rice, and eat filets of fatty salmon—and I sit and eat overbuttered toast and wait for us all to leave. One of the girls comes over and bows and I bow and she bows again. One of the problems with Japan is that it's hard to know when to stop bowing.

"I have bought this rice ball yesterday," she says with a slight British accent, "and I had so much food for dinner and for breakfast"—she waves her hand at her little garrison of plates—"that I am very full. I am embarrassed that this rice ball is already expired." She turns it over to show me that the eat-by hour was three hours ago. "I don't know if it's still good to eat but it should be eaten right away, before more time is lost, and I am ashamed to give you expired *osettai* but you only eat toast for breakfast, and, if it is not insulting to offer you, you would perhaps like it?"

"Of course I would. Thank you." We bow more times than seems strictly necessary.

"I'm Yumi, from Kobe."

"I'm Gideon, from, uh, nowhere at the moment." I feel extremely dorky in this purple fleece headband Max insisted I take with me. It's got kind of a Braquian pattern and it's hideous but I haven't really taken it off since he left.

She laughs. "I would like to hear that story."

The *ryokan* proprietress comes in and says there are two shifts in the car back to the trailhead—this place is a few kilometers out of the way, and even the strictest Japanese walkers don't worry about getting rides off the circuit—and that Mick and I are first.

"Maybe," Yumi says, "you should let us catch up to you."

Mick and I start up the narrow trail. "I'm a slow walker, and you should go up ahead if you want," Mick says. "I have a heart condition, arrhythmia, so I must be careful."

"Oh, I don't mind," I reply. "I'm happy to have company for a while, and your English is excellent, so if it's okay with you we can walk together for a little while."

He smiles. "And maybe you have other reason to walk slow?" We both laugh. He takes out his map, the standard yellow Japanese book all the walkers have. "My favorite part of this is logistics. I have a sense of, how do you say, *orientation*. I like to look at the maps and plan each day."

"Me too!" I say.

Mick looks quite a bit younger than sixty but has bags under his eyes. He talks about his family: two grown kids who still live nearby and come over for dinner a few times a week. He loves to see them but can't understand why they've got no prodigal urges. It might be because they spent so much time living abroad in strange postings, in Holland and Orange County, when the kids were younger; he thinks that as a family they all turned inward, became too reliant on each other.

"They are unusual, this Yumi and Nori from our *ryokan*. My daughter, she would never do this in one million years! She has no urge to travel, no need to go away."

I tell him that my family is the opposite, that both my brother and I went across the country to college, as far as we could legitimately go, and that then I moved to Berlin and he moved to Shanghai.

"How often do you see your mother?"

"More often than a lot of my friends who live in the same country as their parents, actually. She uses all her vacations to come visit us, and the three of us met up twice in Berlin while I was living there, and then once in Shanghai and once in Spain. We went to Gibraltar."

"Gibraltar?"

"It's this big, terrible rock that the British own. It's not important."

He asks if we see our father, too, and I say more rarely. We're wary of traveling with him because historically he's been such a flight risk. I can, in fact, barely remember the last time we successfully completed a full itinerary without his stalking off in anger. On our last attempt at a vacation with him, five or six years before, we woke up at six a.m. to find him stuffing his shirts into his bag. We'd done nothing but humiliate him, he said. (We'd made fun of him for losing a hundred dollars in poker.) We paid no attention to him, kept secrets, he continued. (We'd both strolled away from him when on the phone with our respective girlfriends.) He was having no more of it. It got briefly physical—Micah had to pull him off me—and he stormed out. Neither of us talked to him for months. It turned out, from what we could gather later, that he'd actually just had work obligations at home that he'd been afraid to tell us about.

Our steady, slow pace seems to shore up the candor of the conversation. Mick wants to know all about the Camino. He's very well traveled, but he says he's tired of traveling as a tourist.

"Have you ever been to Shikoku before?" I ask.

He grins. "Never! I've been in fifty countries and never Shikoku.

Nobody comes to Shikoku except for pilgrimage. Oh, also maybe for Dōgō Onsen. Here I will tell you a famous story about *o-henro.* There is a big Japanese electrical company, and in 1960s one truck of theirs hit and killed a young boy. CEO was very upset. He decided to walk *o-henro* to make penance for young boy. Now, today, same company makes three managers walk *o-henro* every single year."

The woman from the *ryokan* careens past in her van. Nori and Yumi wave from the back. Mick explains that they quit the previous day up at the next pass, four or five kilometers on, and are going to be starting ahead of us. We've been dawdling for nothing! Oh, well. We get to the pass ninety minutes later and there's one of the long narrative-looking signs I've been wondering about for only, oh, five or six hundred kilometers.

"What does it say?"

"It tells story of Kōbō Daishi, like all these signs. When O-Daishi-san came to this rock he had been climbing into the mountains, like us, for so long that he began to—" Mick pounds his feet in place, says he can't remember the English. I look it up on my phone. "To stamp one's feet in frustration."

"Yes," Mick says. "Here the Daishi was very frustrated with many mountains, like we are."

Before we can even register the 840-meter pass, we're over the hill and descending to T44, Daihōji. I stop to drop my bag at the *ryokan*—T45 is another "tag" temple, there and back—and head uphill toward T44 a few minutes later. It's on a series of flights graduated into the hillside. I do a brief tour around the main hall and, to my delight, run into Yumi and Nori, who have just finished their extended temple routine—the only reason we were able to catch up with them—and are about to head off to T45. Mick wanders over from the stamp office to say hello. We all stand around and finally the girls ask if I want to come walk with them. I look over at Mick, who waves me off.

A little less than a year later my mom and I will be visiting Micah in Tokyo and I'll meet Mick and his wife for lunch. He'll tell me that in a week he's leaving for Shikoku for his second circuit, with the four or five friends he made on his first. He'll invite me to drop everything and come along, and it'll take me a few minutes to turn him down.

"It's funny," he'll say. "I thought *o-henro* was maybe supposed to help you figure out what to do next, but sometimes *o-henro* itself again *is* what you do next!"

W HY DO YOU HAVE that book?" I point to Nori's copy of the 2008 Moreton, which is held together with duct tape.

"I work in a youth hostel in Osaka. Last year a young American from Texas, Matthew, he is an English teacher in Korea, came in to stay on the night before he made *o-henro*. I told him I was doing it, too, but not all at once—in pieces, just a few days at a time, with Yumi." She invited him to come back when he was finished; she never thought she'd see him again, but exactly forty-five days later he arrived, gave her the beat-up Moreton, and became her boyfriend.

"Why did he decide to come do this?"

"He made similar trip in Spain, maybe you hear of it." I laugh and Nori asks why. I explain at excessive length, tell them all about Tom and how I ended up by myself here.

"What do the old people, the bus people, think of you?" Yumi asks.

"It's hard for me to say. I get the feeling they think I'm out of my mind." But I also think that they're happy that I'm out of my mind enough to do this.

"We get the same thing," Yumi says. "The old people always stop us and give us *osettai* and tell us how wonderful it is that we're doing this at such a young age. They say it's virtuous to do it now, at age thirty, and not when you're old and feel like you really need to do repenting."

I ask Yumi how her English got so good and she says she lived in Nebraska for a year. I raise my eyebrows.

"Hey, you're the one who came to Japan and go straight to Shikoku."

"But isn't all of Japan like this? Rusty tin shacks and tiny rice paddies and pastoral decline?" She punches me on the arm and her sedge hat falls down and covers her face. She walks into a branch. Nori falls off the trail laughing.

"These hats are too big for us," Yumi says.

"I noticed." She has a rough-and-tumble delicacy to her, says she's recently gotten asthma and has to stop sometimes, or walk slowly, and when she does I hang back with her on the shady, half-steep trails.

"Did you meet any other foreign *o-henro-san* to walk with?"

"Yeah, there was this guy JR, a middle-aged American who was kind of hopeless but I came to like him anyway, and he said some things I've been thinking about a lot. He's probably about twenty kilometers behind us. He kept telling me that his toxicity was leaking out through his feet, which smelled terrible."

There's a sign with four characters I've seen with some frequency since I entered Ehime. Yumi says something to Nori in Japanese. "Today is the first time I've been with people who can translate the signs for me."

"This one says, 'Stay away from the poisonous snakes!'"

"First of all, I wish I hadn't known that."

"And second of all," Yumi looks at me, "you think it is obvious advice?"

"Yes, precisely. Also, it's funny. When I was on the Camino, I lied to Tom, who's very afraid of snakes, and said that all the snakes die when they try to cross the Pyrenees, so there are no snakes in Spain. Then we saw one on the path in Galicia and he freaked out."

"You talk about your friend Tom very, very much! You must really miss your friend Tom."

"I do. But I promise you he's extremely happy not to be here with me." He emails me to remind me of that almost every day.

"You must also"—Yumi stops to reseat her sedge hat—"be very happy you met some people who speak English and are not sixty years old and who do not have foot toxin."

"You have no idea."

"What are the differences, do you think," Nori waits for us to ask, "between people who do Camino and people who make Shikoku *o-henro?*"

'Well, it's pretty similar, in some ways." Both sets of people are in moments of crisis of some kind, feeling indecisive and anxious and confused or sad. But in Japan, at least until very recently, the only time you have the freedom to feel that way is between university and a job, or right when you retire. In Spain, it also tends to be for people who just ended long relationships, or who are about to end a long relationship, or who think of it as a transition from youth to adulthood. "It's a more mixed crowd there."

"What about you?"

"I'm afraid if I stopped moving I'd panic."

"One difference," Nori says, "is that in Japan you are not supposed to take too much vacation, or vacation should be about learning, go to museums. In the West you are stressed so you go on a cruise, but here we do not do that. We say it is self-indulgent. But here it is okay to go away if you do something like *o-henro.*"

It's okay to do something self-indulgent if it also hurts. It's okay to go on an adventure when it breaks your feet, or when it's been around for a thousand years. It's okay to go to California for college when you go to Stanford. It's okay to go to Berlin when you have a Fulbright, and okay to stay there because the *New York Times* and *Frieze* agree it's the capital of the now. It's okay to go to Saigon or Tallinn because you have to finish a book. It's okay to move to Shanghai when you work for Apple. It's okay to take off for Shanghai when your brother's there. It's okay to leave your job at Apple and move to Tokyo, as Micah emails me he's about to do, because your girlfriend got a fellowship to study Japanese. It's okay to disappear to Key West or on themed Atlantis cruises to Baja because you've only recently come out and after all it's just biology. It's okay to betray people you love if you're writing a book to set the record straight. It's okay to do most things for the sake of a job, and it's okay to do anything for the sake of a mutual protection racket. All this giving of reasons is exhausting, and the vast majority of them are ex post facto anyway. It would be so much easier and more honest if we could all just let each other get away with saying that we felt like it.

The sun disappears and it sleets, then hails, for seven or eight minutes, and that makes it okay to duck under Yumi's hat, and we all regard the new weather with the kind of idle curiosity people who are very excited to be together can afford, and then it's sunny again. Yumi and Nori both bonk their heads, sedge hats askance, against trees downed across the path.

T45 IS WEDGED into a cleft in a towering pocked-limestone cliff. We descend into it from above, from the harder path, down through a mossy canyon crowded with cedar pillars and dotted here and there with vermilion-bibbed Jizō statues. The cypresses and the cedars rise past the tops of the cliffs. "This is like Mononokeland," Yumi says, which is the sort of thing you expect an adorable Japanese fictional character to say. For the first time in twenty-six days, it occurs to me, I am sure I will be nostalgic for this moment later. Damn Tom and his email predictions.

Yumi invites me to come along with them while they pray. We light the candles and the incense and say the sutras together. A stately wooden ladder that has something to do with the founding myth of this temple leads up to a natural balcony set into a cliff hollow. Nori monkeys up, then takes a dozen pictures from above while Yumi clings to the ladder in terror. From the balcony we can see the snowy summits of Shikoku's forbidding interior.

There are little souvenir and food stalls on the way down to the parking lot, and I buy them molasses-ginger candy as *osettai*. We find a place to get udon for lunch. We linger awhile but decide we ought to get going before it gets cold in the mountains. Yumi and Nori are heading on to a *ryokan* they've reserved another six kilometers toward T46, but we've got eight kilometers back toward T44 first, which somehow today, despite eleven hours of walking, I don't at all mind. I wonder if their *ryokan* has availability but decide I don't want to intrude too much on their time.

We're skating along the trail back toward T44 when around a curve we bump into JR, who looks rested and well and jealous of my company.

"I hope you didn't sleep outside the last two nights, JR. Two mornings ago, when I passed that bridge Kōbō Daishi had to sleep under, there was frost on the windshields, and then again this morning I could see my breath."

"Yeah, I slept in huts, and, uh, yeah, it's been pretty cold."

"Oh, JR." He doesn't have anything to eat, so I give him my last rice ball and tell him I'll wait for him in Matsuyama and we can go to the Dōgō Onsen together. It's the oldest continuously operating *onsen* in Japan, and pretty much the only non-pilgrimage-related reason anybody ever goes to Shikoku. I've been looking forward to it.

The path connecting T44 and T45 is a loop; we took the more difficult mountain trail on our way out and are taking the road to save time on our way back. Nori and Yumi have to call a cab to reach their lodgings by the time dinner is served; the innkeepers are finicky about these things. Yumi turns to me. "When you're finished, will you come to Osaka and stay in Nori's hostel and we can all celebrate, like we did when Matthew came back?"

"Sure, of course. I'd love that."

She hands me her tiny pedometer—she doesn't know how to use it anyway—and says I can give it back to her in a few weeks. I try to use it on my own slow walk back, but it's set for paces half the length of mine.

THE SNOW IN THE MORNING is a lovely break from the rain, and I put on my purple headband and leave at dawn. The path runs up along a busy road and over a high pass, then leaves the road and descends in switchbacks down a long ravine, with waterfalls and panoramic views of Matsuyama and the Inland Sea beyond.

As I bow at the main gate of T46, Yumi calls out my name. "We had so much beer last night we got a late start," she says.

I tell her I'm glad for her hangover.

They like to take their time and look around the temples. At T47, Yasakaji, we lower ourselves into a cellar with thousands of little bronze figurines, the significance of which they don't know. I tell them to make something up. Outside there are two little hallways, one marked "Heaven" and frescoed with cloud-scenes of unearthly delights, the other marked "Hell," with a spiky stone floor and paintings of a bloody hereafter overlorded by bearded and bellicose Mongolians.

"This temple," I say, "has a statue carved by Kōbō Daishi himself, but it's only revealed to the public every fifty years."

"Wow," Nori says. "I can't believe you knew that."

"It's in the Moreton."

"I thought you hated this Moreton-san." Yumi tugs at my sleeve and brings me over to a side hall where there's a special statue she likes to visit at each temple. His name is Binzuru-san and he's a rubicund old wooden man in the lotus position with a monkey face and a knitted cap.

"He's like both a baby and an old man. If you put one yen in his palm, you can rub his body where you need healing on your own body." She rubs his worn foot, then his temples, and I ask if her head hurts. "Not hurts, exactly. Could use fixing!"

We walk down the steps and find Nori waiting for us barefoot on top of a polished granite boulder. The rock has been planed off and has had Buddha's stylized footprints etched into it. Nori explains that if you take your shoes off and stand in the footprint, your foot ailments will be healed. Behind it is a smaller upright stone with an etched handprint. Yumi reads the inscription on the post and turns to me excitedly. If you touch the handprint, it's supposed to be good for your hands and also for your writing. She pushes me forward and says it will help me tell the world that everybody should pick up and go on pilgrimage. I don't have the heart to tell her that I'm less sure of that than I once was, that the self-discovery of austere travel can be as selfish as it can be selfless, and that every quest is also an evasion.

I realize this whole time I've been rubbing the stone.

Yumi smiles. "Don't rub it for too long or I'll expect too much of you."

T48, Sairinji, is our last temple together. Yumi and I go to rub Binzuru-san's head again, and then each of them gives me an *osame-fuda* with their names in Japanese. We embrace and say we'll see each other again in Osaka, when I'm done, and they tell me to be careful at T66, Unpenji, the highest one. They want a report on how bad it's going to be.

I don't watch them walk away, just drag myself through T49, T50, and T51, the last one famous for its grilled *mochi* and for being the home temple of Emon Saburō, the old miser who walked him-self to death on that first pilgrimage to beg Kōbō Daishi's forgiveness. I sit outside of T51 and realize I want a cigarette. I bum one off a lethargic bus-tour driver and sit on a bench on the hillside and look out at sunset over Matsuyama Castle. I watch the last buses of the day pull out and regret the cigarette I just had. I wish I had another.

THE AREA AROUND the Dōgō Onsen has the superfluously re-cuperative feel of a nineteenth-century spa, with damp fami-lies strolling the faux-gaslit arcades in their light cotton robes and cloppy sandals. It's the breezy thick of *sakura* season here, and the old castle town is full of tourists; they observe the pink and white nebu-lae with bittersweet tranquil science. It's dislocating, as it was in Spain, to wander a provincial capital on a day off. The errands of tourists seem so manic and so scattered. But something about the fragility of the *sakura* and the longing I feel in the wake of Yumi and Nori's departure softens me to my erstwhile enemies. Tourism, *pace* my collected rants, isn't just about who's more impressive for having been more elaborately distracted by what. It's also an occasion to share a day felt and perceived and remembered more intensely than the usual routine. A tourist's day is framed by the expectation that its memory will linger. And I, in turn, may never discover or invent the fondness for Shikoku that I have for the Camino, but I can still, even now, recall the outlines of each temple, each convenience store, each business hotel. I'm less and less sure that there really is a distinction between a tourist and a pilgrim. Both are in search of a spell of unusually memorable days. The pilgrim hopes that the experience will change her in some way, but the experience changes you only insofar as all memories change you. The tourist, like the pilgrim, hopes that these moments will linger.

Back at the hostel I write some mellow emails and call my parents to tell them I'm missing them for the seder, though it's been years since I've gone to one at my dad's house. My dad and Brett are drunk and pleased I've called, seem pleasantly surprised to have heard from me. For some reason missing the seder makes me feel actually lonely, not bored-lonely or rejected-lonely but just sad to be by myself. And Passover, for some reason, maybe because of my attachment to the family seder, maybe because of those dead Egyptians, has always made me feel more remorseful than Yom Kippur does. I pace the hostel's common room for a while, finally sit back down at the computer. I write to the woman in Shanghai and say I'm thinking of her on Passover, that I hope she has a nice seder, and that she was entirely right to get so angry, that I've been selfish and domineering and inconsiderate and thoughtless, and I am so sorry. I say I'll understand if she doesn't want to write again.

As I get up from the terminal, the door swings open with a little bumble and wafts my way the perfume of toxicity. "JR," I say without looking around, "I'm here, in the lounge."

He's ragged as usual but smiling. He starts to tell some goose of a story about some guys who picked him up by T47 and took him to lunch, but I tell him to go shower and then we'll debrief. He walks away, still chatting. "Was it sad to say good-bye to those girls? Did you see the *snow*?"

We go and have a nice final dinner—it only takes him eleven restaurants to settle on the first one we passed—and back at the hostel we gave each other a big hug.

"Maybe I'll catch up to you," he says.

"I'll leave you notes. Check all the pilgrim-hut guestbooks," I say.

The next day he sends me a touching email and signs off "Namaste," and that's it for old JR. I'll next hear from him when I check my email on my phone at four in the morning on a Tokyo rooftop at the after-party for some gallery opening. My friend Peter is doing his animatronic-bear dance with a Japanese fashion photographer.

"I've just arrived from T1 to Kyoto," he'll write. "I love the temples here. But I'm having a hard time adjusting to everyday life."

"I couldn't do the temples," I'll write back. I spent my two days in Kyoto waist-deep in sake at a flophouse run by a noise band. "I was pretty templed out, but I dug the gardens. And yeah, as far as everyday life goes, I know exactly what you mean. But, trust me, you'll adjust a lot faster than you'll want to."

D AVID SHIELDS, misrepresenting the work of Paul Elie, writes, "Contemporary culture makes pilgrimage impossible. Experience is always secondhand, planned and described for one's consumption by others in advance. Even the rare, authentically direct experience is spoiled by self-consciousness. We're doomed to an imitation of life."

Of course, life is never an imitation of life; life is simply life. And no experience is any more or less direct than any other one. But the point of view Shields offers is worth considering, more for its assumptions than its shoddy lament. Being self-conscious about an experience means, to Shields, standing at a remove from it. This remove

is created by the fact that we all know, at any given time, that there
is an associated cost, that *we could be doing something else.* Being self-
conscious means recognizing that whatever we are doing is something we have, for the most part, chosen to do—in the light of desires
that so frequently feel alien, desires that seem like obligations—with
some limited knowledge of what's at stake; and though we worry that
perhaps there are costs we have ignored or underestimated, we understand that there is no way to know how we will feel about this
decision down the line. Anything we have chosen to do invites the
specters of all that we haven't chosen—this is the real misery of
choice—and it's futile to think we might now know exactly how to
make the forty-six-year-old versions of ourselves happy with the
costs we've incurred. (Who knows what we will want then?)

What would presumably, then, be something other than an imitation of life would be an experience the cost of which we do not
simultaneously calculate, an experience the consequences of which
we do not simultaneously fear; it would mean the sort of *presentness*
generated by utter certainty. Or, perhaps, by not needing for any
certainty at all. This is what David Foster Wallace was talking about
when he wrote that the smell of cow manure was "blameless," and
what he meant when he praised the glorious unself-consciousness of
tennis players. It is the sort of certainty that would allow us to say,
unapologetically, that we did something because we felt like it, or
because we had to. It would mean feeling as though an act were un-
equivocally justified. Berlin was an experiment in trying to indulge
the freedom of a life where every act was self-justifying. But the only
wholly self-justifying acts are acts of survival and acts of pleasure,
and a life rigged up in those pursuits only deepens the doubt that
attends to all other acts.

The sort of life that is not self-conscious, that is not plagued by
anxiety, and that feels justified and certain on a more sustainable,

fuller basis than survivalism or hedonism—the sort of life that, to Shields, would make pilgrimage possible, the sort of life that would feel *authentic* to that hostel German—is basically a description of the religious life, or, for some people, family life. Actions are justified because you are commanded to do them, and commanded by somebody or other who's got a *plan*. Secular pilgrimage is a little vacation into that sort of plan, but the thing about that vacation is that it has very little to say about what happens next. What it can do is show you that the line between obligation and desire is rarely clear, that what we often label obligations are really desires, and that each step forward is some blurry function of choice and necessity. It can suggest that there might, in the end, not be so great a difference between saying "I felt like it" and saying "I had to."

Nori sends me an email from Osaka. By the end of it I'm surprised her computer hasn't run out of enthusiastic punctuation.

"It is Nori!!! One of two young Japanese women you walked with for two days on *o-henro*!!!! I am back at work in Osaka and I hope your walk still goes well! My boyfriend Matthew comes to visit on Friday and we eat *okonomiyaki* and maybe karaoke afterwards! Do not rush through remaining *o-henro* but Matthew wants to meet and talk about Camino de Santiago and maybe you will be finish by then."

Naturally I do rush, not only because of the party but because of the rain. T53, T54: fetid quarters of a salty town. A random white dude bikes by and stops to acknowledge, briefly, that we are two white dudes in this place.

I study the Moreton while I walk, check and recheck the distances, compute my averages, figure out if I can make it in time or not.

T57, Eifukuji, up a small hill; T58, Senyūji, up a small mountain

that's not, like, on the way to anywhere at all. There's nobody anywhere, not even normal civilian people. There's absolutely no reason
anybody would be outside in this weather, in this province, on this
island.

So there are twenty-five kilometers remaining to T60, Yo-
komineji, which is a *henro-korogashi* and, at seven hundred meters, just
a notorious bitch. It is also, they brag, the last temple to have gotten
an access road, in 1984. That'll take me half a day. Ts 61–64 are in a
row at the base of the mountain and I can mow them all down in the
afternoon. But there's a problem.

I've been keeping up forty or forty-five kilometers a day without
difficulty, but because T66 is up somewhere in the clouds, you've got
to stay overnight right before it if you're going to take it out in a day,
and there's no *ryokan* or hotel at an appropriate distance. There's not
even a hut. So to keep myself on pace to make the party, I either have
to do my forty-click day and then sleep behind a Dumpster or I have
to do two consecutive piddling thirty-click days and miss the party.
I haven't done something so lame as a thirty-click day in two weeks.
I wrestle with this in the rain, find nothing to eat all day but peanuts.

At the *onsen* a little short of T60 I remove my sock and a second
toenail comes with it but the prospect of the party has put me in a
fine mood. I prop up my lost toenail and stage a little photo shoot and
send pictures to Micah and Tom. There's a variety show on TV
where cats climb into cooking pots and I'm immensely entertained.

In the morning the rain's slackened. In fact the rain is so fine that
you wouldn't even know it was raining unless you were already
aware that it's never not raining. Luckily the path to T60 is so pre-
cipitous that it takes me almost immediately above the rain, and I
take my poncho off for the first time in as long as I can remember.
The woods are just destroyed—downed trees, torn and twisted
cedar trunks, thrashed tendrils of upended roots.

Reasons to take a little bit of train: 1. Will allow me more time at the famous Ritsurin Garden in Takamatsu, the fourth-most-famous garden in Japan. 2. It's not like I'm skipping any temples or even any mountains, just a few hours of walking an access road underneath an elevated expressway. 3. I'm going to take the long way round from T88 to T1, the one via T10, so I can revisit in reverse the walk Max and I did, which means in the end the total distance will be about the same.

These are all just excuses.

The descent from T60 is long and gently sloping and really fun in the mist. T61, Kōonji, looks like a sixties Brutalist suburban synagogue and I flee in horror. T62, Hōjuji, and T63, Kichijōji, are little roadside jobs.

I love all the stuff in the second half of *The Armies of the Night* where Mailer talks about how he's worried that if he gets arrested in the October 1967 antiwar march on the Pentagon, he's going to miss this party in New York that he's been looking forward to. Ultimately he reasons that there's no way to climb a moral ladder to its end—for there are no limits to the heights of sacrifice and courage—but the point is to climb past where you thought you could, to climb far enough to nauseate yourself and thus feel, to some extent, made new for at least a little while. He does what he has to to make it back to the party. Or at least that's what I took away from that book: it's important to go to the party.

There's also, it occurs to me, that Zen saying that if you meet the Buddha in the road you should kill him, which I take to mean that if you want to take the train for fifteen kilometers you should just do it.

At T64 I study the Moreton some more, wishing it would give me an answer, wishing it were an accurate, useful guidebook. A retiree, also on foot, comes over and asks if it's the English guidebook. I say yes and try to offload onto him two of the six *osettai* tangerines I got earlier. He's having none of it. I gather that by this point in the circuit the one form of *osettai* you're karmically allowed to refuse is citrus.

"Did you see all the downed trees up by T60?" I ask him.

"Yes. There was big storm here, much snow, on March eight to ten. Trails very messy."

"Oh, I remember." I was in Hiwasa Town then, and it was hailing. It was the same storm that made JR slip and hurt his knee, in the mountains near T12.

"Ah so," the man says. "Very good to have left early days far behind, much better now."

"How did you learn such good English?"

"Long ago, before I retired, I worked for Japanese shipping company. WTC1 building, and then in New Jersey."

I name a company.

"I feel very surprised you guess my company."

"My dad's partner works there, as a chief environmental manager."

"Partner business or partner boyfriend?"

"Boyfriend."

"Ah so," he says. When I email Brett about this later, he'll say that this was a very unusual question for a Japanese man, especially one of his age, and that it almost certainly meant the man was gay.

I get up to go. I square my pack on my shoulders and turn to the retired gay man. "I am going to take the train now. I am skipping fifteen kilometers. I have no excuses, but this is what I am going to do because it is what I *want* to do. It is what I have to do, and it is what I feel like doing."

The retired gay man shrugs. "Good luck."

. . .

T HE YOUNG WOMAN ON TV who delivers the nightly cherry-blossom forecast reaches near-unseemly levels of excitement about the bloom, and indeed when I reach T65, Sankakuji—after the usual four kilometers uphill—it feels like voltaic springtime in a new way, the cherry blossoms pink buttons of ignited ether. In front of me stands T66, Unpenji, which is so high it assumes a topographical-map hue I've not seen Moreton use before.

It's seven hours uphill and feels not unlike that first day on the Camino, but this time instead of the rhythmic buttocks of old people in front of me there's nothing at all but empty path and uncharacteristic sun and the sound of my own breathing. At the top I sit on the little seasonal ski slope and eat my first Japanese ice cream, text Yumi some nonsense. She wants to know how afraid of this climb she should be. I write back that she shouldn't be afraid of the climb but afraid of having it behind her. At the summit there's a thirty-foot statue of what I assume must be Kōbō Daishi, and inside there's a circular staircase with scenic lithographs of each temple. "Oh," I stop at each one and think, "I remember cursorily acknowledging you." But I can also remember everything else I cursorily acknowledged on that particular day.

This little memorial tour, along with the top-tier difficulty of the approach, makes for an easy sense that I'm basically done, that it's all downhill from here. I can't help but feel the first stirrings of that light potent vertigo of conquest that suffused the final few days of the Camino.

This bodes ill. If there's one thing this kind of trip really does, it's lend itself to trite but vital lessons. Your life is for the most part your own responsibility. There's little point to complaining, or at least complaining in an unentertaining way. You ought to choose your companionship rather than default into it. If you can't choose your companionship, work through it. Or, in this case: the hard part isn't the last hurdle but the final flat. I make a note to ask Micah if this is something track coaches actually say.

Kagawa Prefecture, the final one, is the *dōjō* of nirvana, and because it's right across the Inland Sea from Osaka, it's much more densely developed. The temples are practically on top of each other and I figure I can knock down half a dozen in a day. By early morning it's hot out, and I zip off the legs of my pants for the first time. The Japanese are not crazy about this, but then again, I'm also wearing a purple fleece headband and a V-neck T-shirt under my blousy soiled pilgrim's vest. I've long grown accustomed to stares and open laughter in the street.

An hour past T70, while walking under a culvert across from an electronics superstore, I figure out that today is day thirty-five, and that right now—at pretty much exactly this moment—Tom and Nora and David and Alina and I all reached Santiago de Compostela. Now, I've walked just over a thousand kilometers in the time it took me and Tom to walk eight hundred, but nobody's counting, except me. I saunter along, feeling great for another five kilometers, imagining the gloating email I'll write Tom, when I reach back into my bag for the Moreton and realize it's gone. Despite my well-known opinions about the book, this is a disaster, even with only a few days left. I could probably make it on the stickers and signposts alone, but it seems risky, and by now I've made all sorts of important, angry annotations in the book and I'd like to hang on to it.

I turn around, slog back an hour, find the book by the stamp office at T70, hate myself.

This is just a reminder to stay present in these waning days, I tell myself, but I'm mostly just exhausted and irritated until I reach T73 and T74, each up a hillside overlooking, through a glow of late-day cherry-blossom pother, the Seto-Ohashi Bridge, a very awesome eleven-bridge complex that was the first to connect Shikoku and Honshū.

The *ryokan* has wireless, which is unusual, but I'm staying right at T75, Kōbō Daishi's home temple, so they're used to a lot of tourists. There's an email from David the Hungarian, who says that over the weekend he was playing badminton at Lake Balaton and he got a blister; it made him feel connected to me, he jokes. There's also a note from David Levine, who says that he's been behind in the dispatches but has caught up to T40, and he wants to apologize for not having been aware of how difficult it's been. "I kept printing these out and filing them away as if you were sitting at a desk somewhere." I get a few other responses to the dispatches, but I delete each one that begins "It sounds like you're having a wonderful trip!" And, finally, there's my first email in a month from the girl in Shanghai. It's reserved, cautiously chatty, and she asks if I've had any good *osettai* recently. I write back and say that I'm pretty much done with all that. "The plan is to meet Peter in Tokyo with the aim of squandering in one week whatever karma I might've inadvertently accrued on Shikoku."

"You didn't inadvertently accrue karma," she writes, accusative and teasing. "You did so on purpose."

The woman at the *ryokan* tries to charge me tax—a scam nobody's pulled with me yet—and I want to throw her through a rice paper screen, but the last thing I need now is more stuff to repent for.

NOW THAT IT'S PROPER SPRING, I'm seeing more and more pilgrims walking counterclockwise, presumably having started at T88 in the last few days. They look over their shoulders for the signs. Yumi told me there's a horror flick from the late nineties about a woman who walks the pilgrimage backward to resuscitate her dead daughter accidentally opens the gates of hell; I wonder if these guys are concerned. But despite the persistent mild gates-of-hell worry, it keeps me in good spirits to watch the new pilgrims' mixture of expectation, good cheer, and early pain, and I could not be more content to not be them.

At the hovel of a *ryokan* at T80 there are noises upstairs that make me wonder who is being murdered and why, so I get out before dawn even though by now I've got more than enough time to make T1 in time to meet Yumi and Nori and Matthew. I've even got time to stop in the Ritsurin Gardens, which Max had reminisced so fondly about. It's an odd and unassimilable feeling to take a break from a twelve-hundred-kilometer walk to go for a walk. The park is full of rank amateurs, civilian walkers moving with no sense of pace, eating ice cream, feeding koi. I wonder what they think they're going to do with themselves after this pleasant little constitutional.

AT T87 THERE'S A BIG MAP indicating the two routes to T88, Ōkuboji. The old one is less steep and follows the road around the back side of the mountain. The new one summits a gigantic interim mountain before descending to the temple. One of the calligraphers sees me looking at the sign and gestures that I should do the harder one. I figure if there's time for one more superfluous mountain, why not?

At the divergence of the two paths, there's a pilgrim community center, museum, and salon. A man rushes over, takes my pack, gives me tea and crackers, and asks me to spell my name; he instructs his secretary to fill out a certificate of completion.

There's a bench by a vast papier-mâché scale model of Shikoku, with little hut-temples that light up when you push buttons on the side. In broken English, the man asks, "Why are you here?"

I give my standard response. "Well, I did this thing last summer in Spain—" and before I can continue he jumps up and pulls me into a side room. On the wall is a map of the Camino, surrounded by enlarged pictures of *compostelas* and *credenciales* and smiling *peregrinos*. The map is pretty granular, and as I look over the names of those little villages, I'm fresheted with memories: Puente la Reina, where we met young Andy; Lorca, where I lanced Tom's blisters with the chain-smoking Catalan nurses; the long, murderous day into Burgos; the *albergue* pool in Boadilla; our day of national anthems, how close to flawlessly Tom sang "The Star-Spangled Banner"; Sahagún, where Román had to drop out; all the delicious Chinese restaurants and fine boutique hotels; the day I walked toward Melide with Alina in the sparkling, silent, dewy predawn.

The man can tell I want to say something, but all of these memories have left me at a loss. I look at this map and see an eight-hundred-kilometer anthology of anecdotes as absurd as they are meaningful, and I think it would take nearly as long as the Camino itself to tell them all. Sometimes you need to tell yourself you're moving forward in order to just enjoy moving.

"The Camino," he says, "is a UNESCO site."

"I know."

"They try to make *o-henro* into UNESCO site, too, but some people don't want it. The priests."

"I heard."

"Can you tell me the difference between Camino and Shikoku *o-henro*?"

I nod. He takes out a pen and a piece of paper.

"The Camino," I say, "except for about ten kilometers between San Juan and Burgos, is not on asphalt."

He writes that down. "Anything more?"

"When I finished the Camino and got back to real life, I felt a little disappointed. I think most people do. All I had left were memories of equanimity, memories of having committed to this hard, pointless thing and completed it. Memories that contained at once a feeling of decisiveness and a feeling of liberation from the anxiety of decision. I thought that maybe if I did the Shikoku *o-henro* by myself—because it's harder and longer—I'd take something with me that was more than just a memory. But now I think that maybe the memories are enough. Maybe when I next stand in line for cupcakes, if I ever stand in line for cupcakes, I'll remember that there are all sorts of other lives, and that this is something—given the welter of options and authorities around—I'm choosing to do right now, for a variety of reasons both plain and obscure."

"What is *cupcakes*?"

"It's not important. I'm weirdly glad I did this."

"You take hard path over mountain to Ōkuboji, not easy one on road, yes?"

"Yeah, of course."

I leave feeling tentative and a little melancholy, but the route is unprecedentedly steep—as though they needed this final ascent to be semiotically commensurate—and I don't have the energy to think much. The final hundred meters is literally rock climbing, hand over hand over a series of limestone boulders and fragments. The wind blows cold over the exposed rock and I look behind me, toward the whitish blot of the Inland Sea, and in front of me, at the sharp, loose rock, and it feels all of a sudden as the trail narrows that I'm in one of those old cartoons where someone climbs a peak to consult a yogi and the yogi inevitably gives some piece of totally pedestrian advice. I laugh and almost hurtle off the mountain.

At the summit I can see out under the gray storm clouds far into the gray over Takamatsu, the heavy gray over the Goshikidai and Yashima plateaux, the gray extending west toward T66 and out over the sea. It feels perfectly appropriate, somehow, that there's no view but gray, like our climb over the Pyrenees. I turn around and the sign says "T88: Ōkuboji, 1km."

W HEN YOU ARRIVE AT T88 over the superfluous mountain route instead of the pleasant winding-road route, your anxious descent ends mid-temple. You don't have a chance to spy the gate and collect yourself, as you do at the steps in Santiago. You just come around the last switchback and then you're there, right in the thick of it, with the main hall on your right and the Daishi hall on your left and some bus pilgrims milling around.

Nobody comes up and congratulates me, or even seems to notice I've just walked twelve hundred kilometers. For a moment I think I really do wish I'd waited up for JR, arrived here with company, but I know that if I'd arrived here with JR I'd right now be wishing I'd arrived here alone.

T HE SINGLE BEFITTING MONUMENT is a little glass house that's packed with the walking sticks pilgrims leave behind when they finish. In front of the stamp office there's a bin where they collect them for this public interment. I drop the Nordic walking poles at a rakish angle and look back only once as I walk away. I walk down to the clutch of souvenir stands. It's only three in the afternoon and I'm not sure what to do, and then there's a clumsy-looking blond kid coming up to me. "Erik," I say, "from Alaska."

"Gideon, from New Jersey," he says.

He's got a curly adolescent neck beard and a rugby-ball head and is in full pilgrim whites. He's not carrying a bag.

"I heard about you from Moreton on the first day," I tell him, "and I've seen your notes in the guestbooks for weeks." I was two days behind him at the roadside *michi-no-eki* by T24, then three days back at the hut about twelve kilometers past T37. Then I caught up a bit and was only one day back near T45, the last I'd seen of him.

He'd just heard about me at the pilgrim salon; he'd missed me by twenty minutes, and I feel immediate relief I didn't have company for the last part. "I took a few days off in Takamatsu," Erik says, "visiting a friend there, and checking out the last temples in Kagawa Prefecture by bus and train. Now I'm driving to T1 so I can shoot some more footage of my trip for my YouTube channel."

"But you were walking it before, right? This train-and-bus business was just the last few days?"

"Yeah, I walked it through all the hardest parts, but by the time I got to the Dōgō Onsen in Matsuyama I was pretty much done, man. From there it was going to be easy and I didn't think I'd get any more out of walking."

"Right, but that's precisely when it gets hardest! Right when you feel like it's no longer hard, because the hard parts kept it from being truly hard, you know? That's what so much of this was about for me, at least in the end: continuing to walk when both the discomfort *and* the novelty have passed. Like, I don't know, a long-term relationship."

He shrugs. "I just didn't feel like walking anymore."

"Oh, okay, sure, cool."

"Are you going to go to Mount Kōya?" he asks. Mount Kōya is a semiautonomous religious community founded by Kōbō Daishi on a mountaintop two hours southeast of Osaka. It contains, along with about a hundred temples, O-Daishi-san's mausoleum, where he's supposedly not dead but rather in eternal meditation. Pilgrims are supposed to visit him to report on a successful journey. I'd not planned to do it until Yumi and Mick both said it was important.

"I hadn't thought much about it. I guess, maybe. Depends on what else is going on in Osaka. It doesn't feel crucial to me."

But I'll end up going, a few days later, and I'll see Erik there. I'll be dressed in the all-black ensemble I assembled, without much thought save for versatility, in a few hours of shopping in Osaka, and I'll be with a distempered chain-smoking German who was reading Thomas Bernhard's *Extinction* across from me on the train. Erik, however, will still be in his pilgrim whites, now bleached and ironed. We'll stand around and watch the tourists gawk at the mossy pagodas, the incense clouds dissipating into the cool air between the great cedars, the bus *henro* making the après-pilgrim scene. "I wish I still had my stick and sedge hat," Erik will say, "even though that hat never fit me anyway. I wish I had those things to set me apart as a true foot pilgrim from all these masses of regular tourists."

On that day at Mount Ko-ya, four days and a lifetime away, I will wonder what the alternatives might be to Erik, on the one hand, and Yumi, on the other. Erik fought vainly to preserve this sweetly transient experience. But Yumi's spritely credulity, winsome self-deprecation, and chipped-glaze composure on Shikoku had given way, the previous evening at the dinner party I'd so been looking forward to, to a distant hardheadedness, frustrated talk about how tough it was to be thirty-three and single. Matthew, Nori's boyfriend, said the only sensible thing. "The Camino was fun and Shikoku was simply not. It was many, many things, but 'fun' is one of the last words I would use." I will toast him. "But somehow," he finished, "on the very last hour of my circuit, for the first time, I was able to imagine myself doing it again."

Which, on my thirty-ninth day—the same photo-finish victory over Moses on the mountain or Jesus in the wilderness that Tom and I managed into Finisterre; a length that, if days stood for years, might've saved those Egyptians from drowning—is exactly how I, too, for the first time, feel. I remember that guy on the bike in the hut who gave me four *osettai* cigarettes and I walk through the first hints of the cherry blossoms' snowy descent and I think, I now understand that crazy person. Perhaps I ought to just keep going. I could make it back to that hut in two or three days, though going back up over T12 would be less than pleasant.

On page seventy-three of the Moreton, the arrow of inaccurate-map continuity directs you to return to page three, and then page two, and finally page one. Once I'm on page three, I am no longer blazing new ground but instead tracing a path I walked with Max thirty-eight days before. I know I won't see anything new, but there's a buoyancy to this resignation. I think of how my memories of my first circuit would suffuse my second, and my second my third, calling to mind Wallace Stevens: "the merely going round, / Until merely going round is a final good."

Oh! There's the roadside vendor where Max and I almost bought those wonderful-looking strawberries, and there's the gas station where we found a wireless signal strong enough to Skype with Lois. How little acquaintance with a place, in the context of a long and trying time away, can make it seem like a homecoming! How minor the recognitions required. I look out to my right over the Yoshino River Valley toward the once-looming far ridge. I turn away with a memory of alarm, then force myself to brave the old vertigo to look at it once more. I scanned it in those early days in the hopes I might identify which peak held T12, tried to guess how much effort that first ascent would require. At that naïve moment I was so consumed with the proximate difficulty of that single mountain temple that I couldn't conceive of the endless string of far greater difficulties beyond. Here's a road sign. Local Route 12! How I have hated walking on your dangerous gravel shoulders since Matsuyama! I dally a little now, in less of a rush than I've felt the whole time, and pass this familiar stretch, new and made new with all varieties of subsequent acquaintance.

What there is to look forward to along a circumference already traveled is both novelty *and* memory, not a one-off rite but the beginning of a ritual, an act of tradition that grounds you in the continuity of your life. Each future circuit is as rich with anticipation of the new as it is sure with the comfort of the old, and it is a constant reminder that it does not take long for the difficult and new to become comfortable and old. It's a reminder that your future self will look back and find a way to make his life come together. I send Max a picture of the signs to T6 and T7—a picture identical to one I took in the cold and the dark a month earlier—and understand the appeal of perpetuity. For the perpetual pilgrim, the circle is both home and away, the center and the periphery, the familiar and the exotic, the past and the future, all of it at once.

It's a gorgeous morning and the new pilgrims, with the assurance and fear of their first day, stride forward with courage. They appear to me emissaries from the past, with all the excited worry of departure, and I an emissary of the future, with the sorry relief of arrival. But we are bonded nonetheless in this circular confraternity, each a version of the other, and we smile as we pass. I have the privilege and the luxury of knowing that what that far ridge conceals and protects are simply other mountains—and seawalls, and long stretches of nothing, and then more mountains, and dozens of *onsen* and crazy loquat conspiracy theorists and loping New Agey Americans and mile-long tunnels and heroic hand-over-hand ascents, and then, finally, this same ridge, with the same threats and the same exultations now forever both ahead and behind. I am happy not to be these new innocent pilgrims, and I envy their starting out, their fresh unmooring. I raise up my eyes once more toward that mountain and think how good it is to have it far behind me, and how good it also is that it could still be ahead.

Interlude

SHANGHAI/
SAN FRANCISCO

THE PLAN HAD BEEN TO take the boat back to Shanghai, spend a month at Micah's arranging to take the train to Lhasa and then circumambulate Mount Kailash, but the idea of that mountainous circuit no longer had the lustrous promise of pilgrimage. It just sounded like a long, exhausting, dirty walk, and I was drained. I thought about sticking around in Shanghai, but I knew I'd pretty well overstayed my welcome there. Micah and his girlfriend were already packing up to spend some time in the States before moving to Japan. The girl from Shanghai had left Shanghai by then, had finally decided to move on, and though I knew it was probably a terrible idea, I gave some thought to following her. "Don't be an idiot," Micah said. "If she wanted you to do that, she would tell you."

More than anything I missed my friends. I emailed with David Levine, considered going back to Berlin, but Berlin in the late spring and early summer is the last place anybody wants to stay inside and get work done, which was my aim. One night during the bonkers week I spent in Tokyo with my friend Peter, we got back from a karaoke bar at four in the morning and the last thing he said before we wedged ourselves into our business-hotel cubicles was "Just buy a ticket for San Francisco. You can stay on our couch for as long as you want."

Two weeks later Peter, who'd only just barely recovered from our Tokyo trip, picked me up at the airport, and two hours after that I'd already resumed my old routine—the same jog up to Golden Gate Park, the same yoga class, the same seasonal organic produce joint, the same cast of close characters at the same comfortable dives. All of the same baristas still worked at Tartine. The only thing missing was Micah—and our cat, which had long ago moved to Brooklyn, become vegan. Then suddenly, as if conjured by sheer nostalgia, Micah appeared. His girlfriend was going home to Oregon before they moved to Tokyo and he'd decided he might as well overlap with me for a month in San Francisco and a month in New York while he was visiting the States. We resumed our old run as if no time had passed: I still wanted to talk, and he still wanted to run with his headphones on. (We compromised. I talked while he listened to music.) Even our mom came to visit. Unfortunately, our old apartment had passed through several generations of Micah's friends and coworkers into grungy disrepair—though they hadn't bothered to get new furniture, so the place felt alarmingly like a museum documenting our domestic idyll 2005–2007.

"I think I'm going to see if Dad will go to this Rosh Hashanah thing in Ukraine," I said.

He slipped one headphone up over his ear. "What is it, again?"

"I don't really know. I read about it in the encyclopedia of pilgrimage I bought. Forty thousand Hasids go to this village called Uman to celebrate Rosh Hashanah. A famous rabbi told his followers to come visit his grave to say some psalms for the new year."

"I thought you said that after Shikoku you were all pilgrimaged out," he said.

"Yeah, I was, and I am. But it's not a long walk like the other ones." I liked that about it, and not only because I couldn't imagine spending even a week on foot with my dad. I figured it rounded the whole thing out: the Christian one, a line to Santiago in exchange for a get-out-of-purgatory card, was all about the future; the Buddhist one, a circle around Shikoku, was all about the present; and a Jewish one, a dot in the middle of the Old World, would almost certainly be neurotically about the past. The first was about finding a sense of direction. The second was about returning to where you started. The third would be about knowing where we stand. When I'd preliminarily mentioned the idea to my father in the fall he'd seemed excited about coming along.

"You think he'll stick around for the trip and not bolt as usual?"

"Well, I have this idea that the fact that we're there for the book, at least prima facie, will discipline both of us. It gives us a pretext to behave ourselves. I think he'll feel as though he has to rise to the occasion of participating in my professional life, and I think that I'll have to rise to the occasion of not saying something pointlessly insulting or judgmental because I'll be so anxious not to set him off. I have this hope that the artifice of the whole thing will allow us to have some conversations I've been wanting to have with him for a long time." It would be like a David Levine production, where the contrivances of staging made it somehow more real.

"And then you think you could, what, forgive him and move on?"

That's the funny thing. I'd come to realize that there were going to be two big obstacles to my forgiving my father. The first was that he'd already forgiven himself. The second was that I'd pretty much already forgiven him.

This hadn't really hit me until I'd felt so happy to see him again when I was back in New York. For a while I'd had this idea that I was just saying I forgave him as an expedient. This was in part because Tom had been so authoritative about it and in part because my dad had been sick, but mostly because I'd been so caught up in the spirit of the Camino—the sweeping acceptance of our murky, unknowable motivations and those of our fellow sufferers, along with the similarly sweeping forgiveness of the pain and difficulty we've all caused as we've done our best to carry on. I think I'd always imagined that in order to forgive him I'd have to have the straight story, so to speak, from him first, and only then would I be able to offer *specific* forgiveness for the *specific* things he'd done.

But once I'd been in some regular touch with him again, I realized I'd had it backward. The conversations with JR had helped make this clear to me. The forgiveness had to come first, because part of that gesture is reconciling yourself to the fact that there's never going to be any such thing as real, satisfying redress, especially when the person in front of you is no longer the person you've been so mad at and so disappointed in for so long. The truth about the past has relevance only insofar as it might help to reestablish credibility and accountability going forward. David Levine had said that you can acknowledge that someone is in a crisis without letting him off the hook—that you just have to try to sympathize with him as he hangs on it. If my father and I were going to be able to move on with any success, I wanted to feel at once more sympathetic (amid crisis) *and* better prepared to hold him accountable (despite crisis). I'd already forgiven him, but I still didn't think we could move forward until I had some better sense of where I'd stood in the past, which would help me understand where I stood now and where I might stand in the future. I needed a ground that no longer shifted underneath us. And I needed to get that grounding story down, in a way I could point to later and say, "This is how it was."

Moving forward also meant I had to accept the fact that I couldn't trust him with logistics, though he'd offered to take care of everything. That would be setting myself up for disappointment. And the logistics, for their part, ended up being not so much difficult as they were mysterious. A friend who'd grown up Orthodox put me in touch with a shady Hasidic travel agency, and two one-line emails later I was sending a check for thousands of dollars to a post office box in Brooklyn. I made my dad buy his Aeroflot tickets as I stood behind him at his computer.

Micah and I sat in front of the television at our dad's house, the first night both of us had spent there in years. Micah absentmindedly stroked Yoshi, the aging shih tzu. "I think I need you to come with us, Micah."

"But—"

"I really need you to come with us, Micah."

"Okay."

Part IV

UMAN

UMAN

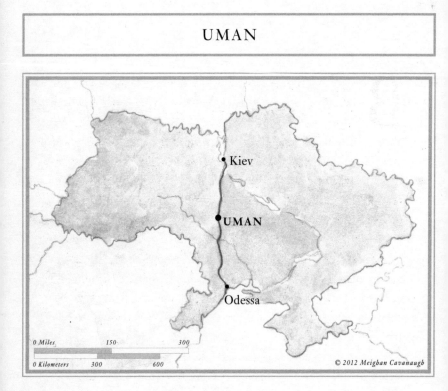

0 Miles   150   300

0 Kilometers   300   600

© 2012 Meighan Cavanaugh

BEFORE MY DAD WAS GAY, which is to say before I knew he was gay, or rather—to try to be painstaking about this from the beginning—before he told me that he knew that I'd known all along that he was gay, he never overpacked. He wasn't particularly judicious, he just rolled light. He wore monochrome T-shirts, sometimes with a breast pocket and sometimes without, over the jeans he'd often raked in. Each year we'd ask him what he wanted for Father's Day, and each year he'd shrug and say he guessed he needed new T-shirts. He did a lot of yard work in those T-shirts, spent much of his free time doing sullen yard work and requisitioning Micah and me for same, and thus wore them out quickly. We gave them to him again and again because whatever it was he might actually have desired was unclear. He accepted the functional gifts with a martyr's resignation.

I will never know what I actually knew then and what I've projected backward in my ongoing attempt to retrofit my youth with added savvy, but I think I can say now that I was not only aware of but actively confused by his sartorial inconsistency. Because on some level he clearly always cared about clothing. He wore stylish suits to synagogue, when he had congregational work, or to officiate at weddings and funerals and bar mitzvahs. He wore narrowly fitted shirts and dieted often. He had a vast harem of ties to suit his blazers, and was fussy about which belts went with which shoes. He took some risks. Around the time he dyed his curly bangs to a sallow wheat color, he bought a pair of high Doc Martens to wear with his suits, though he hedged the bet by blacking out the red stitching with polish. The Doc Martens were pretty cool, actually, and though they didn't quite fit me, I wore them as frequently as he'd let me.

It is worth noting, even if I can recall only one lapse, that this distinction between his professional and his leisure costumes was not absolute. On weekends for many summers he wore a pair of navy Ocean Pacific corduroy shorts he'd had as long as anybody could remember. We begged him to replace them but they were no longer made the way he liked. They were original and *authentic*. What made them *authentic* was that they were woven of no more fabric than a standard handkerchief. It is probably misleading even to call them shorts, as their status as shorts was entirely notional. When people ask me if I had any idea he was gay when I was a kid, I say, "I don't know, but there were hints. His favorite piece of clothing was a codpiece of wide-waled Saran Wrap."

Thus, the day after he told me he knew I knew he might prefer men to women, he went out and bought a pair of Diesel jeans. I was jealous; I didn't have Diesel jeans. This marked the end of his ability to pack light. Now even his least eventful days feature costume changes to rival Freddie Mercury's.

The matter of packing for our trip was thus freighted. There were hundreds of emails. Did we need black hats to fit in among the Hasids? If so, should we look for one of those short bowlers, or one of those broad-brimmed Borsalinos, or try to borrow a *shtreimel*, those high centrifuges of brushed fur? Or did we want to wear a *kittel*, the thin white robe that ushers in the Jewish new year with purity and humility? Even though the sheer number of emails seemed a little extreme, I was really happy that my dad had become so engaged, that he was being such a good sport about a trip that might be terrible, all for the sake of this ridiculous pilgrimage project I'd gotten myself into. It was the most interested he'd been in my life in years, and I was grateful.

Brett was cc'ed on all these emails, and the internet had him worried. The internet always has Brett worried. According to Wikipedia, Brett wrote in a range of colors and fonts, Uman sometimes ran out of water, and with tens of thousands of Hasids we might not even have enough food! He made sure my dad packed some tuna fish and beef jerky, and other high-protein provisions. My dad was afraid he might not have the right converter for his iPhone, and I responded by saying that our time in Uman would be three days of *yuntif*—two days of Rosh Hashanah and one day of Shabbat—throughout which we'd have to observe all the usual prohibitions, no carrying or buying or scrubbing or threshing or flaying, so it probably wouldn't matter all that much if his charger worked.

Brett worried about this *yuntif* business. What if we couldn't find our way around in the dark? Or what if the Ukrainians, perhaps history's most innovative *pogromistes*, used the darkness as cover to rob us of the very iPhones we were worried about charging? Brett's answer to this, he emailed, was that he ought to come along to perform these small tasks when we were not permitted to do so. He's been with my dad long enough to have picked up on some of this stuff; he knows that observant Jews can allow gentiles to help them on the Sabbath. He would be happy, he continued, to be our "Shabbos goy." I saw this and groaned with anticipation of the next email.

"NOOOOOOO," my dad responded four minutes later, "you'll have to be our *Shabbos gay*!!!!"

· · ·

M Y DAD AND I WAITED at the Aeroflot check-in counter at JFK, the only two people in line without *payos*, side curls, and tzitzit, the knotted threads that hang from the waists of Orthodox men. Six Hasids schmoozed in Russified Yiddish as a Hispanic porter pushed their trolley of bulging suitcases.

"Those six guys are gay," my dad said in an exaggeratedly flat, monotonic stage whisper out of the side of his mouth. This is his preferred mode of saying that someone or something is probably gay, or really of saying anything at all. He likes to give his conversations a conspiratorial tenor. It's nice when you're in on the conspiracy.

"Really?" I was a little skeptical. One of the consequences of my dad's coming out at age forty-six, or rather of my dad's having begun to make one decision or another at age forty-six, is that—as he will admit with a funny pride—his gaydar is exuberantly miscalibrated. I once heard him with unshakable confidence call a baby gay.

"You know how I know they're gay?" he continued loudly from the side of his mouth. He gestured to the tottering trolley. "That's all their shoes!"

This is the kind of joke that reminds me that he traces his gay pedigree back to *Will & Grace*, and not, as I might have preferred for him, White and Genet. Maybe, upon second thought, not Genet. But we were traveling to Ukraine to celebrate Rosh Hashanah, and to see if we could take a trip together that would end in candor and not violence, and I had told myself I was going to laugh at these jokes as though I were *Will & Grace*'s live studio audience.

As I came out of the metal detector at security, I turned around to find him gone. I lost it for a moment, afraid he'd bolted already. A moment later I caught sight of him again, letting other people in line go ahead as he squeezed in a quick chat with Brett before he had to abandon his phone to the conveyor belt. He looked as anxious as I was, and on the way to the gate he stopped to buy a bottle of wine. I wished Micah was with us, but it hadn't made sense for him to come back to New York from Tokyo; he'd flown into Kiev the night before and was going to meet us at the airport. I knew he wasn't thrilled that he'd had to leave his girlfriend alone in Tokyo only a week after they'd moved there, so it was a significant gesture that he'd agreed, in the end, to come.

Around us, Hasids were davening their late-afternoon prayers, swaying back and forth with their prayer books in hand; even if you know all the prayers by heart—as all of them certainly do—you're supposed to use the book. They prayed in the waiting area for the nice flights, the ones through Munich and Vienna and Amsterdam, flights with Lufthansa and Continental and other carriers with re-spectable and extensive international safety records. We sat on our bags and waited for our Aeroflot flight to Kiev via Moscow. Moscow is not technically en route to Kiev from pretty much anywhere but the North Pole, but my dad was a Russian major in college and said he'd always wanted to fly Aeroflot, so here we were.

He finished his wine and salad and got off the phone with Brett, with whom he hadn't had the chance to talk since security, so they had at least twenty-one minutes of their lives to catch up on. They've been together for thirteen years—or rather they've been together of-ficially for eight or nine years, were "roommates" for the previous two or three (that particular lie drove me crazy), and for the year or two before that my dad was still married and living at home—and they don't have the easiest time being apart. They solve this with updates at a one-to-one scale, which means they each have to take care not to live at any given time for more minutes than they will have to debrief. It's touching, actually, to see the two of them still so happily obsessed with each other after so long, even if it tends to slow things down.

My dad put his phone away and I put down my book on the life of Rabbi Nachman of Breslov, which I'd asked him to read too. He'd gotten as far as the paragraph in the introduction that said that many of the popular midcentury psychohistories of the great Hasidic sage—the raison d'être of this pilgrimage—suggested he might have been a latent homosexual.

The wine and the fact that he and Brett were now fully caught up made my dad a little less nervous. We were both still jittery, though. "So we have beds in Uman, right? And we know how to find them?" he asked.

"Yeah, I got us food and beds, and I have this map here." I pulled out an envelope a stoned guy had given me at a Japanese restaurant in New York. On the front of the envelope it said "Slava L." There was a letter inside, a Google-translated message in Ukrainian asking Slava L. to provide me and my party with pot in Uman. I had not asked the stoned guy to do this, but it had seemed impolite to refuse the note. He'd gone to the trouble of Google-translating it back and forth several times, as if by this process the translation of the pot request might be incrementally refined. On the back of the note the stoned guy had produced the kind of impeccably detailed and perfectly useless map that people on drugs excel at drawing. It had a main street, some boxes labeled as buildings, a swooshy area where the *mikveh* (the ritual bath) was, and another swooshy area where the ritual of tashlikh would be held. Large stars indicated the *kloiz*, the giant makeshift synagogue, and the Tzion, the grave of Rabbi Nachman. There was absolutely zero information about where the boxes and the swooshes and the stars stood in relation to, say, the highway. It also had soy sauce spilled all over it, in a pattern that seemed vaguely ominous.

"I sorta have this map here," I said. I handed it over. He looked at it, noted the stars and the soy sauce, and flipped it over to the printed side. He began to read the Cyrillic to himself out loud until he realized it was Ukrainian, not Russian.

"What's this?"

"It's a note in Google-translated Ukrainian that a very nice stoned guy wrote to a man named Slava, asking him to sell us marijuana."

"Oh," my dad said. He's afraid of drugs. "Brett printed us some maps too." He took them out; they were professional-looking and in Hebrew. There were five of them, some of which seemed to indicate main roads, and we were both relieved until we took a second look and discovered they were equally as unhinged from the highway and the rest of the city as the amateur map I already had, and that Brett had printed out five different sizes and resolutions of the exact same file.

"We'll find it. You just take the one highway from Kiev to Odessa and there it is, like halfway. When we arrive we're supposed to find Yossi and he'll show us to our rooms."

THIS IS *CRAAAZY*," my dad said. He says "crazy" with a very long "a," really leans into it in a way I've come to do as well, and as he says it he nicks his head forward a little, then floats his furrowed brows with bewilderment. It's the look and the affect that makes me feel the most tenderness for him, which is probably why "crazy" is the descriptor of his I've most helplessly inherited. Micah overuses it, too, just like the three of us all laugh as though we've been shocked into spitting out a mouthful of water.

I've done my best to avoid his other adjectives. The first circle of dubiously overemphatic enthusiasm is "wonderful." Everything with Brett, everything at work, everything with his friends and neighbors and most acquaintances, is always wonderful. Other wonderful things include: most dinners at restaurants, Fort Lauderdale, and Yoshi, the dog.

Things that aren't merely wonderful are "remarkable." Remarkable includes: vacations, parties, and how well everyone has been doing lately. He calls things remarkable with a special intensity: he furrows his brows without the bewildered arch, sets his dark eyes into a stern gaze, and purses his lips. He looks serious and thoughtful, as if it had been a long and painful process that brought him to the conclusion that this remarkable thing is indeed better than wonderful. Oddly, the thing about remarkable things is that he never has further remarks, though occasionally something will be "really remarkable." He'll occasionally pause to try to think of some category even more rarified, but he inevitably gives up.

Things that aren't good enough to occasion wonder are "sorta fun," which generally means that he thinks he likes something but isn't quite sure, or maybe he likes something and is afraid the people around him won't, or is afraid he'll feel ashamed for liking it, or he wants to reserve the possibility he might not like it anymore in the future. "Sorta fun" covers the bulk of the world's trinkets, tchotchkes, baubles, and artworks. It runs the gamut from the work of Léger to the gift he later bought Brett's very sweet aunt Phyllis in Odessa, a snow globe of the *Potemkin* Stairs.

The last important lexical move is "at this point." The implication, I think, is that a lot of things in the past haven't always been great, or maybe he doesn't even remember the past much at all, but *at this point* everything is utterly different. *At this point* he's telling the truth. *At this point* he's going to do what he says he's going to do. *At this point* he's become reliable and transparent. "At this point, things at work are really remarkable." "At this point, I can allow myself to just go out and do something sorta fun."

The shit transpiring on the Aeroflot plane as we boarded was definitely neither wonderful nor sorta fun but it was definitely *craaazy*. Neither of us had ever witnessed so much seat conflict. The Hasids were sitting wherever they liked, refusing to be seated next to a woman, or near a woman, or in a row where anybody might occasionally think about women. They clogged the aisles and took up all the space in the overhead compartments with their hat- and tefillin-boxes, and none of them use deodorant, probably to prevent random women from tearing their *schmattes* off, the way women do. The Aeroflot crew hadn't even tried to board the plane by rows, knowing full well the Hasids wouldn't have given a damn for their secular logic. They never stopped futzing for the whole flight, standing to daven, taking their hats off, smoothing them with lint removers, placing them back in their boxes, taking their coats on and off, arguing, studying Talmud from great codices and pocket paperbacks, a nodding derangement of velvet black discs pitching and yawing and then popping up and down like Whac-a-Mole antagonists, occasionally singing, laying tefillin, always in the damn aisles, a klutzy turbulence of activity. Generally just allowing the Aeroflot flight attendants free rein to indulge their favorite anti-Semitic fantasies. I turned to ask my dad why they tied one arm of their coats behind them when they davened and he said he was wondering that himself. It made me happy to know he felt as confused and irritated as I did.

The major additional hitch was that the people who weren't Hasids were Russians. Across from me was a young Russian woman with breasts that had been put in that morning and a through ticket from Moscow to Dubai. Moscow is slightly out of the way from New York to Kiev; it is very much not on the way from New York to Dubai. The flight attendant was telling her in Russian that her luggage was too big for the overhead compartment—already jammed with Borsalino boxes—and the woman kept replying in English that it was not problem. The attendant finally said that he was going to have to go check the bag and put it underneath. She looked up at him, tucked her iPhone between her freshly promoted breasts, spread out her hands in a gesture of exasperated despair, and said, "You cannot check it because, you see, it's my *carry-on* bag."

"Oh," the man said, as if it had simply been a semantic dispute all along, and shoved aside the hatboxes to make her suitcase fit. Throughout the whole exchange, my dad flirted with the other flight attendant in the Russian he was rapidly remembering after thirty years' disuse. Occasionally he'd switch to Hebrew to talk to the Israeli businessman seated next to him. If he couldn't find the right Russian or Hebrew word, he'd come up with the Spanish or German equivalent.

At long last the Hasids stopped *potchky*ing with their effects long enough for the plane to take off, and as we began to taxi, our seat-back TV screens flicked on. The Russian safety video suggested that in case of emergency you ought to clutch a swaddled infant to your enormous bosom before making a melodramatic final gesture of woeful resignation. The screen shifted to show a camera feed from just below the nose of the aircraft. We were passing over what was either the tarmac or the Belt Parkway or perhaps already the Atlantic; it was monochrome and low-res.

My dad leaned across the aisle and spoke to me once more out of the side of his mouth. "You know, they used to have these nose cameras on all flights, but then, just before you were born—when was that, 1980 or so?—there was this DC-10, American flight 191, I think, which had an engine-pylon problem as it took off out of O'Hare, and all two hundred seventy-something people aboard watched themselves plummet to their deaths in a field by a trailer park. I thought they took those cameras out of all planes, but I guess not in Russia."

We both looked at our seat-back monitors, which for all we could tell were showing Long Island screaming toward us. He crinkled up his nose and spit-laughed a little bit at how awful that must have been, and also how funny. I found myself laughing too. My long-dormant memory of his encyclopedic command of historic aviation disasters, especially in the context of his courage in immediately attempting to speak languages he hasn't spoken in years—as well as his clear sense of assurance and strength and pleasure despite his anxiety about what this trip might mean for us—made me feel a sweet, simple, childish, overwhelming love for the man who was sitting there and grinning sheepishly and acting in some obscure but wonderful—no, *really remarkable*—way like my father. This was not something I'd been expecting, and I had to look away for a second before I teared up.

I looked back and he was more serious now. "I believe it was the worst aviation disaster of all time on American soil." (When I got on the internet I couldn't help fact-checking all of this—I have, largely thanks to my dad's predilections, a terrible fact-checking habit—and he'd been almost frighteningly accurate.) Max was an engineer and amateur pilot; Micah inherited the love of aviation misfires, too, and in the car on the way to Odessa, as we fled horrible Uman in joy, they would spend an hour, while I sat and made notes and breathed slowly, talking about the TV show *Seconds From Disaster*.

IN THE FIRST-CLASS LOUNGE IN the Moscow airport on our layover—my near-constant travel over the previous three years afforded me access to these places—my dad took out his little Flip camera to record some people drowsily checking their email. I warned him that people in transit to Transnistria or Ingushetia might have reasons not to feel so great about being taped, even if the tape was only in the service of providing Brett with a map the size of the territory. I was a little apprehensive about saying something, as far more trivial things than this have been known to make him upset. But I was more apprehensive about the guy who looked as though he'd punched a few holes in Grozny. My dad put down the camera and drank some free vodka, and we got in line to board our connection to Kiev.

Of the hundred and fifty people on our flight to Kiev, there were a hundred and forty-six Hasids; now, made slaphappy by their proximity to Uman, they broke out into near-constant chants of UMAN UMAN ROSH HASHANAH UMAN UMAN ROSH HASHA-NAH. My dad was sitting mid-plane in the real thick of the scrum, and I was in the back row with the two other non–black hats: an exchange student from rural Shaanxi province, off to Kharkiv for God knows what reason, and a Chechen looking over some PowerPoint files. Though I was in the only *treyf* row in the whole plane, and needless to say was wearing neither *payos* nor even a yarmulke, the flight attendants gave me a kosher meal. It was a little horrifying to discover that, despite my jeans and uncovered head, I was recognizable to an Aeroflot flight attendant as just another Jew; I felt like Woody Allen in the scene with Grammy Hall. But then I looked over at the mixed offal the Chechen was eating and decided I'd lucked out.

In the Kiev airport the entire shtetl Diaspora had reconvened and was celebrating with song and pushiness. Israel, we heard, had organized a hundred and ten charter flights for this, or maybe it was a hundred and twenty, two hundred. My dad and I found ourselves standing next to an American who'd been on the plane with us from New York; he saw my dad's rainbow-emblazoned luggage tag forced upright from his overpacked bag and noticed he was from New Jersey. He introduced himself as Aaron, as most of the people we met in the coming days would, and said he lived nearby in Jersey.

"So, have you ever been to Uman before?"

"No," I said. "This is our first time."

"You're going to go back home with *payos*, I'm telling you! It's an amazing experience here. Just wait until tashlikh: tens of thousands of fellow Jews lined up at the stream at the end of the first day of Rosh Hashanah, tossing their sins into the water to be carried away by the current, wishing for renewal of self and spirit on the site of a terrible pogrom. It'll change your life. Just remember, if there's one thing you can't miss here, it's tashlikh."

The guy didn't have *payos* himself, and only a small yarmulke instead of a big black hat. "So, are you, then," my dad asked, "Modern Orthodox? As opposed to Hasidic, I mean."

"No! I'm ultra-religious, ultra-ultra-religious, and just because I don't look like the blackhats doesn't mean I'm not a true Breslower. The thing about Uman is that it doesn't matter here. No matter what you look like, we're all the same." I took out my phone to see if there was an open wireless network around. On the international pilgrimage circuit there are some conversations you've had enough times.

Aaron said something about his kids and my dad looked over and commented that he wasn't wearing a ring. My dad had taken off his own ring, the one he wears in anticipation of the legal marriage he expects before too long.

"We don't wear them," Aaron said. "We don't wear any jewelry at all. We consider it the garb of a woman." He paused. "And besides, we don't want to look married!" He winked.

"That's what I thought," replied my dad, with old sympathy.

"Nah, nah, I'm just joking. I wanted to get a rise out of you."

Around us a group of dreadlocked Israelis started up with the UMAN UMAN ROSH HASHANAH chant again.

My dad continued. "So, Aaron, is it tough to be away from your family?" Of the estimated twenty-five to forty-five thousand Jews who come to Uman each year, there are no more than maybe forty women, and they're not allowed to go anywhere or do anything. Once again I knew exactly what the answer to this was going to be, so I went back to trying to check email on my phone. Against everyone's good advice, I'd sent a "Good *yuntif*" email to the girl who was no longer in Shanghai, and was wondering if she'd written back while I was on the plane.

"No way! It's a vacation. Okay, well, not exactly a vacation, but it's a religious reason to tell my wife and three kids that I need to be away. You know, to go and pray for our family so that we have a good and successful year."

This shit was always the same, but right away it seemed different than the not-a-vacation lines I'd heard all along the Camino and circling Shikoku. It *was* different. It was already clear, if only by the costumes, that the journey to Uman was much closer to the medieval end of the pilgrimage spectrum than the contemporary one. These might have been people in crisis, but—and this was obvious from Aaron's strained humor about his family—they suffered from a surfeit of authority, not a lack of one. These were pilgrims who had a perfectly good idea what their lives looked like at home; their hours were micromanaged by scriptural obligation from sunrise to sleep. In fact, one of the things about ultra-observant Jews is that there is no gray area: unless you are explicitly *commanded* to do something, you are actually *prohibited* from doing it. They were here to go beyond the fields for three days a year, to take a short and uniquely authorized break from the responsibilities of home, such that they might return to their seamlessly circumscribed lives with renewed vigor in compliance.

We got through customs after an hour of elbowing and teeth gnashing and met Micah in the arrivals area. He'd already picked up

the rental car, had the tire fixed, and gotten directions to the highway to Uman. Our dad went to the bathroom.

"How'd everything go?" Micah looked a little concerned.

"Well, Dad thinks he got cruised by a Hasid already. But everything seems fine. Weirdly, almost ominously fine."

IT PROVED EASY ENOUGH to find Uman itself, which sits on the
Kiev–Odessa road past hundreds of kilometers of wheat and desic-
cated sunflower stalks, and Micah managed to drive the whole four
hours into the Ukrainian night without getting shaken down by any
cops. Once we got off the highway and into the dark streets, though,
we found that neither the soy-sauce-stained stoned-person map nor
the vast array of identical Hebrew mini-maps from Brett helped us
find Pushkin Street, the main drag through Rosh Hashanah Towne.
Lone people walked quickly with zombie purpose through the underlit alleys of Uman, equal parts squalid Ukrainian village and
blighted Soviet city, and you had to be practically on top of them
before you could tell if it was a Jew hurrying to safety or a Cossack
hurrying to murder. Everybody knows from the rich anecdotal
tradition of oral Jewish-persecution history—pre-, mid-, and post-
Holocaust—that the Ukrainians were the absolute worse, worse than
the Poles and worse than the Hungarians. The Romanians gave the
Ukrainians a run for their money. But, in the end, the Ukrainians—
the worst. I said that we should stop somebody and ask where the
Jews were. Micah thought that was a bad idea, said we'd be better off
if we had our dad ask a passerby in Russian where the pogrom was.
We all spit-laughed nervously.

We drove around for an hour until we finally parked the car near
where the stoned guy had drawn a police barricade. On the map it

was a crenellated line defending the Jews from soy-sauce hostilities. It turned out the difficulty in finding Pushkin Street lay in the fact that it's the chief artery of, and sole entrance to/exit from, what's hard to describe as anything other than a ghetto. The ghetto began at the police barricade—dozens of parked taxis and minivans advertising local Hasidic tourist destinations (Medzhybizh, Kholodets)—and then descended through dust, past hulking and decrepit Soviet tower blocks, to dead-end at a muddy river.

And that short stretch from the police to the water was bonkers. Even at ten at night the dusty path was so thick with people, all newly arrived from Israel, France, Brooklyn, and New Jersey, that foot traffic had been reduced to a near standstill. Where the soy-sauce map indicated a "market" the sides of the streets were lined with stalls where locals hawked cheap plastic toys, fruit, water, and inflatable mattresses. The Ukrainian peddlers bargained in the impressive smattering of Hebrew they'd managed to pick up over the last twenty years of their Rosh Hashanah–based economy. Breslower mantras—like the ubiquitous UMAN UMAN ROSH HASHANAH UMAN UMAN ROSH HASHANAH—had been set to trance beats blaring from bureau-sized speakers, and unwashed Israeli hippies danced arm in arm with unwashed blackhats from Borough Park. (The hippie dervishes are notorious for holding up Tel Aviv traffic with their impromptu devotional raves; the videos are a minor YouTube phenomenon.)

Men handed out little pamphlet psalteries as we angled our way past the tents of local schlock, bottled water, and electro beats. "It's like the Jewish Woodstock," I heard somebody say. Someone else called it "the Jewish Burning Man."

"It's like Halloween in the Castro," Micah said.

"I think you're even more right than you realize," my dad said.

We were slamdanced up and down Pushkin Street—or Rehov

Pushkina, as it's called in Hebrew, Hebrew being the lingua franca of the whole bash—periodically referring, for lack of a better option, to the soy-sauce map, until we were finally directed to the Scheiner Property, where I was supposed to find Yossi. For some reason it had not occurred to me that among forty thousand Hasids packed into a tower-blocked Ukrainian ghetto it might be a little difficult to find a person called Yossi. (I had not realized until I got to Uman that all of these people are actually named Shlomo and Moishe and Shmuel and all the other fools of Chełm I'd thought Isaac Bashevis Singer invented for comedic effect.)

We got past the for-hire Ukrainian commandos guarding the gate to the free-food tent and walked up to the most competent-looking guy we could find, Nahum from New Jersey. We asked if he knew a Yossi, a question we'd been vainly putting to random Hasids for hours. "You guys lookin' for Yossi?" he said.

"Yeah," we said.

"I flew over on Yossi's chartered plane. I'm part of the entourage. Follow me to that white tent." The back of his shirt said JERSEY DISCOUNT TILE and had an address in Edison.

As my dad dropped back to answer a text from Brett, Micah edged up to Nahum. "My mom's redoing her kitchen," he said under his breath. "Can you get her a good deal on tiles?"

"Can I get her a good deal on tiles? Nobody anywhere can get her a better deal on tiles. Here's my card," he said, and winked. "Call me after the holidays and we'll see what we can do."

He led us into the free-nosh area to wait for Yossi. It was tumbling with jet-lagged blackhats trying to get up to the buffet; the air was a flatulent mixture of *schwitz* and acrid stewed kasha, and everywhere bits of beany auburn stew found itself dribbled and caught in broad fans of curly beard. We stood off to one side, beardless, like three Jeremiahs contemplating the destruction of the food tent.

A hippie Hasid jam band started to play behind us, and we could no longer hear anything at all over the pious din. Micah looked at me. My dad looked at me. I looked at the ground. I was exhausted and this was awful. My dad, sensing my misery and wanting to make me feel a little better, finally said, "I'm not sure how I'd feel if you brought us here as a vacation, but we're here for your book, so it's okay." He meant well, and it was consonant with the not-really-vacation vacation that pilgrimage is supposed to be, but in the moment it made the whole thing seem even more burdensome. What made me feel even queasier than the kasha or the *payos* or the jam band or my dad's and Micah's discomfort was the prospect of beginning the conversations I'd brought us here to try to have.

I didn't have time to respond to my dad before Nahum emerged from the free-for-all, grabbed us, and led us through a series of steamy cooking tents to command HQ, at the center of the multi-tented complex. It was an unfurnished cinder-block bunker with a few computers and conference tables lit by a single hanging bulb; some young men idled at the monitors while others reported to their subordinates via walkie-talkies and BlackBerrys. Nahum introduced us to Yossi, who didn't look like a Hasid at all. He wore an understated pink yarmulke and resembled a small-time arms dealer, or an Ecstasy smuggler of waning ambition. He was a squat guy at the conference table in the center of the room, and when we told him my name he peeled off three laminated cards, each of which said "Bed/Food," and handed them to us, told us to have fun, and turned back to his BlackBerry. Later on, we'd hear that nine years ago Yossi "didn't have a pot to piss in," but that God had given him a fortune and he'd understood his calling to be the logistics of Uman. Now, for a few months a year, this is all he does. Throughout the next few days he would stand on a table before mealtimes, the only person in all of Uman in a slick gray suit, and try to tell one parable or another, about redemption or charity or forgiveness—he figured his generosity had bought him some homiletic air time—but the blackhats paid him no mind, chanted down his sermons with their mantras.

Nahum radioed for a kid named Baruch to come show us to our room.

O UR ROOM WAS ON THE first floor of one of the Soviet tower blocks, up off Rehov Pushkina near the police barricade. It was immaculate and bunked to the hilt. When I'd made reservations through the Breslower travel agency in Brooklyn, I'd been warned that I'd be sharing a room with several other people and would have to respect their observance of the holiday. The Ukrainian tenants had stacked up their wicker furniture under floral sheets in the corner and had removed whatever there might have been of value. I was told that what we paid for four days here covered their rent for the year, and that the usual tenants were the folks sitting outside on the low stone walls, sleeping in their cars and idly grilling.

Baruch was in his early twenties, from Crown Heights, and wasn't sure he was into this whole thing. "I'm not usually quite so religious, but I'm a photographer, so I thought I'd come do some shooting here, but I'm so busy working for Yossi that I won't get any time to take pictures before *yuntif* starts. Anyway"—he swept his arm around the room—"this is the place, and Yossi said his only rule is 'Don't jizz on the walls.'" The walls were ablaze with hot-maroon swirls in glittered vinyl; the motif was the fractal bloodstain.

"The walls," Micah said, "look like someone already jizzed on them. And that someone is the premiere iTunes-generated acid artist of his generation."

As Baruch was finishing up telling us to be sure to keep the doors locked and our valuables on us—there are a lot of *ganefim*,

thieves, around, he said—a guy who looked and talked like Bobby
Baccalieri from *The Sopranos* walked in. The first thing my dad ever
notices about anybody is his weight, and I could tell he was thinking
that this was the heaviest Jew he'd ever seen. The guy introduced
himself as yet another Aaron, but said we should call him Ari. He'd
grown up in Borough Park but that had gotten too Lubavitch for him,
so now he lived in Flatbush and davened at an Orthodox shul there.
He didn't have *payos* and his yarmulke looked like a pudgy kid's cartoon beanie. His soft child's voice had a loose fuggedaboutit taking
the tops off his words, each lipping broadly into the next. This was
his fifth year in Uman, and he'd only missed one since he started
coming. That was two years ago, the week after he'd gotten married,
when his wife made him stay home for some reason. Now he insisted
on returning. "Yeah, I got a wife waitin' for me at home. I ain't a
lonely guy."

We asked him what he liked about it here, especially since he
wasn't a blackhat. "You gotta wait and see for yuhselfs. It's different
for errybody, but you'll know when you feel it, trus' me. People just
feel sumthin', maybe not right away, maybe not the first time they're
here, but you will. You will. Maybe in three months you wake up at
home in your bed and understand that this was sumthin' special. It's
never easy comin' here, you gotta deal with the flights and bein' away
from yuh family and gettin' robbed by the cabbies and the cops and
then stayin' in a place like this . . ." He looks around. "Well, actually,
for Uman, this place is downright five-star. *Five-stah*. Even so, it ain't
easy gettin' here or bein' here, but that's how the rebbe, Reb Nachman, bless his memory, wanted it to be. I just spent six hours looking
for Yossi to get into this room. In the end it's worth it. Just tashlikh
alone, you never forget it. You know what they do?"

Micah looked to me, as if I'd prepared for this. We shook our
heads. We're both terrible Jews, especially considering our pedigree.

We never know anything about anything, though Micah had somehow already signed up to teach Sunday school at the only synagogue in Tokyo. "The rabbi was a middle-aged gay dude," Micah said. "I was helpless to resist."

"So the tashlikh, right, it's when you empty yuh pockets of crumbs, like yuh sins, and you toss them into the stream. The moving water takes them away with it.

"Here, dey do it in this lake down the bottom of the hill, a lake that once ran red with the blood of Jews. That's why the rebbe, Reb Nachman, came here to die, two hundred years ago this Sukkas." He pronounced the upcoming harvest holiday the Ashkenazic way, with a sibilant flourish. "They had this pogrom, in the 1760s or sumthin', where they killed thirty-five thousand of us. The rebbe chose to die here, and to tell his followers to come celebrate every Rosh Hashanah by his grave, so that those Jews would always be remembered. So that even in a town with no Jews left, these people would have someone to say kaddish for them.

"The Ukrainians, they don't like us much here." He giggled. "Every year sumbody gets whacked."

Micah looked up with a start. "Somebody gets whacked?"

"Yeah, every year there's a guy gets whacked." Ari excused himself to go to the bathroom.

My dad went to root around in his bag but I asked him and Micah to sit down with me for a minute. I'd been preparing this for months but hadn't expected to have to say what I wanted to say so early. My voice sounded tremulous and tinny.

"Look, when we were back in that terrible free-food tent with the fluorescent glare and the kasha-fart smell and the horrible hippie-Hasid jam band playing and the thousands of people climbing all over each other as though it were their last meal, Dad turned to me and said he was glad that this wasn't a vacation.

"And I guess I just wanted to say to you two that this isn't a vacation for me, either. I feel just as alienated from what's going on as you do, and I feel just as ashamed and apologetic and confused about the ways in which I might be identified with these people, how uncomfortable I am with that idea. But in all this traveling and reading I keep coming back to the idea that pilgrimage has always been a pretext. It's a way to have a trip with some higher motive.

"My purposes in being here aren't the same as everybody else's. In fact, I can't say I really know what these Hasids are doing here and why. Or, rather, I think I know why they're here—to have a few days away from their families and their infinitesimally structured lives—and it's just not a celebration that really applies to us. We're not returning to the same sorts of lives they are. I don't think they want us to feel included, and I don't think we want to feel included. But the important thing for me is that I want us to take this seriously in our own way, as a time to talk about forgiveness and renewal." This sounded a little more practiced than I'd wanted it to sound, but I'd been thinking about how to put all this for months.

I wanted to use this time out of time to have conversations we'd never had. I'd never have anticipated this—and had never even imagined this as part of the pilgrimage project in the beginning—but this was becoming the most important trip for me, even though it was the one whose rituals I was least interested in, and the one least likely to result in weight loss. On the Camino and on Shikoku I was more interested in the form of the ritual than in the content; here I didn't care nearly as much about the form as I did about the content.

In the ten days between Rosh Hashanah and Yom Kippur, the Day of Atonement, Jews are commanded by God to ask forgiveness of those we've hurt. Judaism holds that God himself cannot forgive our wrongs against other people. People go on the Camino—an experience that on some basic level makes you confront the fact that you're doing what you want even if you're not sure why, and even if you're pretending otherwise—to forgive themselves for the decisions they've made, to acknowledge and accept that they've been doing the best they can. Part of what this process does is help us forgive others, others who aren't there. I didn't need my dad to be there with me on the Camino to forgive him in that way. But in order for us to move on now, it was necessary for us to stand before each other. I wanted to hear about how painful his life had been, I wanted to feel sorry myself, at least in part so that I would have an excuse—or, perhaps better, an occasion—to know, in an urgent and specific way, that it had been okay to forgive him in general, and I wanted us both to remember where we'd stood, at which fixed points, when we said what I hoped we would say.

In these ten days, Jews ask to be "inscribed in the book of life" for the coming year, and that had always been a powerful image for me. I wanted to ask forgiveness, to offer it, and then to inscribe it. Being here in this dot, not on a line, not on a circle, not in motion at all, not seeking out strangers, meant a commitment to conversations I'd for so long been afraid to have, admissions I wasn't sure I wanted to hear. But we were here now, and if only for the sake of those inscriptions, I told myself, I needed to follow through.

"I want this to mean something to us, even if what it means to us isn't anything like what it means to these forty-thousand weirdos with *payos*."

"Well said," my dad responded, and it felt as though he'd really listened. "I don't care about all these guys, either—and I hate the fact that other people would identify me with them—but I, too, look forward to taking it seriously in our own way."

Micah had listened, too, and hadn't even once told me to shut up, but then again, Micah had been prepped for this. Still, it is hard not to prep Micah not to tell me to shut up.

Ari flushed the toilet and came back into the living room. The front of his shirt was soaked through to the skin. "Let me show you guys how to use the shower, okay? It's a little complicated. I tried it once to see and I got whacked."

MICAH AND I WENT TO SLEEP on a pull-out couch big enough for one and a half people, and Micah, who has been mistaken for the older brother since he was twelve and I was fifteen, is already big enough for one and a half people. He mummified himself in the blanket and I was left with a sweatshirt wrapped around my feet. Our dad had decided to go back out again. He didn't say more and we were asleep by the time he returned. The other people staying in the room with us came in late but couldn't figure out how to operate the nineteenth-century dead-bolt key, so Micah had to get up three or four times to let them in.

The morning was going to be our last chance to check email for a few days—the holiday started, and electronics ended, at sundown—so we went over to Yossi's compound to use his wireless network. People shoved and grasped for free coffee and dry biscuits; the brute incivility of the spectacle made Micah indignant. "And I'm used to living in China," he said with a scowl. We brought coffee out to our dad, who was talking to Brett on the phone in the street.

The big event of the day, we'd heard, was at the Tzion, Rabbi Nachman's grave, at noon. Rabbi Nachman was a great-grandson of the Baal Shem Tov, the founder of Hasidism. The three generations following the death of the Baal Shem Tov saw the Hasidic movement—populist, ebullient, mystical, messianic—splinter into all of the sects that jostle up against each other in Brooklyn today, each of which has had its own rabbinic lineage; the Breslowers, however, have promoted no leading rabbi since Nachman himself, and have thus been called the "dead Hasids." Before his death in 1810, Nachman told his followers that if they came to visit his tomb on the occasion of Rosh Hashanah and repeated ten particular psalms, he would grant them redemption in the world to come. The pilgrimage ran continuously through the Russian Revolution and was banned under the Soviets, though occasionally someone would smuggle himself here despite the danger. Since the collapse of the Soviet Union the pilgrimage has become hugely, ahistorically popular. Some pilgrims wander into the makeshift grave building to say the psalms at their leisure, but everybody I'd talked to recommended we join the thousands who meet to do it together at noon before the start of the holiday.

We were carried along by the crowd down the street toward the site, past the Ukrainian security forces with GRYPHON written on their backs and their arms—my dad taught me the Cyrillic alphabet on the plane—and paramilitary commandos in fatigues and red berets. We weren't the only ones taking advantage of the final few hours of electricity; practically everybody had an iPhone or BlackBerry or Flip camera out to document the madness. I was worried about how I was going to be able to take notes come sundown—writing is work, and is thus prohibited—and I knew my dad was worried about how he'd be able to keep in touch with Brett. Micah seemed up for the novelty as long as he could sneak off to break it on occasion. His girlfriend had said she'd understand if he couldn't be in touch.

Thousands of Jews jammed the street in front of the Tzion. We stood shoulder-to-shoulder with them, elbowing out a place to stand, trying to brace ourselves against the press of the crowd behind us. On the tin roof of the Tzion stood a fiery yellowed ghost of a Hasidic rabbi with a flaming gray beard, long and bony with black-marble eyes set deep into hollowed sockets, skin like sandalwood. He was attempting to lead the unruly crowd, doing his best to train the choruses of enthusiasm in a collective direction. He shouted chants into a megaphone as the bored Ukrainian commando by his side stared out into the middle distance, occasionally tapping his baton down on the eave as pilgrims tried to climb up out of the crowd and onto the roof. On a wire above us were Hebrew signs, which my dad said read "No great, no small, all friends."

He did his side-of-mouth stage stammer: "I walked around last night for a while and I couldn't find an LGBT tent anywhere." I couldn't tell if he was joking. For a second I was a little ruffled by this, wanting there to be one moment in his life that wasn't first and foremost about his being gay. But I took a deep breath and reminded myself that this was all really alien to all of us and he was just looking for a way in.

The rabbi indicated that now was the time to read the ten psalms. The psalms, which Rabbi Nachman called the Tikkun HaKlali, or the "general remedy," are, when said at his grave and accompanied by donations to charity, supposed to gain a kind of forgiveness in general—like the no-questions-asked unilateral forgiveness of the Camino. Beyond that, though, they were supposed to gain very particular forgiveness for the sins of nocturnal emissions or masturbation or pretty much any sexual activity besides the strictly conjugal sort. (Some biographers, it turns out, have speculated about Nachman's sexual orientation, particularly because of his likening of having sex with one's wife to the suffering of circumcision.) Nachman taught that wanton sexual activity was the source not only of evil in the world but of depression, with which he consistently struggled as an adolescent. From the historical record, it seems as though his response to depression was just to take off, first from the village of his youth to another part of Galicia, and later on an extended pilgrimage via Istanbul to Palestine, but his teachings are also unusual insofar as they demand what is, for Jews, a radical asceticism. At any rate, I was probably just primed for these sorts of correspondences, but as I'd read about the tradition of the Tikkun HaKlali, I couldn't help seeing an uncanny resemblance to what I was also seeking here. The first step was the general remedy, the broad forgiveness, which had begun more than a year ago on the Camino. The second step took up the particulars, the specific grievances at hand, which in our case also was an issue of sexuality, or at least the deception that attended to sexuality. First the acceptance, then the accountability.

I'd been given the idea that the Tikkun HaKlali and tashlikh were the two most inspired, inspiring events of the celebration here, but it was hard to get much out of what was going on. Nothing seemed unified or collective; everybody, from what I could tell, was just racing through the psalms at his own pace, not even chanting, rushing to finish so the merit would be accrued and people could get back to the important business of milling around taking pre-*yuntif* videos of everybody else milling around.

Or maybe that was just me. Maybe I'd grown too accustomed to meeting the kinds of demands that created one community—the sort that required nothing besides showing up and committing to something hard but singular—and too lazy or afraid or skeptical of the demands of a different sort. The community here in Uman was, in contrast to those on the Camino or Shikoku, being not created but sustained. It's not the kind of community that lets you just show up, not the kind of ritual that immediately affords you the comfort of feeling a part of what William James called "a wider self through which saving experiences come." You had to know the prayers, have associations with these particular psalms, understand the tradition that brought you to this godforsaken place and would bring you back year after year.

It wasn't some one-shot effort that might just help you feel a better sense of control over your life, or might help you reconcile yourself to the control you do have—or might, at the very least, leave you with a memory of what it was like not to worry about the costs of your decisions every minute of every day. The journey to Uman is not about changing your life. It's about coming to terms with the authority of the past in the context of some release from the religious authority of the present. It's one ecstatic part of the ongoing struggle by which an individual works out his relationship to the authority of his particular tradition. The idea is to make you okay with the life you have, the life you've inherited. You return home from the joyous, oceanic merger that is Rosh Hashanah Uman to affirm that life, to choose it anew. You return home from Santiago, with any luck, feeling slightly better equipped to decide if you're able to affirm it or not.

What makes the Camino both exhilarating and impossible is that it holds out this promise of change. If you're not careful, it seduces you into thinking in terms of a grand gesture of renunciation, of the angel Damiel striding through that Berlin Wall and into final freedom. The trip to Uman, however, is part of an ongoing struggle, what Turner identified as part of a "lifelong drama." Unfortunately, it was also an ongoing struggle in pursuit of, among other things, an ideal of sexual purity I despised, both on principle and on behalf of my dad, and the misogyny and xenophobia and everything that went along with those sorts of beliefs. What I was thus confronting here was also not a religious life or ritual I wanted for myself, and I couldn't help but feel as though this trip wasn't about these men finding ways to accommodate rigid lives so much as contorting themselves to fit into somebody else's idea of what a life is. At the same time, I could recognize some obvious sources of my alienation. I couldn't stop thinking of the old joke where a secular Jewish woman is sitting on a bench next to a guy with a black hat and a black coat. She turns to him and says, "You Hasids live in the Middle Ages. Your practices are superstitious and silly and an embarrassment to the rest of us." The man turns back and says, "I'm sorry, ma'am, I'm actually Amish." The woman pauses and replies, "Oh, how wonderful that you've been able to maintain your traditions!"

I turned to Micah and our dad, asked if they wanted to get out of the crush and find lunch. We pushed back against the throng toward the main road and the ghetto's single exit. We navigated the police barricade and found a little Ukrainian grocer. As we opened the door, a passing Hasid snarled at us, wagged his finger, and said, "Not kosher!" We closed the door behind us, bought hard local salami and bread, and went across the street to sit on a park bench and eat our lunch. A group of Hasids passed us on their way out of the ghetto and Micah leaned over to cover up the salami. We felt judged and ashamed in front of a group of people we judged and were ashamed of. But we felt judged and ashamed together, the three of us, and sitting there eating *treyf* on a park bench outside the ghetto had a kind of wagon-circling effect. We felt huddled together and protective and close in a way that felt new, or felt new insofar as it felt old.

A BOUT SIX WEEKS after my dad had come out to me, or whatever it was that he thought he was doing when I was nineteen, he'd come to visit me in Munich, where I was for a summer, spending a little time learning German between long intervals of mopey self-pity and turgid letter-writing. The woman I was writing the turgid letters to had lent me a copy of *Giovanni's Room*, which I'd heavily marked up—to the great and lasting chagrin of that particular woman—before passing it along to my dad. He read it in one sitting on a train we took to visit Davos, Switzerland, where Max had been born. (Max's father contracted tuberculosis on his honeymoon.) I remember virtually nothing of his visit except that when we returned to Munich we used the book as a way to begin a conversation about what he had wanted from life. I recall only one scene, of the two of us walking through the English Garden; I asked him, through tears, if he'd regretted having a family, and he'd said of course not.

But that was a long time ago, and his story had changed so many times since then. Back then, as I remember, he told me he hadn't even known he was gay until he was well into his thirties. Later he told Micah he'd known when he was nine years old but had never had the courage to accept it. In recent years he'd hinted about old boyfriends, first loves. I wanted some clarity about all of this. I wanted to understand what he regretted and what he didn't, what injury and resentment he might possibly have avoided. I thought it might help me sort out my own worries about regret, my own fears of resentment. And I wanted to have a fixed record of it all, something inscribed in the book of my life, something that Micah and my notes would defend, that I could point to later and say, "Look, this is what you said; this is what you admitted to; this is my attempt to hold us both accountable as we forgive each other and move forward."

I wasn't sure I was going to be able to initiate these conversations myself. I have a way of, say, asking a stranger for directions and seeming as though I'm calling him an idiot. Micah, on the other hand, can tell someone to fuck themselves and one wide goofy smile later he's pipette-nursing their kittens. A big part of the reason I'd begged Micah to come along on this trip, at a moment of transition and massive inconvenience in his own life, was to be the one to ask.

We packed up the rest of our salami, locked it into the car, and began to walk back down through the Rehov Pushkina market, past Yossi's tent city and the Soviet tower blocks full of pilgrims. The soy-sauce map seemed to indicate that if we followed Pushkina to the end, past the *kloiz* synagogue and toward the river, we'd come to the popular *mikveh* spot, the ritual bath. We followed the path down and around the side of a hill to a little flooded quarry, the water slately mirroring the sky. The adventuresome—mostly young, mostly Israeli, mostly dreadlocked—stripped and jumped in from the bare rocks, splashing around and playing grab-ass before performing the three prescribed ritual dunks. They clambered back naked onto the bank and smoothed their *payos*, wrestled for towels. Observant women visit the bath once a month, but it's something men have few opportunities to do, and we'd heard from somebody that the *mikveh* here saw round-the-clock activity. My dad thought two of them were cute.

We followed the path beside the river bog and walked for a while. Micah looked over. "I thought you said this wasn't a walking pilgrimage," he said. "For a non-walking pilgrimage, we're sure doing a lot of walking."

"It's conducive to good conversation. Shut up."

"You shut up." Micah punched me.

"Boys!" my dad said.

A Ukrainian came over in a raft with a little outboard motor and told us it cost ten dollars five minutes. My dad asked in Russian where the guy took people for ten dollars five minutes.

He gestured across to the far bank. "To other side."

"What's over there?"

"He says it's nicer," my dad said.

We thanked him and kept walking. We were alone, far from the great crowds on the ghetto ridge above us, our only company the occasional stray Hasid or dreadlocked Israeli davening or getting high alone in the little brush-obscured coves along the embankment. Micah decided now was the time to get started.

"How's Mario?" Micah asked. Mario was our dad's roommate and best friend in college, a half-German half-Peruvian, and I think both of us had always wondered if maybe the two of them had been involved—not because there was evidence that they had been, but because we never had any idea what to think about anything. We'd heard a lot about Mario as kids but he hadn't been mentioned in a while. This happened with some frequency over the course of our childhood: our dad would have a particularly intense relationship with a male friend, they'd spend huge amounts of time together, and then all of a sudden he'd never be mentioned again. If we asked after the vanished friend he'd get evasive.

"Mario doesn't talk to me anymore."

"What happened?" Micah was going to have to do all the talking. I felt a clenched nausea. I didn't want him to feel interrogated and cut us off. I was afraid I'd ruin the whole trip. Actually, I was afraid *he'd* ruin the trip. I was worried we would fail. The only thing I was more worried about was that we'd succeed. I didn't know if I wanted to know this stuff or not, where any of it would lead, if anywhere at all, though of course this was the stuff I'd been wondering about for years.

"He always made a lot of gay jokes, all the time faggot this and faggot that, in college and afterward, and finally I thought I had to say something. A few years ago I had a few glasses of wine in Fort Lauderdale and I called him and right away I just told him."

"What did he do?"

"He hung up the phone and I have not heard from him since."

There was a curtness in the way he said this, but no fury, almost a sense of embarrassment.

"Does Brett have experiences like that?"

"Sure, of course, but in Brett's case it's much worse because it's his family. At least my family has always been supportive." He told a long and detailed story about a huge family reunion that Brett's father was planning in Chicago. The invitation arrived and Brett hid it because Dad hadn't been invited. In thirteen years Brett's dad had never acknowledged their relationship, and it made both of them feel terrible. Our dad never knew what to do about it, whether to support

Brett in breaking off communication with his dad or whether to offer to help Brett acknowledge his father's limitations and figure out how to have some relationship with him, however muted.

Over Thanksgiving three months later I'd meet up with my dad and Brett in Tokyo to visit Micah, and Brett would say that he'd finally told his dad that if the Christmas card didn't come addressed to both of them this year he was going to mark it "Return to Sender." A month later I was at their house in New Jersey for a Christmas party, and that day a card came addressed to both of them for the first time.

"At least they don't seem to send those letters anymore," my dad said.

"What letters?" It's possible this was me talking now.

"The same old stuff Brett's dad has always sent, the kind that his mom used to send, about how they pray to Jesus for Brett to change, salvation of his soul, that sort of thing."

"Brett still gets letters like that?" Brett is forty-eight years old. He lived with a man for nine years in his twenties, then married a woman—with whom he never had children, and with whom he's still close—for the next seven. He treats his hair with Sun-In and lies about it and has a shy boyish charm. Micah sends him obnoxious Mother's Day cards that he loves and puts on the mantel next to the pictures of Yoshi and the backstage shot—my dad paid for a pass—of him with the Go-Go's.

"Not so much anymore."

None of us had been paying any real attention to where we were going—if I had any direction at all, it was to keep us tarrying way out here in the fields, away from the crowds of dancing Hasids and the trance mantras—but I'd noticed we were inadvertently trailing some young Israeli guys. We picked our way across a stubbled plain, tuft grass and hillocks jagged with bits of old masonry. The Israelis had stopped a hundred yards ahead of us to look at a large plinth painted white and identified with a stone placard. We kept up in their direction but I slowed us down. I stopped but did not quite turn all the way toward him.

"So this might sound like a failure of imagination on my part, especially given that there are obviously millions of people out there who love to hate homosexuals, many of them just over the next hill, but I'm starting to realize now that I don't really think I've ever thought there was anybody we knew or had anything to do with that disapproved so venomously. It just doesn't ever occur to me." I'd lived in San Francisco for years, a few blocks from the Castro, and then Berlin, and it seemed as though pretty much everybody was gay everywhere all the time. "And I guess I knew in some vague, abstract way, that Brett got letters like that from his parents, or at least used to, but I'm not sure I ever thought about what that meant or how it must feel. And I don't think I ever knew that there were people in your own life, like Mario, who'd stopped talking to you."

I felt as though I were walking slowly across a thin and narrow bridge. The way the words hung limp in the air before me made them sound like the words of someone very near to losing control. It felt important to get this right.

"What I'm saying is that I don't think I ever had a very good sense for how hard, for lack of a better way of putting it, your life has been. And I'm sorry, Dad."

I looked around me, and I stopped to write this down.

WE CAME UP UPON the white plinth. The placard we'd seen at a distance was a Hebrew grave marker. Our dad translated it as he read it out loud, saying that this marked the spot where Rabbi Nachman's remains had been found, before they were relocated to the Tzion. The Israelis we'd been following were stopped at a different marker a few yards away, and we walked over to them.

Our dad began to read the Hebrew there but he was confused by an unusual phrase, and as he read along the Israelis helped him translate. The word he'd been tripped up on was "mass grave," and it turned out that this entire field marked the old Jewish cemetery, which had ultimately been used as a mass grave—first after the big eighteenth-century pogrom that brought the rebbe to die here, and then again after a Soviet pogrom in the thirties. Three thousand Jews were buried in the uneven ground along which we'd made our slow way uphill.

One of the Israelis was wearing a white knit yarmulke that looked like a snowboarder's beanie; they'd been selling them in the market on the street, and Dad had bought one for Brett. (Brett loved it, didn't seem to mind it implicated him in a messianic cult.) Along the side it read, in black Hebrew block letters, NA NACH NACHMA NACHMAN M'UMAN, the closest thing the Breslowers have to a motto—part mantra and part millenarian sloganeering. It's untranslatable, and my dad asked the Israeli for an explanation. As he began to recite his response in measured broken English his pupils dilated and his eyes began to glow with an icy amber.

"It is not mantra, it is science. It's from the Zohar and it begins with a word that is one letter, then is two letters, then three, then four, then five." (In Hebrew, this is the case.) The Zohar was the founding text of Jewish mysticism, a creation of thirteenth-century Spain that identified itself as by Rabbi Simeon bar Yochai, a second-century teacher and mystic who Breslowers believe was reincarnated as Rabbi Nachman. The Israeli went on into a lot of complicated numerology, but the long and short of it is that there were five great rabbis in history and Nachman was the fifth. He predicted that he would be the last great rabbi, the last "master of prayer," before the coming of the messiah, when we would all step out of history and into eternity, the reverse of Damiel's traversal of the Berlin Wall. His flame, Reb Nachman said, would burn until the coming of *moshiach*, and all the inscriptions and the *Na na na* chanting were meant to be the symbols of his followers' contribution to the hastening of the messianic age. The rituals of the present would usher in a future in which all the deeds and misdeeds of the past would be redeemed. But we'd been in a serious conversation, so it was hard to concentrate now on the coming of the messiah. The Israeli decided we weren't going to get it and wandered off, back in the direction of the *mikveh*.

So who was Bart?" Micah didn't really remember Bart but I'd asked him to ask this.

"Bart was a remarkable guy and a really, really good friend of mine. He died in 1991."

That meant I must've been eight or nine the one time my dad took me along to meet Bart. This was somewhere near Tompkins Square Park. What I recalled was a shaggy shock of blue hair, and feelings of both elation and terror: on the one hand thrilled to be old enough to be taken along one night to the city to meet a guy with blue hair, and on the other frightened of the jagged dark in the Alphabet City of the late eighties. In my memory Bart looked like Warhol, but maybe that was just part of the dream pedigree I had for my dad, the one that looked to White and Genet and not *Will & Grace*. But I did think that my dad once said he'd gone with Bart to sell drugs to Allen Ginsberg, so maybe in this case my retrospective fantasy—that if he'd had a secret life, it could at least have been an exciting one, something worth escaping his surface life for—was accurate. I remembered hearing for the first time about AIDS, and I remembered my dad walking around for some months, maybe years, as though accompanied by ghosts. It was selfish and obscene for me to look back and want his secrets, the secrets I'd come here to try to clear up, to have hidden amazing things: it meant I have at best ignored and at worst aestheticized the fact of what must have been unimaginable pain. Like any gay man of his age, he'd watched a great number of his close friends die of AIDS, but unlike many of those men, he was not able to talk about it to the people closest to him, the people he lived with. Maybe the reason he liked *Will & Grace* and not so much White and Genet—though, now that I think of it, I did give him *The Married Man* once and he told me it was the best novel he'd ever read—was that all he wants now is to be normal and happy. He wanted to marry Brett and drink boxed wine and take Yoshi out for walks and watch *Mamma Mia!* until their DVD player caught fire. I myself had never been less than loathsome on the subject of *Mamma Mia!* and I felt terrible about it, but I didn't want to digress into overemphatic apology, and I would stand by my derision of *Mamma Mia!*

It was around the time that Bart died of AIDS that things began to get really bad. That was when my dad had dyed his bangs platinum, which didn't go over so well with the congregation he then served and would not serve much longer. This was around the time that in a fifth- or six-grade art class I made a painting of a male seraph sealed in a black box in the center of an otherwise Edenic scene and wrote, in black block letters across the top, WHO ARE YOU FORCING INTO THE CLOSET? A nasty debate ensued over whether it could go up on the middle-school wall. I can only imagine that my dad had gone to see *Angels in America*, talked about it at home. It is, however, also possible that this episode lends credence to his idea that I knew all along. He talked about theater a lot back then and gave me John Simon's reviews to read when he thought they were particularly savage. They were confusing for a ten-year-old. But I liked waking up in the morning to clippings he'd left under my door. Sometimes he said he'd wished he'd been an actor, had become a rabbi less for the liturgical than for the performative aspects of the job, and because he'd so much liked spending time in Israel and speaking Hebrew. This was also around the time my dad started to seem arbitrary and punitive, when he would come home late and throw all my CDs down the stairs because there was unfolded laundry on the dining room table. I began then to understand there were sealed-off swaths of my dad's time, and that the patterns of his emotional climate could neither be predicted nor accounted for.

"Bart was the first person I ever told I was gay. That was in 1986. I was taking social-work classes one night a week in New York. It was raining and I was headed downtown in a cab. The cabbie asked if I minded if we picked up a guy standing in the rain. He got in the cab and looked at me and knew right away, and we went out for coffee. He was the first person I could talk to openly." Again, it's hard to get his stories straight (again: *so to speak*). When he told me, at nineteen, that he knew I already knew he might prefer men, the backstory went like this: in the early to mid-nineties he discovered he was bisexual but chose to live with this knowledge and remain in his marriage. In 1997 or 1998, after meeting Brett, he began to envision a different sort of life. It was time for him to do something for himself for a change, put himself first. This meant the license to make up for lost time. There was a lifetime of Palm Springs poolside drag parties to catch up on.

After five or six years he was telling a new version, or hinting at one. There were salacious allusions to the loss of his virginity, wistful ones to his first love. But these comments felt more like boasts than invitations to further inquiry. Under the pretense of closeness it expanded the distance between us. His unexplored asides reminded me of how much I didn't know, how much had happened that had nothing to do with me. "I had a boyfriend who sold drugs to John

Lennon. Someday I'll tell you about that," he'd say, and then smile and trail off. These conversations made me angry. No, more than that, they made me feel stupid, gullible, excluded. He'd deceived me, deceived us, and then everything he ever said could only appear in that light. His clumsy attempts to clue us in only ever deepened my sense of deception. The implication of this second story was that he'd been with men before and then decided—in a way that somehow suggested a proleptic sacrifice—to martyr himself with a straight life. Twenty years later he found the strength to live once more for himself. His stories always ended with this new resolve, a moment in which he at last was able to swear off his burdensome obligations.

I told people, when they asked me about my expectations for Rosh Hashanah in Uman, that what I thought was going to happen—what I wanted to best-case-scenario happen—was to hear the third version of his story, the one where Micah and I found out he'd been with men all along. I wanted to hear this in part because I wanted to feel undeceived. Of course, though, there's no such thing as making yourself undeceived; I suppose I wanted the deception confirmed. Contained. Laid bare. There had always been rumors. My freshman year in high school I heard thirdhand from a classmate that my father had told someone he was gay, or maybe had been seen at a gay fund-raiser. What was worse than not knowing was that other people did somehow.

"I told Max in 1988. I went to Philadelphia on business and I stopped into his office at the thermocouple plant when I knew I only had ten minutes to talk. I told him and I walked right out before he could really respond. He didn't know what to say. He didn't say he knew all along. I think he was stunned."

"Did Max seem accepting?"

"I don't know. I didn't give him a chance to say anything. I told my mother a few months later. By then Bart was taking me out and introducing me to people, showing me around, taking me to the Roxy."

"So you and Bart were involved, then?" I tried to keep my voice even.

"No! Never. That first time I met him, over coffee, I made a pass, but he looked at me and said I was *craaaazy*, that *he'd* have to be crazy, that I had a wife and two little kids at home. He didn't want to get involved with that. So we were only ever friends, which was better anyway, because what I needed then was a friend I could talk to about things I'd never talked to anybody about."

"I want to know how you were feeling then. Did you wake up in the morning at home and look around you and think, This is not really my life?" I thought of David Byrne, *This is not my beautiful house... this is not my beautiful wife.*

"No. I wanted that life too. I wanted to be married. I loved you guys, and I loved your mother, and I know you don't believe me but I still love your mother. I never thought about doing anything differently."

"But didn't you feel regrets? Don't you feel regrets now? Wasn't it hard to live this double life?" I was baiting him a little. It seemed important to me, had seemed important to me for a long time, to know he regretted everything, he was sorry for everything, he wished it had been otherwise. I do not know how to account for this but there was some part of me that wanted to hear he regretted we'd been born.

"Gay guys compartmentalize. It's just what you have to do. No, it wasn't that hard, mostly, and I really have no regrets at all. At that point in my life I had no way to imagine anything else. In 1974 there was simply no openly gay role model in my life that might have shown me a way to live differently. And I never didn't want to be married. I never didn't want to have my family. I'd always wanted a family."

"So, what made you finally stop? What made you decide it was time to come out. Also, wait a second, what's 1974?"

"I wanted to give your mother her life back." Micah and I exchanged our long-practiced well-that's-bullshit look. The one thing we knew we were absolutely not going to talk about was our mom, because whatever he was possibly going to say was going to make us angry. "And I wanted to do something for myself. I wanted to put myself first."

"But weren't you already putting yourself first, at least half the time? In your New York life? In whatever was going on in the other compartment? Weren't you number one there?"

"I guess I wanted to put myself first *successfully*."

"And you couldn't have done that before? And you never regretted not having done that before?"

"No, really, Gideon. I am not lying to you. I couldn't and didn't."

We stood over fragments of Jewish gravestones strewn amid the clumps of dead grass. This was all a little much, the broken gravestones, the pogrom detritus. I was surprised. I'd always imagined this was going to be a conversation about his regrets, about the psychic strain of having committed to a life that didn't feel like yours, that didn't feel like what you'd wanted or chosen for yourself. I was prepared to be sympathetic to him—the volatility, the punitive tendencies, the absences—if I could hear from him that he'd been driven out of his mind by the suspicion that his real life was happening elsewhere. If he'd had two lives, I could have been at the very center of one and at the very periphery of the other, and I would have known to take only the first one personally.

But my dad was making it clear that he did not feel as though his real life had been elsewhere. I had suggested it must have been hard to have two lives, and he'd agreed, but he didn't actually have two lives. Nobody has two lives, just like nobody lives an imitation life.

He had one life, a real life, and in that one life he'd told a lot of lies and kept a lot of secrets, and it was never clear if I was—if we were— at the center or on the margin. I'd never wanted to think of him as a liar. I'd never wanted to feel like someone who could be so easily lied to. I'd wanted him to have regretted a lot of things because that might also have meant he hadn't lied about a lot of things, and if he regretted them, it meant he was acknowledging he hadn't made the best decisions—even if he continued to think of the consequences of those decisions in terms of his own life, not in terms of ours.

But I could hardly deal with his regret, either. If he was a liar, I was an idiot; but if he was regretful, Micah and I had been burdens. It would be better to admit I'd been deceived, deceived by the person in the world I most wanted to be like—the navigator who knew all the long-cut (mileage-saving, time-adding) hypotenuses on local back roads; the only parent who was willing to drive around on empty unplowed streets after a blizzard to pick up all of our friends on the way to the secret sledding hill he'd found; the former college radio DJ who'd always been so endearingly baffled by the part in "MacArthur Park" (the Donna Summer version, of course) where someone leaves a cake out in the rain; the news junkie who came to dinner with labeled manila folders for each of us, full of relevant and absurd clippings from the five daily newspapers and three weekly magazines he read; the theatergoer who loved the savagery of this John Simon guy and took me to off-off-Broadway productions in dingy Greenwich Village basements when the other suburban parents made the thirty-minute trip into New York once a year to go skating at Rockefeller Center; the rabbi who seemed so proud and calm and authoritative giving demanding High Holiday sermons in which he alluded to the lyrics of Queen and Procol Harum, who made me so proud to be the rabbi's son, progeny of moral authority, near to a moral center, even if I had so little practical knowledge of

Judaism—than to continue to feel as though my existence as the rabbi's son had thwarted his chance at having the life he deserved. I did not want to have to imagine my childhood and adolescence as an obstacle. I wanted to be able to think of his happy gay life now in terms other than contrastive freedom.

We paused under a lone shade tree and looked at a few sheared-off gravestones with Hebrew names. We picked our way over the uneven ground. Micah had grown completely quiet. He's got other issues, or maybe he doesn't have any issues at all. He doesn't remember as much as I do. He's much quicker to let go of things.

"But, Dad, wait a second." I felt as though we'd skipped something here, that whatever had actually been going on—this other life we'd started to talk about—was being acknowledged without being admitted. If he wasn't going to talk about regret, then we were going to talk about lies.

"You said that Bart was the first person you ever told you were gay. But didn't you have relationships with men before that?"

"Well, there were always physical things. Bart would take me out and I'd find gratification. After a certain point you just get tired of masturbation, you know? But there was nothing emotional, nothing serious. It was all just physical. After all, don't forget, I was married."

I hadn't forgotten. This felt so unfair. If your dad casually admits to having serially cheated on your mom for your entire childhood with other women, you have the right to be furious. If your dad casually admits to having serially cheated on your mom for your entire childhood with men, you're supposed to be sympathetic. Or I felt as though *I* had to be sympathetic. He was such a convincing martyr. I hadn't been allowed—hadn't allowed myself—to be furious for so long, because I'd believed the story of sacrifice my dad told. I wanted to feel furious now, but all I could feel was a surprising sense of gratitude. I felt as though these casual admissions had *fixed* something for me, both in the sense of repair and in the sense of the record I'd come to get, and I was somehow finally understanding where I stood in relation to him.

"No, I mean, that's interesting," I said, eager to keep this going, "but that wasn't quite what I meant. I thought once when you were visiting me in Berlin you made some comment about your first boyfriend, your first love. And a minute ago I thought you said something about 1974."

"Oh, well, that was before my marriage. That was Rocky."

My dad stopped and smiled his least melodramatic smile. The imminent unveiling of these memories made the moment seem staged, as if he'd been given a script and asked to play the part of a father overcome with nostalgia. He looked engulfed, totally convincing. I didn't know if I wanted to hear what was coming. When so much has been kept secret, it's impossible to know what you do and what you don't want to know, what ought to be shared and what might best be kept to oneself.

"I was twenty-one and in Jerusalem alone. I'd wanted to go abroad to Russia but it was hard to do that in 1974, and my plans fell through at the last minute. So I scrambled and went to Israel instead. If I'd gone to Russia, I probably would've ended up in the CIA or the State Department or something, but as it was I went to Israel and I met Rocky, and I loved Hebrew and I loved Israel and I thought, I'll just stay here and become a rabbi. Rocky was in his forties. He was an ophthalmologist. He once fitted Golda Meir for contact lenses." My dad laughed.

"Where did you guys meet?"

"At the Turkish bathhouse, which was the only thing like a gay scene in Jerusalem in the seventies. You could go and, you know, have sex with young Arab boys." I hadn't known that. Micah, I am willing to guess, hadn't known that.

"Rocky had money, and he had this great apartment, an entire floor on the fourth floor of a building on King David Street, right near the YMCA and HUC," the reform rabbinical seminary where my dad met my mom a year or two later. "He had such nice things, such beautiful furniture, wonderful rugs. Exquisite taste. I was a kid and away from home and he took care of me." My dad looked so sweet and serene as he remembered this other place, this thing it's tempting to call a previous life. We all kept stumbling on the shards of pogrom gravestones underfoot.

"When did it end?"

"I started rabbinical school the next year and met your mother and that's what I wanted then, so I broke it off with Rocky."

"And there was really no way for you to imagine living a gay life then? No role model?"

"It was unimaginable to me." I wondered why Rocky himself didn't count.

"How did he take it when you broke up with him?"

"To be honest with you, I can't remember. I hadn't made any promises to him. I was really just a kid. But then"—he paused—"I went and saw him once, years later, maybe fifteen years later, I looked him up when I was back in Jerusalem." We'd gone to Israel as a family in 1988, when I was eight and Micah was five. Micah had been run over in the street by a kid on a bike. "I can't remember what we said to each other, though."

"I'm sad that you were never able to tell us these stories. I'm sorry you weren't able to tell them to us growing up." I was a little shaky, but it was a lot easier to hear stories that predated my mom than the other ones he'd been telling. We'd gone back past the *mikveh* and were walking by a low-slung trailer soliciting donations for a "Fond Rising for the Monuments to Victims of Holohost." I wanted to hear these stories, didn't want to hear these stories, felt bad about needing to hear them, felt bad about not wanting to hear them, doubted that even this third version of his life was totally honest, angry to have to feel doubt, very sorry for my mom—sorry for my mom both because of what she went through and because it felt like a kind of betrayal to feel so good that talking to him about all this stuff made *him* feel so good.

It is nothing special that my dad had a life separate from me, or that he kept secrets; this is something all parents do—straight ones, scrupulous ones—and it's what we grapple with, to varying degrees of success, our whole lives. What's unusual about my relationship to my dad's life is not that there were things about it I didn't know because he was gay. It's that I was able to indulge the fantasy that he kept secrets only *because* he was gay, that if he had been able to be openly gay he would've shared his entire life with me and I always would have known exactly where I stood. At a certain point other people have to understand that parents keep secrets, that parents close parts of themselves off to their children, because that is what parents do.

What was I getting out of learning this now? In part, I wanted to hear him tell a story about his life in which he claimed some responsibility for the way things had turned out, rather than a story in which he was first in thrall to social mores and later in thrall to biological urges, in which the pretexts had shifted but the irresponsibility had remained. In which he'd never simply said, "I did it because I felt like it." I wanted him to be a father who provided an example of how to live a life that he could describe as more than just a series of obligations to others, a life in which he did more than just hurt others under the cover of conflicting obligations. We follow St. James to the end of the world, and follow Kōbō Daishi in his path around that horrible island, because we want to associate ourselves with their absurd decisiveness. We want to inherit from them the ability to make our own absurd decisions, even when that means taking the damn train to the karaoke party. But we also want to know that when people get hurt it's because they had to be hurt. We also want to be reassured that the eight innocent sons of Emon Saburō had to die in order for justice to reign. That the promises he made had to be broken, that he could not possibly have done what he said he was going to do.

This longing for his decisiveness helped explain my preoccupation with the history of his sexuality. There are very few examples in modern adult life of the successful instantaneous transformation, the switch that is flicked to make everything new—the fantasy of the transformative arrival in Santiago—but the example of *coming out* is one of them. Which I think is why I'd for so long kept such careful tabs on what story he was telling whom when: I wanted to nail down the moment of his coming out, with the hope that if I could pinpoint that transformation I could . . . I don't know what I could do, I would just feel better, would be able to look to him as a model of resolve. I wanted to identify the moment that he decided to live for himself despite the costs involved. I wanted to know where he stood.

I wanted him to have been able to say, "I did this because I felt like it." I wanted that example. But I didn't want him to stop saying, "I did it because I had to." I wanted that example too. It is an intolerable conflict to want your father to have been resolute and unapologetic and also need him to have not hurt you, to want to take nothing personally and everything personally.

What I was finally coming to understand here was that there was no such moment, no grand gesture of repudiation, no final grace, no scene of coming through the Wall, nothing you can do now that makes all future cost considerations fall away, no way to know what you might regret. There was just a long muddle in which he'd had terribly conflicting desires and had been doing his best to resolve them. I still do not believe he's ever reckoned with the costs—or perhaps he's reckoned with the costs *he* paid, but not the costs borne by others. But in Uman I accepted, in a way that felt new, that he had been in a crisis, and that he had also been doing what he wanted.

I'd drawn exactly the wrong lesson from his surfeit of contradictory stories. I thought it was just his standard obfuscation. But it was just his ongoing and incomplete attempt to tell a story about his life that made everything make sense.

There is no such thing as knowing, once and for all, where you stand with someone. Life has no fixed points. But pilgrimage does; that is the point. And the fixed points of a pilgrimage allow people to exist for each other in motion. There is no such thing as coming out.

In Tokyo, three months later, we'll be having a great time—a *really remarkable* time—at Thanksgiving dinner and I'll ask Brett what he thinks about the idea of coming out.

"I'm forty-eight," he'll say, "and I've been in the process of coming out for thirty years."

B ACK AT THE ROOM we sat around and relaxed from our walk and watched our other roommates—Uri, Ezi, and Shlomo— primp for the beginning of Rosh Hashanah. All three of them had grown up in very religious homes in Lakewood, a mostly Orthodox community down near the Jersey shore. It was hard to assimilate the fact that these guys were more or less my age and had grown up maybe forty minutes away from where I did. We might've driven by them on the parkway, hoped they were Amish. They'd strayed during their twenties—all three into drug and alcohol addictions—and then returned to the faith in the form of the Breslower tradition.

Uri had a long crescent of a jaw shaded with a thin beard. He had a lubricious spiel, the apostolic bustle and the nebbishy patter of the late adopter, and once he heard that it was our first time in Uman he saw his mission this Rosh Hashanah as our conversion to the faith. It was his fifth trip here. On his second trip he asked God for a wife and now he's married.

"See, the thing is," Uri said, "I grew up thinking that God was stern, that God beat you, that God disapproved, but what Reb Nachman made me understand is that God is love. God is like your father. God is like your father and he loves you and you can ask him for things. You can just talk right to him and he'll respond, because he loves you, and he wants you to come to him. That's why we have free will, so we can go to Hashem on our own."

He handed me a copy of a self-published book called *The Garden of Emuna*. "Everything you need to know is in this book right here. It'll answer all your questions. It's by a great rabbi, Rabbi Lazer Brody, who's American but he lives in Israel and he's here in Uman right now. He's incredible, blows my mind—just wait till you hear him speak, you'll just die, I'm tellin' you."

I looked down at the cover. "By Rabbi Shalom Arush," it said, "and translated from the Hebrew by Rabbi Lazer Brody."

Uri turned to Shlomo, who had a broad, relaxed 1920s low-life slouch, as though he were leaning against a gas lamp running numbers, and asked if he should wear his nice black shoes.

"I brought the nice black shoes all the way from Brooklyn but now I dunno I should wear the nice shoes. Whaddaya think, Shlomo? Do I wear the black shoes or the shoes I wore on the plane? Can I even wear these black shoes with this brown belt?"

"I'm just wearin' sneakuhs," Shlomo said, eager to get going to daven. Ezi, who had a tattoo across the width of his upper back that said ADDICTED, and whose email address indicated the length of his sobriety, was putting on his shirt. Ezi had recently moved back to Lakewood from LA, where he'd been in rehab.

"Do I wear this hat?" Uri picked up his Borsalino out of its box, smoothed the felt. "If I wear the hat, what am I going to do with it during dinner? Just, uh, put it on a bench or sumthin'?"

"You just put it right on that bench, no problem," Shlomo said.

Uri stopped futzing with his hat and took in the blood-fractal wallpaper for the first time. "Hey, that's pretty cool!"

The sun was going down and Shlomo was running out of patience. "You think that's pretty cool, Uri? You know where it'd be cool? It'd be cool in a nightclub, maybe, if you put some lights on it, maybe a disco ball. Maybe you'd like that, some lights and a disco ball. You wanna be in a nightclub right now? You wanna go to a nightclub? I bet these Ukrainians got some nightclubs."

Later I learned that the word "nightclub" was Hasidic code for "the secular life" or "Sodom." If the live option for all young Poles, according to our short-lived friend Anya on the Camino, was Catholicism versus alcoholism, the live option here was *payos* versus nightclubs. A young Hasid told me that he felt at home in the Breslower tradition because it let you think outside the box. "Like, these things?" he wound and then unfurled his *payos*. "Other people wear them, and they just do it because they're told to. They don't think outside the box." I asked him why he wore them, then. "I got them for a reason. They look silly to the world of men, so they define what I can and can't do, like go into a nightclub. You think I could get into a nightclub with these guys? Pshaw."

"And what about a tie?" Uri again, experiencing real sartorial *tsuris*. "Do I wear a tie? Are you guys wearin' ties? I can't decide I wanna wear a tie or not."

My dad had been observing the whole scene with delight. "This is like watching *The Real Hasids of New Jersey*." Everybody laughed.

Ari, the heavyset guy who'd told us that every year somebody gets whacked, then got whacked himself by the shower, pottered in from his private room in the back and weighed in on the tie issue. He was tired of waiting, though, and said he was going to daven with his brother and would catch us at dinner in Yossi's tent.

Finally Uri had his hat on, no tie, and was ready. "Okay, we're going to daven now, you guys, down at the Tzion. You guys wanna come daven with us? It'll be good there, lots of good energy for the first night down by Reb Nachman's grave. You'll love it. Best place to start, where I started myself. Then we'll go daven elsewhere, maybe hit up the *kloiz* or this other little spot I know about. You guys should come let us take you around."

We left and walked past some displaced Ukrainians. Shlomo paused for a moment to check the tilt of his Borsalino in the tinted window of a late-model Lada.

We walked down through dusty Rehov Pushkina, where the Ukrainian schlock souk was reluctantly closing down for the holiday. Shlomo knew a shortcut between two of the tower blocks, their crumbling tiled facades glowing a pale copper in the crepuscular light, and we approached the Tzion from the back just as the sun fell below the horizon. Right away a bunch of guys grabbed Uri and Shlomo for a minyan, the ten adult men you need to begin to pray, and we stood back as they davened. The whole rickety building swayed with people. We stood outside, unsure of where to go or what to do. Under a large awning to our left rotund Hasids stood on benches and chanted "NA NACH NACHMA NACHMAN M'UMAN" over and over, louder each time until the tent trembled with a terrific din and the men here assembled were frothy and ex-ultant with mantric insistence. The three of us decided we'd try to get into the building itself. A Hasid in a wheelchair rolled over Micah's foot. Inside, Hasids literally bounced off the walls, climbed the columns and shimmied along beams, hung upside down from the ceiling, swayed and shoved and hollered song.

The yellowy ghost rabbi from the day before, with the flaming gray beard and the sandalwood skin, stood on a raised platform conducting the chants. One chant would start—"RABBI NACHMAN AYN KAMOCHA BA'OLAM"—and he'd let it lather up through a few dozen repetitions of increasing fervor, then put out his arm and wave his hand up and down while yelling "SHEKET SHEKET KULAM—SHUT UP, EVERYBODY"—and then as the crowd began to quiet he would point to one of the men in the overfull monkey house and that man would propose the next chant, which the rabbi would then begin to lead. Micah turned and yelled into my ear, "Man, the Knicks need to get a crowd like this."

The crowd started to chant a line I actually knew and liked, from long ago, a quote attributed to Nachman himself. "KOL HA'OLAM KULO GESHER TZAR ME'OD, VEHAI'IKAR LO LEFACHED KLAL." All the world is a very narrow bridge, and the most important thing is not to be afraid.

M ICAH WORRIED WE WERE GOING to die in a fire or stampede, so we fought our way to the exit; under the awning outside, Hasids alone or in pairs were taking breaks from davening to smoke. We hadn't known you were allowed to smoke on *yuntif*, so we asked Uri, who'd just finished davening here and was trying to assess where the davening was going to be good next. He wanted to make sure he davened at all the best spots, so he was a little distracted, but he said you were allowed to smoke on *yuntif* as long as you didn't light a match; it was kosher if you lit your own cigarette with the cigarette of another. (The original cigarette had to be lit by a Ukrainian.) They had to keep smoking so the fire wouldn't go out. I seemed to recall the image had been used in that novel where the

Ukrainian guy funny-talked like a foreigner while he took the Jew around to think hard about the "Victims of Holohost."

Uri waved us over and said he'd gotten a good tip and we had to leave. On the way to the *kloiz* he kept up the hard sell.

"What I forgot to tell you guys before is that even if you don't know the prayers, you should just talk to God in your own language. That's what God likes best, when you do that. I know it seems silly. But just talk to him. Sing to your father. He's your father and he loves you."

He turned to our actual father. "Look, what makes you happiest in the world? Isn't it when your boys"—he gestured helpfully to us— "come to you and say, Dad, we love you, and we're grateful to you. Thanks for everything you've done for us, we'll do anything for you." Our dad nodded.

"And wouldn't that make you want to do anything in the world for them? If they told you about their love and their gratitude?"

The three of us stopped and looked at each other. I wondered whether I should tell him, right then, of my love and gratitude.

But Uri kept going. "Or imagine you had two employees, one who complained all the time and the other who did whatever you asked with a smile. Wouldn't you like the second one better?" God had gone from being a father to a small-business owner. "It's all in Rabbi Lazer Brody's book, the book I gave you, you gotta read it."

We got to the *kloiz* just as the reportedly good davening was ending. "I know a great little place," Uri said. "Keep following me." Shlomo and Ezi trailed behind a bit. "What's your issue, man? What don't you get?"

"Look, I can't say I know too much about Jewish prayer—much less than I should, for sure—but I just never thought that it was about the hope for miraculous intercession," I said.

"It's whatever you want it to be, Gideon, just like your father. Sometimes you ask for something and your father doesn't give it to you, but he has his reasons. You have to trust that Hashem"—literally, "the name," or what religious Jews call God—"knows what's best, and that he's looking out for you, and that everything he does is for a reason. You just need to show him your love and trust."

"Got it. But how, then, do you handle the problem of theodicy?"

"Theodicy? Wassat?"

"You know, like, the existence of evil in a world putatively created by a just and omnipotent God."

"Whaddaya mean?"

"Well, uh." I waved over toward the mass grave we'd been walking around on all day.

"Oh, like the Holocaust and pogroms and stuff? Let me explain it to you." He went on, at great length, to not provide a satisfactory account of the existence of evil in a divinely created world. We got to the next spot to daven and they didn't have the required ten men for a minyan, so then they led us back down an alley and then behind the food tent to where Yossi's group was praying. We traipsed through a little mint patch on our way to the back of the building. We stood as they all davened mintily, then went off to dinner.

NOBODY IN THE TENT WANTED to sit with us at dinner. We were the only people in civilian clothes; we might as well have been invisible. Even heavyset Ari, who'd been so friendly back in the tower block, got up to switch tables when we sat down. He said we shouldn't take it personally, but he remembered he'd promised to sit with this guy he knew from back in Flatbush. We said it was okay. We didn't really care to sit with anybody else, anyway.

Yossi got up and gave a long speech about "vitility," but the hungry and rambunctious Hasids made a show of not listening. In his brushed-aluminum suit and pink shirt, Yossi looked almost as out of place as we did. We set to eating, gefilte fish and beet-red horseradish and challah with hummus. The Hasids who'd been forced to share our table didn't look at us as they passed the dishes. We scanned the room.

A scrubbed redhead with an auburn beard and a lily-white *kittel* came over and introduced himself as Ace, held his hands behind his back, and leaned in close. His eyes had the same amber light as the messianic Israeli at the mass grave, but he was amiable and clean and charismatic, and nobody else was talking to us. A quiet boy in a black suit stood at his elbow, also with his hands held behind his back. Ace said he lived near Monsey, New York, and ran a drug and alcohol counseling program for troubled youths. He paused to caress his *payos*, which were long and streaming and arrested in luxurious curl with some Hasidic brilliantine.

"I don't look like such a weirdo in real life!" he said. "In real life I go around in secret." He tucked the *payos* up underneath his yarmulke, where we were supposed to pretend they'd been successfully disappeared.

"I've got four kids at home, including a two-week-old! My wife had a baby two weeks ago."

"Mazel tov," we said.

"Thanks. It's hard to leave my wife with a newborn and three other kids—all of them under the age of seven—but I tell my wife I come here to pray for the family for the year, so she can't complain. It's for the good of everybody, and it gives me a chance to get away." He winked, smoothed out his *kittel*.

"I love meeting new people here and introducing them to everybody, so come find me later on and I'll show you around, find you some cool people to talk to. Rabbi Lazer Brody, he wrote this great book, and he's talking tomorrow. I'll come find you for that." Translated, I thought. Jesus.

We'd had more than enough vacationing-proselyte Hasid for the moment, so we got up after the fish and before the soup and went off on our own. We'd had a draining day, and were happy to wander around while everybody else was inside eating. We found an open room with sweet tea on brass taps and I began to relax for the first time. It was quiet and mellow, and the three of us seemed at ease.

We went to sleep while the others were still out, at dinner or whatever went on after dinner. We'd heard there was a lot of drinking, which was interesting, because we'd also heard half the people here were recovering alcoholics. Micah mummified himself in the lone blanket again. At one thirty in the morning we woke to the sounds of the others fruitlessly spinning the medieval key in the disengaged lock, then pounding on the heavy wooden door. Micah got up and let them in with a gruff good night. Then they couldn't figure out how to relock the door behind them, so we got up and pushed them aside to do it. The door relocked but then the key wouldn't budge; they'd busted the lock somehow in spinning it from the other side. All of this was happening in the dark, of course, since we couldn't turn on any lights. One lone candle, lit before *yuntif* in case we needed to light the stove, shone from the kitchen. I wished Brett had come along as a Shabbos gay.

We tried for twenty minutes, but the lock was irreparably broken and we were stuck inside. Uri and Ezi had brought a friend home and he had to go jump off the balcony, about a ten-foot drop into an unlit courtyard. Ari started to get pretty freaked out, as he could barely fit through even a standard unlocked door and was terrified he'd die in a fire.

"If you think you're going to die in a fire," Micah said, exasperated, "you should let me put the candle out!"

"No, you can't do that, not allowed."

"I'm a Reform Jew, Ari, and I don't care."

"Yeah, but I care, and you can't do that."

"Go to bed, Ari, and we'll figure this out in the morning. We'll get a Ukrainian to call the landlord and they'll come and fix the lock and get us out."

"If there's a fire, I'm not going to make it out alive, you guys."

"Go to bed, Ari," Micah said. Uri and Ezi and Shlomo were already snoring.

IN THE MORNING SHLOMO, Uri, and Ezi got up, put on their hats, and jumped off the balcony to go daven. We weren't in a rush to do anything, so we sat around and tried to figure out what to do about the lock. Somebody finally managed to get hold of a Ukrainian who could fix it, but it was going to take a few hours for him to show up. Ari was dejected, all tricked out in a Jewish-newsie cap and a new white embroidered shirt for the holiday. He'd come thousands of miles to celebrate Rosh Hashanah in Uman and now he was a prisoner in a sublet Soviet tower block. And there was still that lit candle in the kitchen. He wasn't complaining, though.

"You guys just go on ahead, and Hashem will be okay if I just celebrate the holiday here by myself." We offered to find a minyan for him and bring everybody back, but he said we shouldn't worry, that he didn't want to ruin anybody else's holiday. He just hoped the lock would be fixed in time for him to hear the shofar blast that rings in the new year, or at the very least to get down to the lake in time for tashlikh, which he'd been talking about nonstop for two days.

The three of us went back to the coffee-tent riot and checked our email on our phones in the porta-potties—somebody had forgotten to turn the wireless off, or maybe had left it on deliberately—where

I also camped out for a little while in the kasha stink, trying to remember all the stuff I'd wanted to write down in my notebook. When
I emerged from the porta-potty there was a line and I think the
queued Hasids knew I'd been jotting. My dad found a couple of taste-
less slabs of nondairy holiday marble cake and said he wanted to take
them back to Ari so he had something to eat. It was a really nice
thought, exactly the sort of thing—on a small scale—that made him
such an attentive and comforting rabbi to congregants in need. It's
also exactly the sort of thing that later causes him to wonder where
all of his time for himself has gone.

Back at the crib we yelled through the front window to Ari, who
padded over to the ledge to accept the cake slabs through the window. Then we went around back to climb up through the balcony.
There were three Ukrainian cops crashed out in a patrol car to make
sure nobody broke in while the lock was busted, and my dad chatted
briefly with them in Russian; they looked at the way we were dressed
and asked if we were tourists.

"Are we tourists?" my dad asked.

"Oh, come on, don't get him started on this," Micah said, turning
to me. "The whole thing about a *pilgrim* is that he's not a *tourist* blah
blah blah."

I turned toward the little jerk. "First of all, we are *definitely* tourists here. Second of all, I think that by this point I don't buy that
distinction anymore." I'd had the notion that a tourist goes off in
search of diversion, while a pilgrim is after something *serious*. But we
weren't really there to engage with the actual pilgrimage so much,
which meant there wasn't really a way to describe us but as tourists,
but we were still there after something serious. Plenty of pilgrims
are just after diversion, and plenty of tourists are after something
serious, and sometimes when you think you're after diversion you're
after something serious, and sometimes something you saw as a di-

version at the time ends up feeling serious later, and vice versa in all those cases. I was just flattering myself when I used to defend the pilgrim against the charge of tourism.

Neither my dad nor Micah was listening anymore. We climbed hand over hand up the jagged bricks and in through the window to Ari's room. Ari, despite his faith that Hashem knew what he was doing in breaking the lock, was bummed out. It was getting on toward noon and it looked as though he was going to miss the sound of the shofar.

Micah asked if maybe there was a way we could get Ari down off the balcony but I couldn't see how it would ever work. First he'd have to climb up and out of a waist-high window, then jump down from a ten-foot ledge, and this was a person who has his work cut out for him strolling down an empty corridor.

My dad agreed with Micah. "Ari," he yelled from the ground below the balcony, "come here and we're going to get you out."

Ari thanked him in a still, small voice from inside but said he didn't think he could.

Micah stood on the balcony and leaned over the lip of the window. "Come on, Ari," he said. "We can help you do this."

The idea of hoisting himself out a window and then jumping off a balcony terrified him, but his burning desire to hear the shofar—and, furthermore, not die in a *yuntif*-candle fire—was enough to drive him to try. We found a few crates of curling Ukrainian Christmas-themed wallpaper for him to stand on as he lifted one haunch, then the other, up onto the narrow sill. The crates bowed but didn't break, and I braced him from behind as Micah caught his feet and helped him swing them over, then leaned into his hip as he eased Ari down onto the tar-paper balcony. Ari looked down to see how far it was to the ground, looked up again immediately, and drew the back of his hand against his forehead.

He was committed now, mostly because it was going to be just as hard to retreat back inside through the window. My dad and I jumped down first, falling to our hands as we landed in unison, and turned toward the wall. The Ukrainian cops looked up from their watchful naps, elbowed each other, picked up their phones. Micah stood in front of Ari on the balcony and held his upper arms as he turned around; we stood on the ground below and each leaned in to shoulder a hindquarter. The Ukrainian cops were practically selling tickets. One of them had his camera out and was leaping around like a paparazzo. The other guy was on his phone, probably giving a play-by-play on Ukrainian radio. Three tourists in jeans and sweatshirts and tiny yarmulkes helping to lower a husky Hasid in a white caftan from the crumbling balcony of a tower block.

Micah began to lose control from above and Ari started to fall; we pressed hard with our shoulders up against his bulk until the last minute, when we jumped out of the way just in time for Ari to land on the ground in a great cloud of dust. He patted himself down to make sure nothing was broken, then looked up to see what he'd done. He broke into a wide smile.

"I can't believe you guys! What mensches. Shucks. You saved my Rosh Hashanah! Everybody else was going to just leave me here, all those other guys off davening, and you came back and brought me marble cake and helped me jump off a balcony. I never ever jumped off a balcony before." He enfolded the three of us in a massive and awkward hug, and we all clapped him on the back a few times.

"I think Hashem brought you guys here to Uman so that you could help get me out of that apartment so that I could hear the sound of the shofar that rings in the new year." He waddled off so he wouldn't miss it, and the three of us stood around with the hysterical Ukrainian cops to bask in the experience.

We walked back out past the barricade to the car to pick up our leftover salami en route to Uman's Sofia Park, its lone tourist destination. I turned to Micah and my dad. "I know I must sound like a crazy person saying this, but it's kinda hard not to feel somewhat as though Ari was right, that we were brought here to make sure he could hear the sound of the shofar." They were quick to agree but we left it at that. It was also hard not to feel grateful to Ari for allowing the three of us a break from thinking about ourselves and each other.

We stopped back into the non-kosher mini-mart to buy something to drink with our salami. Micah and my dad, who share a taste for the bizarre and disgusting exotic juices of the world, settled on a green apple–starfruit blend that proved, as I predicted, undrinkable. They drank it anyway, taunting me with sips. We stood by the car near the police barricade, on the border of the temporary ghetto, eating the last of our Ukrainian salami, and heard, in a stagger from all directions, the long, wild trumpet announcement that a new year was at hand.

JUST INSIDE THE ENTRANCE TO the park there was a little medieval-style Ukrainian coach with a peacock, a monkey, and an old petted-out shar-pei chained to a NA NACH NACHMA banner; you could take your picture with the coach and the animals for ten or twenty Ukrainian hryvnias. There was also a little extended golf cart you could hire to take you around, and my dad was pretty sure the driver was checking him out. We walked along a little river sickly abloom with lime algae and noticed a guy we'd seen leaving the ghetto behind us; he'd taken his yarmulke off just as we had, before we stopped off for the gross juice and car-warmed salami. My dad said he thought we were in the cruising part of the park and I asked him how he figured. First he pointed to the guy who followed us out of the ghetto, and then he pointed to the one other guy visible anywhere. He was sitting alone on a bench unconcernedly reading a newspaper.

"Unless you think," Micah said, "that *every* part of *any* park is the cruising part, I don't buy it. I think there's a much better chance the guy behind us is a Mossad agent. I mean, we stand out among the Hasids, and we keep sneaking off to spend long periods of time in porta-potties, and we go to the car to eat pork. Also, Ari told us that the place was crawling with Mossad to make sure we wouldn't get whacked." The Mossad agent kept turning up in front of us as we came around corners.

At seven a.m. New Jersey time our dad wandered off to call Brett and wake him up—Brett has a hard time getting out of bed—and Micah and I got our first hasty chance to talk alone.

"I was pretty happy with that conversation yesterday," I said. "I mean, we found out a lot of stuff we'd never known before, and the whole thing seemed to make him so happy, and I know some of it was bullshit but I think most of it was honest, or at least honest as he truly sees it. What'd you think?"

Micah's brow furrowed a little bit and he looked for a second like our dad. "I don't know. I guess I was partially surprised and partially satisfied, but there was so much he said, about Max and Bubbe's divorce and stuff, that I don't believe. There are all these real issues that he pretends don't exist, or he pretends they only have to do with his being gay, when that isn't the case at all. And then he really lamed out when I asked him about the problems we'd had with him over the past few years, and all he had to say was that one line about how he takes full responsibility for everything that went wrong, but then couldn't even remember what had actually happened or why we'd ever been angry." Micah had pressed him, but all he'd been able to say was "I'm really sorry, but I think some of that stuff was so painful that I really just blacked it out."

Micah finished: "I think I wanted a little more from him than that. I mean, I believe him that he just blacks that stuff out—I think it's how he's always dealt with things—but it was hard to feel good about his taking responsibility when he couldn't even remember what he'd done to hurt us."

In the past I'd been the one to get angry and Micah had been the one to get sad, and one time our mom said that sometimes she'd wished I'd allow myself to get more sad and Micah would allow himself to get more angry. Micah didn't seem angry, exactly, now, but he did seem a little steeled, and I was feeling soft. Micah could tell. He could also tell that I was feeling soft in a way that seemed self-satisfied and risky.

"Your problem"—he corrected himself—"*one* of your problems, is that your hopes and expectations are consistently unreasonable. You think there's going to be one moment where everything is finally going to be okay, once and for all. I know you had this idea that we would come here to Uman for Rosh Hashanah and we'd have all these conversations and finally learn the truth about his life, and that he'd finally admit his deceptions and apologize for them. Or maybe he'd admit he had regrets and it would help us better sympathize with him in a way that would make the issue of forgiveness moot. Or maybe that you'd finally be able to figure out the exact moment where he betrayed himself so that you could, I don't know, allow him to be a real father again but this time by counterexample or something. And what happened? He did admit a lot of his deceptions but it didn't even really occur to him to stop and say, 'Oh, and sorry about those twenty years of lying and sneaking around.' Not only that, he went so far as to say he didn't have any regrets about any of it at all.

"What I find sorta weird is that you don't seem to recognize how contradictory your impulses are. On the one hand, of course you don't want to hear that he regretted having a family, but on the other hand there's some part of you that came here to hear he regretted everything. It's, like, you have this idea about his life where if only he'd done the honest, courageous thing and come out when he was our age or whatever, he would have been so happy and never would have been resentful and never would have caused all this pain for Mom or for us or for Max. *But we wouldn't even be around then.* You seem to forget that somehow, or maybe even want it. You kept pushing him to say that he regretted having us because you want to trace everything to one mistake he made one time that messed everything up afterward. But you know what? *He's happy now.* That was the bottom line of everything he said yesterday. *He's happy now.* Period. Nothing got messed up, at least for him. He got everything he wanted. He had a family, and he had us, and now he has Brett and he has Yoshi. He *won*.

"I don't think you're admitting to yourself that a big part of all of this for you is just justifying your own choices. You tell yourself that he made this one big mistake that you're not going to make, and then you use that as an excuse to do whatever you feel like all the time. Or it's like you have this idea that if you do your penance in advance, you'll then deserve to be happy later. You think to yourself, Okay, if I'm restless and all over the place now, and if I go on these long, punishing quests, I'll deserve to have some feeling of purpose bestowed on me afterward, I'll really deserve whatever I end up choosing when I leave Santiago, and it doesn't matter whom I'm abandoning or whose life I'm fucking with—like that girl in Shanghai—because I have this attitude that nothing right now matters as much as making sure I'm not regretful in the future, that I'm living a life that connects all the future points in a predictable way. But you can never know what you'll regret in the future, and you'll still find a way to connect the unpredictable points. It seems like putting everything in terms of fear of regret—of your fifty-year-old self—is just a way to evade responsibility for the decisions your thirty-year-old self has to deal with. You have this fantasy of having a fixed quantity of restlessness inside you that you can use up somehow for the sake of the future, instead of accepting that the restlessness just means you're having a hard time right now. Or, to put it slightly differently, having a *great* time right now. I mean, you like to complain about how adrift you felt living in Berlin, but I can tell by the way you talk about it, especially now that you haven't been there in a while, that you loved your life there."

What he was saying was that all of it had been real. A lot of it had been hard and a lot of it had been great but it had all been equally real, and the stories we tell in retrospect rarely resemble the stories we hope we might tell one day.

THE MOSSAD AGENT FOLLOWED US back to the ghetto for lunch. Toward the end of the meal, Ace, the guy who thought he was able to hide his yards of *payos* underneath his yarmulke, came back over to rap at us some more.

"I work with these kids with histories of drug and alcohol abuse and I'm always like, 'Look, if a guy invites you over to his house for Shabbos dinner, you can't leave a line of coke on his bathroom sink.'" What addict was in the habit of leaving lines of coke around for the serendipitous pleasure of the next bathroom visitor? Maybe that was beside the point.

"What we need to understand in the period between Rosh Hashanah and Yom Kippur is that God gives us the gift of forgetting," Ace went on. "I love to think about the story of the parting of the Red Sea. God parted the Red Sea for the Israelites to pass through, but then he brought the waters back together again, and the Torah says the waters were calm, as if they had never been disturbed. That's what God can do. He can make the waters calm."

"But those calm waters were full of dead Egyptians," Micah said. Tom had said something about dead Egyptians once. Dead Egyptians seemed to be popping up a lot.

Ace wasn't interested in dead Egyptians. "Okay, well, the other way to think of it is in terms of inspiration. Inspiring things happen in life, and it's our job to try to remember what that inspiration was like, to try to take it with us. So, like in the Red Sea example, there was this major thing that God did in parting those waters, and then he closed them up again. There was a great, inspiring moment and then the inspiration went away, and you couldn't even tell it had happened, and it's up to us to have a seder every year to remind ourselves about that moment even when we feel uninspired."

My dad, who hadn't been listening, now leaned over to say, "Ace, I'd like to ask you a question, but you don't have to answer it if it makes you uncomfortable."

"My friend, I deal with teens who are addicted to drugs and to alcohol: nothing you say will make me uncomfortable."

"Is there some kind of underground, uh"—my dad assumed his side-mouth stage whisper—"gay scene here?"

The color drained from Ace's cheeks, down the ruddy spouts of his *payos*. "That's not something I'd know about."

He looked away, composed himself, came back on message. "Rabbi Lazer Brody, he wrote this book—"

"*Translated* this book," I said.

"What?" Ace asked.

"The book you're about to tell us about, *The Garden of Emuna*. Rabbi Lazer Brody *translated* it, okay? He didn't write it."

"Yeah, sure, wrote, translated, whatever. Anyway, he's talking in a little while, and you should go hear him." It was a good time to take a break, anyway. We were getting on one another's nerves. Micah and I had had a twenty-five-minute argument about whether it makes sense to call the Hasids "rude." He said they were boorish and I said they just had a shoving-based etiquette.

"I'll bring my pal Avi over to bring you to the talk. Hold on a sec."

My dad had wandered off and we saw him by the main tent flap, talking to Shlomo and another young guy. A few minutes later he came back and stage-whispered that he'd just come out to Shlomo.

"We were talking to Shlomo's friend over there, and he asked if I was married, and I said that I'd been married for twenty-four years"—an overstatement of a mere fifteen percent—"and he looked at me and said, 'And what's the guy's name?' I smiled and said, 'His name is Brett.' Shlomo looked astonished. Shlomo's friend looked over at Shlomo and said, 'I'm glad I don't gotta sleep in a room with this guy!' And I said to him, 'Don't worry, you're not my type.' And he said, 'Who's your type?' I said, 'Shlomo.' Shlomo turned red but then gave me a hug. It was really, really remarkable. Shlomo and I have become pretty good friends at this point." He went off to the porta-potty to call Brett.

"So you think that was true or what?" I asked Micah.

"Who knows? I got no idea. Maybe, maybe not. Certainly could be. I think he's just trying to tell us he feels comfortable."

ACE BROUGHT AVI OVER and we set out to hear celebrated translator Rabbi Lazer Brody. My dad was still in the porta-potty on the phone with Brett but Micah and I agreed that they'd go nap at the apartment and meet me back at Scheiner at six to walk down to tashlikh together. We'd decided that we'd had enough here and would skip town first thing in the morning.

Avi was twenty-five and lived with his parents in Queens and

was in some sort of health-care-device trade; most of the people we
met were peddlers of one thing or another, tiles or real estate. He was
wearing a sumptuous eggshell-and-cerulean caftan and didn't have
payos. He asked me what I was doing here and I said I was interested
in the varieties of the pilgrimage experience.

"There are other pilgrimages?"

"Yeah, sure, tons."

"Other Jewish ones?"

"Not so many, actually. There hasn't really been a Jewish pilgrimage tradition since the destruction of the Second Temple,
though there are sites in the Maghreb where Jews go to pray at the
tombs of famous rabbis, like here. Maybe it's because pilgrimage has
largely been for sedentary people, so the Jews of the Diaspora didn't
have much use for it. The last thing they needed was yet another
reason to keep moving."

"So you went on other pilgrimages, like for other religions?" I
nodded. "Like what?"

"Well, it all started when my friend Tom dragged me on this one
medieval walk across Spain, which dates back a thousand years and
has become really popular with a secular crowd over the last few
decades."

"Why's that?"

"There are a lot of reasons, and that's part of what this book is
about, figuring out what it means to want to make a pilgrimage, and
then what it feels like to be on it, and what it does and doesn't do to
your life afterward, but it all has something to do with leaving your
home, leaving comfort and responsibility behind, and putting yourself and your usual desires aside to concentrate on doing this difficult,
painful trip that a lot of other people have done for a long time, and
to be in the company of other sufferers who are doing it now. While

you're on it, everything feels so simple, even if you're in pain, and you make these instant friendships based on a shared sense of need and vulnerability, and it's a sense of need and vulnerability that are beyond explaining—there's no real need to be able to say why you hurt or why you're doing it, you just sort of trust that everyone is doing it for some reason or another and that's enough." It occurred to me it was strange that I'd brought my father to do exactly that—to explain himself—and what he'd ended up showing me was that these explanations are always evolving. "Anyway, it's kinda hard to put it in a brief way."

Avi thought for a second. "So what you're saying is, like, it's become a thing, and now it's a thing. Like, a thing people do."

"Yes, that's precisely it. It's become a thing, and now it's a thing people do."

"Sounds fun."

"Yeah, it is."

We walked down one of the ghetto alleys to a four-story brick building guarded by another Ukrainian commando. Avi flashed an entry pass. "Rabbi Lazer Brody runs a pretty exclusive compound over here. You're lucky you're with me, to get you in. It's not for everybody."

"What's so special about him?"

"He gives practical advice, like advice about daily life. It's what I think this religion needs: a dose of practicality. It's good for everybody, his teachings. Soldiers, real estate people, businessmen, women. He shows how it's all in the Torah, from agriculture to the internet. He teaches about *emunah*, faith, and how everything happens for a reason, for Hashem's reason."

We ran into somebody Avi knew, a guy named Steve who was the most seam-burstingly closeted guy I'd met so far in Uman. He'd been walking around all day getting *bruchos*, rabbinical blessings, and had just had his palm read by a famous sage. Avi asked him what the palm reader had said.

"He looked at my hand and said I had a good business future but that the most important thing for me was that I get married right away. He said it didn't even matter who the girl was. He said, 'Don't worry about finding a beautiful or intelligent wife, just go back to Crown Heights and get married as soon as you possibly can.'" We went inside to hear the rabbi talk.

Rabbi Lazer Brody sat at the front of the room looking like a mean Chagall dude, the kind who floats above the room with his neck crooked, with rough-cut cheekbones and skin a burnt sienna and eyes black with holy smolder behind floating cascades of shimmering *payos*. There was very little worth reporting about his talk, which was an ad hoc mixture of hucksterism, self-promotional rabbinic geneal-ogy, inane sports analogies, casual misogyny, scatological humor, and militant Israeli politics. It was like watching Avigdor Lieberman and Rick Warren do a Bobby McFerrin duet. I tried to pay attention until he said that he'd successfully sold fifty thousand copies of *The Garden of Emuna* to the IDF and made sure they were in all Israeli tanks, so the next Lebanon war would be a little different. I began looking around and came to the conclusion that the thing about *payos* was that they were a very silly haircut that took a long time to grow, so it was an easy sort of status symbol to define a hierarchy. I briefly made the mistake of trying to pay attention again and now he was recommend-ing the men never talk to their wives about spirituality but instead give them a copy of his book *Women's Wisdom*.

There was a lot of stuff about God the father, about how God the father shows his love for you by withdrawing his presence from you, the way a father takes steps back as his toddler learns to walk. But God the father will never actually desert you, and if he's taking those steps back it's so you can come to him of your own free will, so you can walk into his arms, but if you fall en route he'll catch you, because he would never let anything bad happen to you. It's like, when you have a bad business deal, and you're so upset, it's just that you don't understand that Hashem has his purposes and everything will be okay in the end. A woman had breast cancer and she bought a hundred of his CDs and gave them out in her town and when she went back to the doctor they couldn't find the tumor anymore. A Jew is not a Jew if he's not smiling.

It was a mixture of inoffensive pedestrian self-help alongside some bad, pernicious stuff, and I didn't want to have anything to do with it, but with all this talk about Hashem's purposes and the mysterious ways of God, I kept thinking back to the sense we'd all had that morning of having been put in Uman in order to help spring Ari from his tower-block captivity, and how warm it made us feel to do that, but beyond that, how much better it was to enjoy, with as much arrogance as humility, the idea that we'd been *put here* to do it. It gave an otherwise kind of trivial series of events, in a place we never actually wanted to be, the glamour and reason of destiny, and it made the whole trip glow with sense and importance. It made us feel both active (*we* had been elected for this purpose) and acted upon (we had been *elected* for this purpose).

We all want and need opportunities to feel this way, to feel as though everything has been willed and purposeful and would be so willed again, ways to feel as though our lives are out of our personal control yet also special, designed to work out for the best. Some of us believe what a militant flimflamming lunatic like translator Rabbi Lazer Brody tells us, which is that everything—pain, difficulty, sadness, failure—makes sense according to some secret divine tabulation we can never know, that all of this is for the best according to some perspective that obtains outside of history and individual desire. On this account, we need to do whatever we can to gain the grace of that divinity, and not everyone can be chosen—like, say, gay people. Sins make sense because they divide the deserving from the dismissed, and they present you with a choice: they allow you to return to God of your own volition. That is what being in Uman is about, a people in history coming together to remind itself through the rehearsal of its ritual tradition that after sadness and tragedy and sin there is comfort and continuity, that you can go down to the lake for tashlikh and take your sins from your pocket and toss them away and try harder next year to live up to the image of God.

The secular inheritance of pilgrimages such as the Camino and Shikoku suggest another option. They promise coherence not from the perspective of the infinite but from the finite. You've allowed for the fact from the beginning that at times it will be difficult and painful, but it is all part of the process. The meaning of the experience itself can be sorted out later, or indefinitely deferred. But, in the moment: My heel is coming apart and two toenails have fallen off *but it's all part of this experience.* I had to break into a mountain temple and sleep in the freezing terror of the dark *but that's what makes this journey what it is.* When you get to the end and look back with the thrill of triumph, the fact of having simply endured, you can no longer imagine anything having happened in even a slightly different way. I hated ninety percent of my hours on Shikoku and still, in the end, couldn't help feeling glad I'd done it.

By pilgrimage's end, all of the pain and all of the misery are granted their place in the retrospective order of things. This, I think, is what Nietzsche meant when he wrote of the eternal return: the sense of confident resignation that says, right now, no matter how bad things have been, I have endured and am enduring, and thus could not ask for anything to have been different. It's what Camus meant when he said we had to imagine that Sisyphus was happy, or maybe how Dorothea Brooke seems to feel at the end of *Middlemarch*. The difference is in the source of authority. In Uman, we are told by divine decree this has all been worth it. On the Camino, you're the only authority by which things can be made to make sense. As Rilke wrote, "Temples are no longer known. It is we who secretly save up / these extravagances of the heart."

But the thing about this sense of order is that it's provisional, this sense of coherence that it's evanescent. This makes it a bounded experiment in the *as if*, a few weeks of coming to terms with difficulty and disappointment—and *cost*—in terms of their necessary existence. It's a vacation to a land where life has meaning—the meaning of moving forward, of getting to Santiago—and things, in the broadest sense of the term, make sense, in the broadest sense of the term. Its fixed points allow you to deal with the fact that everyone is in motion.

It's so easy to feel this way on the road *because* it's provisional. This is its strength and its limitation. It is to be used and discarded. Its remove from the past, from conflict, from real life affords you the chance to form relationships with wonderful people from whom you expect nothing, whom you begrudge nothing, whom you owe nothing, people who haven't ever had the chance to hurt you, and probably won't, and if they do or you do you just walk away, you stay in motion. The stakes of *communitas* are low because everything is taking place in the present. The grace comes easy. And the sense of coherence that seemed so vital and inalienable while you were on the Camino, the sense that you're simply spending your hours the way you're spending them and, for the moment, not worrying too much about the costs, disperses into the air like incense the moment you're no longer on the way.

But a life cannot be lived, at least by most people, walking up and down the Camino, or walking the circuit of Shikoku until death.

The real trick, then, is to find some way to recall these feelings of grace and coherence and meaning and forgiveness—for what we gain with this coherence is the ability to forgive, ourselves and others—when the *as if* has run its course, when Santiago is achieved and you are returned to a world where all is conflict and nothing makes itself plain to us, where there is no hope for miraculous intercession and the people you love most will hurt and disappoint you and you, in turn, will hurt and disappoint them. Where the ground is shifting and we rarely know where we stand. And where often your own fantasy of fixity—as had happened with the girl in Shanghai—will doom you to feel ever more unstable. If you're able to believe that there is a God and that God acts in the world, if it has never occurred to you that this makes theodicy a problem, if you have that true gift that is faith, you ought to count yourself inordinately blessed. For the rest of us, there is one Camino or another, and then, perhaps more important, there is the memory of that Camino. These are brief encounters with radical acceptance that we do our best to secretly save up in our hearts.

IN UMAN, THOUGH, there is no injunction to be present. Unlike the Camino or Shikoku, which take place outside of time, this pilgrimage exists in all times at once: the present and the past and a hint of the messianic future have been made simultaneous. The past has been invited to dwell in the present as the Hasids invite the redemption of the future; the community that comes together here attempts to reckon as one with the traumas of the past as they await redemption. Thus the Jews at Uman have made a custom of performing tashlikh, the emptying of one's sins from one's pockets and the act of tossing them away into a swift current, here where the water ran red with the blood of thirty thousand Jews. I'd thought from the beginning that part of what makes this whole experience so moving for the pilgrims is that it takes place in the courtyard of the murderers, that it affirms the strength of Jewish life in a place of centuries of hostility. "Every year somebody gets whacked," Ari said, and there was something about that that made him proud.

But when we got to tashlikh it seemed as though it was more than just waving the continuity of Jewish tradition in the face of some rural Ukrainians, people no more anti-Semitic than your average French intellectual. It's far broader than simple defiance. It's that all of this is enacted, enacted annually in the season of forgiveness in a place that would seem to defy all forgiveness, a site that should make it impossible to believe that anybody may radically accept that anything at all happens for any reason.

There are ten thousand Jews, twenty thousand Jews, stadium numbers of Jews in waves and streams, mottled crowds of white and black singing and swaying and throwing bits of bread over the concrete flanks and into the brownish-green muck of a Chernobylian pool, every once in a while breaking into a solemn holler for minutes at a time, all of them begging forgiveness from God in a wilderness from which God had withdrawn. What David the Hungarian had said in jest about the Camino was even truer here. Perhaps, in moments like these, it is not God who forgives us but we who forgive God.

When we forgive God the father, we are acknowledging that God's motives may be obscure to us but they make sense to God; it'll all ultimately cohere from the perspective of the messianic era, and in the meantime we need to have faith. When we forgive our actual fathers, we are acknowledging that their motives may be obscure to us but they probably make as little sense to them; some of it will ultimately cohere and some of it won't, and in the meantime we need to have reasonable expectations and try as hard as we can to hold them accountable.

My dad hadn't come to tashlikh. I waited by Yossi's tent and Micah walked up slowly by himself. He said Dad said he needed to stay back and guard the stuff at the tower block; the lock hadn't been fixed yet and it was starting to get dark. I was sure the nice Ukrainian cops were still there, and after all, it was just clothing, and the lock would be fixed within the hour. Micah was afraid I'd be angry, or sad. Even after his skepticism about what this had accomplished, now he was worried that the fact that Dad hadn't come to tashlikh was going to undo all the good that had made the last few days the first genuinely good time we'd spent with him in just about as long as either of us could remember.

Micah and I stood close to each other on the shores of the lake and listened to the Hasids bellowing into the once bloody void.

"I was sitting there during translator Rabbi Lazer Brody's talk, and listening to him go on about how everything happens for a reason, for God's reason. And I was thinking about what you said this afternoon, about how I'd justified my own restlessness in part by not wanting to repeat what was a really simplistic view of Dad's life, which is that he made this bad decision and then regretted it and then resented us and ultimately created a lot of pain. I think there are a lot of reasons I wanted to accept that version of Dad's story. The way Dad has come to look at his life is that he suffered a lot at the hands of others—not being able to live openly as a gay man— and that then, once he made the decision to come out and live for himself, he *deserved* to do whatever he wanted whenever he wanted.

"And I think that I collaborated in upholding that fantasy because I had this idea it would make things easier for us—that if I could convince myself that it was true, that he really did *deserve* to do whatever he wanted, then we wouldn't have to feel bad, we wouldn't have to feel neglected or spurned or angry, because we would understand that it had all been justified. I always wanted him to have a *reason* for doing something instead of having an *excuse* for doing it. If he'd lived this life of regret, he would've genuinely had a *reason*—that is, a legitimate motive—for disappearing to Key West and frittering away all that money that had been saved for your college tuition.

"But what he made clear to us in that conversation was that he'd been doing just as he pleased the entire time—sleeping with whomever while keeping up a marriage and family life that was important to him. I've been thinking, Well, in that case he didn't *deserve* anything."

What we'd finally gotten from him was his admission that he did all of these things because he wanted to do them. If there's a meaningful difference between the idea of a reason and the idea of an excuse, if there's a meaningful difference between "I felt like it" and "I had to," it has something to do with the authority you invoke and the costs you're prepared to acknowledge. For so long the stories he told were excuses. They were varieties of "This is what I was forced to do"—by sexual mores when he was married, or by implacable biological urges when he wasn't married anymore. These stories allowed him to evade moral responsibility, to act as though the costs of his decisions—the pain that they caused—weren't attributable to him, and could be written off. His language was the language of obligation, never the language of decision. And then, because he'd sacrificed so much out of obligation, he'd later deserved to do what he wanted without paying any attention to the costs. To have a reason is to understand the costs of a decision and make it anyway.

What pilgrimage does, I think, is complicate this distinction between a reason and an excuse. The story of a pilgrimage is so often the transition from "This is what I *had* to do"—something commanded—to "This is what I *wanted* to do"—something chosen. The pilgrim comes to understand that sometimes the only way to fulfill our desires is to hear them as demands. After all, we are driven by our desires, and when you press the question, the distinction between the active and the passive breaks down. Maybe in Berlin I wasn't distracting myself from anything. Maybe what I wanted to do with my time there was take long walks deep into the former East, go out dancing as much as I could, sit in front of the Turkish bakery with Alix talking about Rancière as the U-Bahn screeched by, settle deep into long nights at Bar Drei with David, and manage just enough mostly unfulfilling experimentation to know that self-congratulatory promiscuity and the attempt to live out Genet's ethics of betrayal—which culminated, with the girl from Shanghai, in a small disaster I'm still not over—didn't solve any of my problems; I look back and know I wouldn't give up a second of it. After all, I had the rest of my life to read *Middlemarch*, which I finally did on my iPhone in New York as I waited in line for tacos. The experiences that made so little sense at the time have come to assume the steadiness of a line, the line of what I did, the line that brings me here.

The neutral word "pretext"—as opposed to the loaded words "reason" and "excuse"—suspends, for the moment, the question of moral responsibility, and makes way for the final fact that, as Wittgenstein says, we just do what we do. We're all going to find pretexts for doing what we're going to do anyway, for having our adventures and doing our *demmij* along a road in northern Spain, or in a broken-into temple in rural western Japan. There is no such thing as the life we deserve, just like there is no such thing as a prophylactic against regret. There is the life we live. There is the series of crises we do our best to muddle through. No sacrifice now will make the future effortless or the pain we will inevitably cause easier for others to forgive. The thing that can be so hard about my dad's life, about anyone's life, is that he caused so much pain and is somehow happy now. He is happy and has come to tell a story in which the pain he caused was worth it. But we all do our best, and we hurt some people and get hurt by others and what's as terrible as it is wonderful is that we endure, we endure and find ways of looking back and, if we are able to manage the trick of perspective, if we are able to hold on to our memories of Santiago, we find a way for it to have made sense.

And in the end what's important is not that our dad did what he wanted to do, or what he felt he had to do, but simply what he did. The person who did what he did was no longer quite the same person who was there with us in Uman; the person we had long been angry at was not exactly the person we were now surprised and delighted to be having a good time with. The Ukrainians speaking Hebrew and selling bottled water up the hill were not the Ukrainians who had committed these atrocities. But we still have to try to make sure that the stories we tell ourselves about how it all made sense in the end are stories that include the pain as well as the triumph, the dead Egyptians as well as the triumphant Israelites. The stories we tell will conflict with the stories told by people we love, but the only way to learn how to tell new ones—to wean us from fixity—is to listen to those of others. I had caused the woman in Shanghai pain because I hadn't listened very well to what she was trying to tell me about us. Minor as that experience may have been—and I am sure she has long forgotten about me—there was something about it, something about her, that allowed me to tell this story here. I know that some of it will cause my father pain, and because I love him it will also cause me pain. But I also know that I have contorted myself in the attempt to accept a particular version of our family romance for too long, and that in order to proceed with the wonderful—no, remarkable—relationship I hope to have with him, I need to feel as though I've made my version clear. This was and had been a time to revisit the trauma of the past with the hope that, if we manage to honor it, it might lessen its grip on the present and allow for a new future. For so long we'd had no idea where we stood, and now we realized we were much closer to him than we'd ever thought we'd be.

I turn to Micah and speak over the hollering din. "I'm a little disappointed that Dad didn't come down to tashlikh, but I'm not mad. You were right that nothing is ever going to be totally okay, but all that feels relevant now is the idea that on some level he's been doing his best all along, and we don't have to forgive him because he deserves it, we forgive him because we love him, and we forgive him because we can. I came here in part wanting him to apologize, and even though he didn't, really, it feels somehow even more important that *we* apologized, that he might not have come to us but we went to him, and somehow that's made it easier and more satisfying to forgive him than if he'd asked."

"Yeah, I feel the same way," Micah said. "This has been surprisingly great, and in the end we're probably all better off if we try to forget about those dead Egyptians. At least until next year."

Epilogue

KIEV/BERLIN

REGRETS ARE JUST MEMORIES that come unsummoned, and do us more harm than good. We'd had more than enough of the past for the time being, and the next morning as Ari and Uri and Ezi went to find the best spot to daven we ran to the car with our suitcases and fled Uman. We drove to Odessa and it felt great to be a mere tourist at last. We went to the *Potemkin* Stairs and the market, took the clanking streetcar along the seaside promenade of decrepit sanatoria, ate *varenyky* and drank ill-advised amounts of vodka. We drove back to Kiev, visited the underground monasteries, and helped our dad find the one gay bar in town. We were actively creating new memories, memories we'd want to summon, to complicate the story the old ones told. It was the only pilgrimage with no postpartum melancholy. Quite the opposite, in fact. The minute we left Uman we began a very fun vacation, and that was more than enough for all of us. The only moment of anxiety was when Micah said something about Max, but even that passed, and a month later my dad emailed to say that, because of things Micah and I had said, he'd insisted he and Max get together and find a way to talk some stuff out.

Micah flew to Tokyo and my dad flew to New York and I got on the train from Kiev to Berlin, a weepy twenty-four hours in a compartment by myself. I wasn't going back for good. I just hoped to have a few months in which I might take advantage of the time and the space Berlin offered. It would be the first time I ever spent in Berlin in which I felt as though I only stayed out until dawn when I really wanted to, never because I felt as though I had to. I mostly stayed inside and went to bed early and tried to turn all of this pretext into a text, a text that would, with some qualification, recommend some pilgrimages to some people. When I went out I met Emilie and David and we would sit on the cold pool deck of the Soho House like old, rich people from Munich, sharing a joint, taking bets on how long a Soho House would even last here. Emilie looked at her pink cocktail. "I'm drinking something called a Bubble Wap." She laughed. "Maybe I should be embarrassed about it, but I've been here long enough that it's just fine with me."

I had arrived in Berlin at six in the morning on Yom Kippur, and I went right to David's. I brought him a pack of the red Gauloises he likes, and he blearily made coffee. I told David how good it had felt to create, or exploit, this pretext for forgiveness, and how great it was to be able to have the new memories that would allow me to imagine a future not wholly dominated by the past. David went back to sleep and I wrote an email to the girl in Shanghai, saying it was now Yom Kippur and that I wanted to say I was still sorry. Then I wrote an email to my dad in which I said that it was now Yom Kippur and I wanted to say I was sorry for the wrongs I'd done him, that I hoped he could forgive me. A few minutes later Micah, home in Tokyo, wrote him a sweet email, too. We were nervous when it took him a day to write back.

> Dear Gideon and Micah,
>   Your messages touched me very deeply. I wanted to write back immediately but found I wanted to simply bask in them a little longer. I hope this year is for both of you, individually and together,

what I want for myself—a year of creativity and peace. I hope that my flaws which have caused you pain are lessened, and that you will forgive me for all the things I have done wrong. I love you very, very much. Thank you for accepting me back into your remarkable lives. You are both wonderful children. I will try even harder this year to live up to your hopes.

Love,
Dad

Acknowledgments

Without whom not: Tom Bissell. David Levine, Alix Rule, Emilie Trice. Max Kraus. In a way, Delia Chiu is responsible for all of this.

Without whom not (work category): Tina Bennett, Becky Saletan, Jynne Martin. Svetlana Katz, Elaine Trevorrow.

Lively and irreplaceable companionship en route: In Berlin, Maxime, Ignacio, Zhivago, Carson, Lars, Gregor, Hannes, Frederika, Kevolution, Nicholson, Alexa, Thilo, Cecile. In Spain, Ben, Andy, Kiyomi, Tim, Wiebke, Bill, Stephen, Thomas, David, Alina, Nora, Nico, Sebastian, Lisa, Román, Karo, Geneviève. In Shanghai, Sophia, Eric, Taylor, Emery, Sean, Alanna, Steve, Yo-Yo and Tim and the profoundly ineffectual staff of the Shama Xu Jia Hui, Clock2, Ocfober, the Official Best Cabbie in Shanghai, and Taylor's Uighur liaison. In Japan, JR, Yumi, Nori, Mick. In Ukraine, Nahum, Baruch, Shlomo, Ari, Ari, Ari, Uri, Ezi, Ace, Avi, Ari.

The girl from Shanghai.

Thank you to Andrew Leland, Prue Peiffer, Oana Marian, and Gregor Quack for opportunities to read aloud from the manuscript in progress.

Thanks so much to Elena Lappin, Adam Freudenheim, Gesche Ipsen and everyone at ONE and Pushkin Press for their care and attention to this UK edition.

The late Oliver Statler's book on the Shikoku o-henro, *Japanese Pilgrimage*, is a nice read, though long out of print, as is Ian Reader's academic study, *Making Pilgrimages* (a nice read that is, not out of print). Nancy Frey's dissertation about the Camino is useful. Lee Hoinacki's memoir has its moments. I am indebted to Jack Hitt's *Off the Road: A Modern-Day Walk Down the Pilgrim's Route into Spain* and Susan Tennant's recent translation of Takamure Itsue's 1918 account of her strange journey. Arthur Green's biography of Rabbi Nachman, *Tormented Master*, is a classic.

Incommensurate thanks to the helpful readers of various emails/chapters/drafts at various stages: Laura Adler, Anna Altman, Michael Ames, Rachel Aviv, Angie Baecker, Lauren Bans, Jordan Bass, Cathy Bishop, Simone Blaser, Victoria Camblin, Michael Chabon, Delia Chiu, Harriet Clark, Chelsea Clinton, Josh Cohen, Corina Copp, Chris Cox, Caleb Crain, Chris Crane, Dave Croke, Nina Curley, Gordon Dahlquist, Anne Diebel, Susan Dineen, Kiyomi Doi, Rachel Doyle, Florian Duijsens, Clark Durant, Dave Eggers, Arnie Eisen, Omer Fast, Laura and Yoni Fine, Katie Founds, Peter Freed, Keith Gessen, June Glasson (as well as Sirikanya "Pim" Lapcharoensap Glasson), Chris Glazek, Jason Glick, Gary Greenberg, Lily Gurton-Wachter, Steve Hely, Samantha Henig, Sheila Heti, Lauren Hilgers, Eli Horowitz, JJ Hurvich, Benita Hussain, Menachem Kaiser, Angie Keefer, Jonas Hassen Khemiri, Colleen Kinder, Dave Kneebone, Trevor Koski, Henrik Kuhlmann, Nick Kulish, Dave Lampson, Rattawut Lapcharoensap, Josephine Lau, Mi Lee, Andrew Leland, Ben Lerner, Lawrence Levi, Rose Lichter-Marck, Sam Lipsyte, Lauren LoPrete, Christian Lorentzen, Jessica Loudis, Sara Marcus, Katherine Marino, Ralph Martin, Brian McMullen, Tom Meaney, Josh

Meltzer, Marc Mezvinsky, Rebecca Milner, Stosh Mintek, Christian
English Montegut, Sara Nadel, Jason Nadler, Jordan Nassar, Saskia
Neuman, Alana Newhouse, Rachel Nolan, Ethan Nosowsky, Alex
Nydahl, Chris Onstad, Eugene Park, Richard Parks, Chris Parris-
Lamb, Jen Percy, Allison Phillips, Alex Provan, Michelle Quint, Ian
Reader, Max Rosenberg, Anna Saulwick, Gary Shteyngart, Choire
Sicha, Aria Sloss, Christine Smallwood, Ian Spiro, Liza St. James,
Noah Strote, Evan Swisher, Peter Terzian, Louisa Thomas, Emilie
Trice, Steve Yelderman, Jacob Young, Nicole Walker, Bill Wasik,
John Williams, Margaux Williamson, Gus Winkes, Emily Witt, Ben
Wizner, Annie Julia Wyman, Wesley Yang, Chris Ying, Webster
Younce, Molly Young.

I owe Bill Wasik a whole lot.

Reiterated incommensurate thanks to the unbegrudging readers
of multiple emails/chapters/drafts at *multiple* stages: Rachel Aviv,
Tom Bissell, Delia Chiu, Harriet Clark, Peter Freed, Gary Green-
berg, Sheila Heti, Trevor Koski, Dave Lampson, Rattawut Lapcha-
roensap, Andrew Leland, David Levine, Rose Lichter-Marck, Ralph
Martin, Michelle Quint, Alix Rule, Louisa Thomas, Emily Witt,
Ben Wizner. Ralph Martin knew this was going to be a book before
I did. Before Tom did, even.

Family: Susan Anshanslin; Marjorie Kagan; Max and Lois Kraus;
David Kraus and Debbie Soverinsky; Karen, Nathan, and Noah
Levin; Sarafina Midzik and family; Bob Miller and family; Rebecca
Golden and family; Susan Mamis. Sydnie "Little Dodo" Yao Reed
for her research, preposterous linguistic gifts, extreme patience, un-
justified kindness to Micah, and special way with *emoji*. I would like
to single out Gert Lewis, because periodically an email-dispatch
recipient would look over the names on the cc list and write to me,
"You send emails this long, dirty, and absurd to your *grandma*?" Yes,
I did send such emails to my grandma, and she was an excellent sport

about it. I'm very sad that Harvey Kagan, whose ring I wear, and Ed Lewis did not see this book. I wish Richard Rorty had lived to see it and shrug. May their memories be blessings.

Again: Becky Saletan, probably the smartest and most honest editor anyone has ever had the pleasure to work with anywhere. I could not feel luckier or more grateful. And I haven't the faintest idea what I'd do without the brilliant agency of Tina Bennett. And, again, Jynne Martin!

David Levine. Alix Rule.

Tom Bissell, the most generous writer I've ever known, who's promised to do the Camino again with me next summer.

Peter Freed.

Truly unable to thank enough, ever: Harriet Clark.

Dad, Brett. Yoshi.

Mom.

Micah.